OPEN KITCHEN

OPEN KITCHEN

INSPIRED FOOD FOR CASUAL GATHERINGS

SUSAN SPUNGEN

AVERY
an imprint of Penguin Random House
New York

AVERY

an imprint of Penguin Random House LLC
penguinrandomhouse.com

Most Avery books are available at special quantity discounts
for bulk purchase for sales promotions, premiums, fund-raising,
and educational needs. Special books or book excerpts
also can be created to fit specific needs. For details, write
SpecialMarkets@penguinrandomhouse.com.

Library of Congress Cataloging-in-Publication Data

Names: Spungen, Susan, author.
Title: Open kitchen : inspired food for casual gatherings /
    Susan Spungen.
Description: New York : Avery, an imprint of Penguin Random
    House , 2020. |
    Includes index.
Identifiers: LCCN 2019030080 (print) | LCCN 2019030081
    (ebook) | ISBN
    9780525536673 (hardcover) | ISBN 9780525536680 (ebook)
Subjects: LCSH: Cooking. | LCGFT: Cookbooks.
Classification: LCC TX714 .S6748 2020 (print) | LCC TX714
    (ebook) | DDC
    641.5—dc23
LC record available at https://lccn.loc.gov/2019030080
LC ebook record available at https://lccn.loc.gov/2019030081
p.   cm.

Printed in China

10 9 8 7 6 5 4 3 2 1

Book design by Ashley Tucker

To my husband and BFF, Steve

CONTENTS

INTRODUCTION

A few years ago, I came across the word *sprezzatura*. Not only did I love the way it sounded, I was intrigued by its translation, which, simply put, means "studied nonchalance." It deeply resonated with me because that is what I always aim for when I cook—and especially when having people over. I want my food to be deeply satisfying, a little special, a little surprising but not seem like it's trying too hard. I want my friends to feel cared for and considered, but I don't want them to feel bad, as if I went to too much trouble for them (sometimes people do!). So even though I may have put a considerable amount of work into preparing a meal, I want it to seem effortless and uncontrived but still elegant and a little undone, like a messy bun on a beautiful girl or a guy's shirttail sticking out just so.

This idea translates to a kitchen strategy that involves breaking down my prep into stages, so I can spread it out over a day or two (or three) so that in the end it feels kind of nonchalant for me too. Doing everything all at once for a meal usually results in a sink full of pots and pans, and if it's just me, it can be hard to keep up. I like getting some of the work—and the cleanup—done well ahead of time. The one thing a professional home cook like me has over the ordinary home cook is years of experience as a restaurant chef, a caterer, a food editor, and a food stylist. These experiences have taught me how to "mise" things out (that's French for getting all your prep ready) in the best way possible. I know what I can do ahead of time and what I need to leave for

the last minute—that final toss of the salad, sprinkle of herbs, drizzling of sauce—the things that incidentally make things look beautiful and taste their best and freshest. This innate sense of timing takes time and experience to learn, but in this book, I guide you through each recipe with tips that tell you what you can do when—beyond what the recipe itself tells you. My hope is that, armed with this more granular guidance on how to get ahead, you will develop your intuition and have more fun cooking, with some of the stress taken out of the equation. I hope it will help you get a beautiful meal on the table without too much last-minute fuss.

This is not a book about make-ahead food, even though some of it is, but rather about the concept of "get-ahead cooking." Once you discover the joy of getting ahead, you will become a planner even if you never were before. If you want to be in the moment with your guests and join the party, it's absolutely essential to start thinking and cooking this way. In fact, the recipes themselves are engineered specifically to make cooking for a party easier, whether it's for four or fourteen. You won't find things that need to be finished *à la minute* standing at the stove. Your oven is your best friend when it comes to getting ahead, and it is used often in this book; whether it's to warm the French Beef Stew (page 101) you made two days ago, gently reheat the Italian-ish Ribs (page 95) you cooked the day before that, or to bake off the Quac 'n Cheese (page 269) or Winter

Vegetable Lasagna (page 201) you assembled yesterday, sending delicious aromas through the house and giving you a hands-off hour to do other things, be it setting the table or taking a shower. Your choice.

I really love cooking for people, and I do it often. Cooking makes me happy, and it's a way I can make other people happy too. I feel like I've really given something of myself, and because it is usually so enthusiastically appreciated, it is an incredibly rewarding experience. The by-product of all of this is that you've created a shared experience that will be remembered for a long time by everyone involved.

Being a professional recipe developer means there are days when I'm cooking enough for a huge crowd and there's no one there to enjoy it, at least not in the moment. It's an occupational hazard I struggle with.

In my old days, cooking in the test kitchens of *Martha Stewart Living*, where I was once the top banana, I was grateful for the "little kitchen," aka the pantry, where everyone in our office stopped for a cup of coffee, or a pretzel log, or, yes, a little gossip or venting over the water cooler. All day long, my staff and I would plop our creations down on the counter and watch them disappear (and sometimes not—those recipes didn't make the cut), but it would have felt really weird to be cooking tons of food all day long and have no one there to eat it. What would be the point?

I studiously avoid the word *entertaining*, as the stuffy stereotypes it conjures up are a bit dated. I used to cater parties in New York when I was younger—often cooking in Park Avenue apartments (where I used the service entrance leading directly to the kitchen) and stodgy houses in Southampton where we had to choose which of six sets of china we were going to serve on. The tables were set with linens and crystal and silver. Things have changed, thankfully. I guess they never were like that in my world. This book is *not* about that kind of entertaining. The pressure is off and the doilies are long gone. My husband, Steve, and I have a lot of nice things we collect and like to use to serve food on, but our quirky tastes run more to handmade ceramics, especially Japanese ones. The food looks handmade too, so

they complement each other. It's all more wabi-sabi than fancy-schmancy. Matching up the food you cook with a beautiful platter or bowl is half the fun and makes everything look more special.

We like to gather friends around our table as often as possible, and as casually as possible. Like so many people, we have an open kitchen, which has made me embrace get-ahead cooking more than ever before. As if the kitchen wasn't already everyone's favorite gathering place, when people come to our house, they are standing around our open kitchen, which is what it was designed for! Our "dining room" is a long table right next to the back side of our stove (which is on a peninsula), which we often use as a buffet.

Most of the food in this book is designed to be made at least partly, if not completely, ahead of time, and to be served family style, by which I mean on shareable platters and bowls—whether they are set on a buffet or passed around the table. Quite a few recipes are meant to be served at room temperature—something to consider when assembling a menu (for more on menus, see page 354)—and others can be served straight from the oven or from a simmering pot on the stove. I try to minimize last-minute grand gestures like sautéing fish on the stovetop or anything else messy, smelly, or that requires too much concentration when you're already hosting and should be having fun yourself.

You'll notice that a bunch of recipes have a "Project" tab at the top of the page. This is just a heads up that that particular recipe may take a little more time to prepare than some of the others in the book, but it has the distinct advantage of being done completely ahead of time.

Although this book is not organized seasonally, I cannot help but indulge my proclivity for highly seasonal cooking, because that's what inspires me and drives my creativity. This isn't to say that every recipe in the book depends on access to a backyard garden, a CSA, or a farmer's market—though they are everywhere!—there are plenty that take advantage of and draw inspiration from seasonless everyday foods found in any supermarket. Building and balancing flavors is something that can be done any time of year. You will find just a few recipes that are so highly seasonal that you might be able to make them for only two or three weeks of the year—I can't leave these recipes out, because I want to inspire you to shop with the seasons—and when you find those gems, you'll know just what to do with them. But I always try to give substitutions for highly seasonal ingredients. In the winter, at least on the East Coast, that is what we have to work with.

You'll also notice that there are a lot of vegetable-based recipes and dishes that are easily made vegetarian with the omission of one nonessential but perhaps flavor-enhancing ingredient, like a bit of pancetta. I am not a vegetarian, but I eat plenty of vegetarian meals and have plenty of vegetarian friends whom I don't want to neglect when having people over for a meal. Like a lot of people, I've cut down on the amount of meat I eat, and I also just really love vegetables and am always finding new ways to use them. That said, this is not a healthy cooking book, per se—I like a little luxury, especially when feeding friends—but I want my guests to go home feeling nourished in body and soul and indulged but not weighed down. There are many things I want to give my friends when I feed them—a food coma is not one of them. I am not a fan of gratuitous richness—it's easy to make things taste good with lots of fat and salt, but I prefer to coax out flavors in more balanced ways.

I'm not gonna lie—cooking good food does take some planning and work. I don't want to make promises of effortlessness—I just want to help you get closer to that, and to the *appearance* of effortlessness. But it's pleasure that fuels the work. Going to the farmer's market, going to the fish market to see what looks good, being creative in the kitchen—all of these joyful things happen while you are making this "effort."

Cooking is how you learn to be a good cook. Just like anything else, cooking is a practice, so as you keep cooking you'll find yourself getting more and more comfortable and better and better at it. You won't get better at cooking just by *reading* this book—you need to get yourself into the kitchen and cook, without fear of failure, because there really is no such thing.

PANTRY:
CREATING YOUR KITCHEN'S PALETTE

Since I was trained as an artist, and fell into being a cook quite by accident, I still approach cooking with an artist's sensibility, as that's how I first learned to create. I layer on flavors, textures, and colors, often coming up with ideas, and even epiphanies, in my head, long before I step foot in the kitchen. One of the biggest lessons I learned as an art student is to know when to stop—when a work is "done." That lesson of restraint is one that translates well to cooking too. A heavy hand leads to muddled flavors or overly rich food, both things I aim to avoid. For me, a recipe often starts with an inspiration, and I build from there. The ingredients I like to cook with are like an artist's palette, and yeah, they are all stored in my "pantry," which is more like all over my kitchen. I have a separate pantry just for my baking projects and ingredients, a drawer very close to my stove full of most of my spices, another deep drawer just below my "station" where I keep bottles of oils, extracts, salts, and more spices. I like to be well stocked with all kinds of spices, condiments, grains, seeds, oils, and vinegars, so that when inspiration strikes, I have everything I need close at hand. I am not attempting to give you an encyclopedic list of all the ingredients I use, only the ones that may be less familiar to you or those that need a little bit of extra explanation.

Salt

I generally use two kinds of salt in my kitchen: Diamond Crystal kosher salt for everyday cooking and seasoning and Maldon flaky sea salt for finishing dishes, salads, and desserts. If you currently are using fine salt in your kitchen, rather than trying to convert the amounts you should use (less), just buy yourself a box of kosher salt. My recipes and many other published recipes use Diamond Crystal as the standard. Different brands can be very different in volume, so always add salt slowly and taste as you go. You can always put more in, but you can't take it out!

Black Pepper

It is so basic to cooking you may wonder why I am mentioning it, but please—grind black pepper yourself! Never buy pre-ground because it is terrible—it has a strange flavor and it is just not the same. If you don't have a good peppermill, get one—but I really like the disposable ones you can buy in the supermarket too. I prefer the ones that have a choice of three grinds. If I need a lot of black pepper for something, I grind it in a spice mill to save time and elbow grease. In most cases, I don't give measurements for pepper in this book, as it is hard to measure if you are grinding it, and I would never ask you to do that. If you are seasoning meat or fish, aim for a light, even coating over the surface. I never use white pepper.

Parmigiano-Reggiano Cheese

I always have a chunk of Parmigiano-Reggiano cheese in my fridge. Sometimes it's more of a dried-up rind, but those are useful too (see Ribollita en Croute; page 195). I consider it as basic to my pantry as salt, olive oil, lemons, and butter. When it's very fresh, it is a good eating cheese, and it finds its way into many of my recipes. It has become ubiquitous, which doesn't lessen its appeal. If you don't have a cheese department where it is cut fresh, look for Cryovac-packed wedges, which will be the freshest.

Breadcrumbs

I use breadcrumbs to top many baked dishes to give them an irresistible crunch. I always keep panko breadcrumbs on hand, because they really deliver in the crunch department, but sometimes I prefer homemade breadcrumbs.

Tahini

Tahini is to sesame seeds what peanut butter is to peanuts, in case you were wondering, but brands can vary wildly in taste and texture—all may seem a bit bitter when tasted straight, but that bitterness will be softened by the time they are baked into Black and White Tahini Swirl Cookies (page 301), swirled into a sauce to drape over Za'atar Tofu Bowls (page 183— I can drink this stuff), or whisked into a creamy dressing for Green Bean Salad with Tahini and Quinoa (page 213). I love Seed + Mill tahini, but shop around to find one you like and start using it!

Black Garlic

Black garlic is everything raw garlic is not—sweet and mellow. This fermented version of a most common kitchen staple adds a smooth umami note and subtle sweetness to dishes, especially when added to a long-cooked braise like Korean Short Ribs (page 97). The Roasted and Black Garlic Aioli (page 145) used in the Winter Grand Aioli (page 143) ascends to heights previously unknown. Once you have some on hand, experiment with different ways to use it—in a stir-fry, perhaps, or a vinaigrette, or try adding some to Fried Black Rice (page 161). Like so many of my pantry favorites, black garlic keeps for a very long time!

Harissa

Harissa, the North African red pepper paste, has become as common as ketchup in the United States and is used as a condiment and in sauces in some of the same ways. Ingredients for homemade harissa are more challenging to source than the sauce itself, so rather than give you a recipe, I urge you to seek it out and keep some on hand—it lasts forever! There are a lot of different brands and types out there, and they vary in flavor, heat level, and consistency. One of my favorites, Mina Harissa, comes in mild and hot, is easy to order or find on a supermarket shelf. I like the mild variety for certain dishes, because you can use more of it!

Preserved Lemons

Preserved lemons are easy to make, if you can wait a month or more for them to be ready, but they are relatively easy to find and definitely easy to order. They have a strong smell and flavor, and a little goes a long way, but they add a salty, citric umami punch to whatever they touch. New York Shuk makes a preserved lemon paste that has become one of my favorite new ingredients. It makes it easy to add a dab to vinaigrettes, pan sauces, marinades, dips, cocktails, and even desserts. If you are using whole preserved lemons, discard the pulp and finely chop the skin to add to your recipes.

Fresh Herbs

I use a lot of herbs in my cooking, and in the summer I plant many varieties in pots on my deck just outside my kitchen door. It's the only way to get my hands on more obscure herbs that I like to use such as shiso, summer savory, Thai basil, chervil, anise hyssop, cutting celery, lemon verbena, and lovage. The list goes on, but you get the idea. I also plant edible flowers like nasturtiums (the leaves are tasty and beautiful too), chamomile, and violas. I tell myself I'm saving a lot of money (I'm not, really) by planting them instead of buying bunches when I need them, but they give me a lot of pleasure both in the kitchen and on the deck. I love to run my hands through the fragrant plants when I'm sitting outside, pluck a few to throw into an alfresco meal, and, well, just look at them! I also grow all of the regulars, including thyme, rosemary, sage, tarragon, chives, and parsley, and those are mostly what I call for in my recipes, but if you have a garden (and I encourage you to start one, even if it's a tiny windowsill garden), please feel free to experiment with different herbs and use two or three when I've only called for one.

Za'atar

Za'atar, as you probably know by now, is a seasoning mix, usually a powdery green with whole sesame seeds, that usually contains dried za'atar (an herb not common in the United States but similar to thyme and marjoram), toasted sesame seeds, sumac (see below), and salt. Ingredients and ratios vary according to region or maker. Its current popularity makes it pretty easy to find, if not in a store, then definitely online. I urge you to get some and keep it on hand to use in Za'atar Chicken Thighs (page 119) or Za'atar Tofu Bowls (page 183) or simply to sprinkle on hummus, warm bread, labneh, salads, and roasted vegetables.

Sumac

Sumac is a beautiful deep red, almost purple, powdery spice made from the dried and ground berries of the sumac shrub. You've likely had it every time you've been to a Middle Eastern restaurant and have been served a plate of hummus. Maybe you thought it was paprika, but it was sumac. Think of it as powdered lemon flavor—a sprinkle will add a little fruity acidity to whatever it touches. Its gorgeous color enhances a simple plate of Burrata with Pickled Cherries, Sumac, and Basil (page 69).

Aleppo Pepper

This is a mild fruity red pepper that I always keep on hand. I love the warmly spicy flavor and that I can use it more liberally than typical red peppers that pack a lot more heat.

Herbes de Provence

I always have a little crock of the good stuff—you know, the one that comes in a little ceramic pot with French writing on it? I've tried other mixtures, and they just aren't the same. I love fresh herbs, but I do not look down my nose at dried herbs, especially these.

Herbes de Provence is usually a combination of summer savory, marjoram, rosemary, thyme, oregano, and lavender. They add a flavor—especially to grilled or roasted chicken and lamb—that is distinctive. I call this my default seasoning—especially in summer, when we often stay late at the beach and grab something to throw on the grill on the way home. I often combine it with chopped fresh rosemary or thyme.

Labneh

There isn't a huge difference between thick Greek yogurt and labneh, and they can be used interchangeably in my recipes. Technically labneh is "yogurt cheese," strained in a cheesecloth-lined sieve to be even thicker than the thickest Greek yogurt. My local supermarket sells tubs of labneh, which is not necessarily thicker than yogurt, but definitely creamier and a little less tangy. If you see it, buy it! It makes a great dip all by itself, drizzled with olive oil and sprinkled with za'atar, or used as a base for roasted vegetables like Roasted Beets with their Greens over Labneh (page 206).

Demi-glace Concentrate

Even though I never went to cooking school, early on in my culinary career, I was fortunate enough to work alongside a couple of chefs who were classically trained, so I learned about proper sauce- and stock-making techniques, in particular veal demi-glace, a very concentrated stock made from veal bones, which is simmered for a really long time, strained, and then reduced by half or more (hence the name). At the end, it's a delicious and very concentrated flavor bomb that is so full of collagen you can cut it with a knife when cold. I like to have it around to add to pan sauces, braises, and soups for an extra flavor boost. It lasts forever in the fridge. Williams-Sonoma makes very good ones. It may seem a bit expensive, but when you realize how many meals you can use it in, the price seems totally worth it. You can also find Demi-Glace Gold in little plastic containers in many supermarkets or on Amazon; they are made by a company called More Than Gourmet.

Duck Fat

Small tubs or jars of duck fat are pretty available these days, as the demand for this wonderful cooking fat increases. It's usually found in the meat section of the supermarket or at the butcher's counter in a specialty store. Of course, you can render it yourself if you happen to be cooking duck—just strain it and store it in the freezer—and it will last a long time. It is my fat of choice when cooking potatoes—it adds a bit of ducky flavor and also creates incomparable crispiness. Try it in Duck Fat Oven Fries (page 279) or Crispy Semolina Potatoes (page 275).

Dried Porcini Mushrooms

I'm a big fan of dried porcini, and use them often to add a little deep, earthy, mushroomy flavor to a dish, like in Ribolitta en Croute (page 195), or in Modern Chicken and Dumplings (page 117), Osso Buco Sugo (page 103), or Baked Pici with Sausage Ragù (page 83). They are usually sold in 1-ounce bags, and often in the produce sections of supermarkets. The quality can vary, of course, but it's usually based on the size and wholeness of the mushrooms, They will consistently have good flavor.

Flour

A few words about flour. The measurements in this book are given by volume. Eventually American cooks will be converting to weights, I'm sure, but for the moment, this is how it is. It is crucially important to measure flour properly, but unfortunately, not all recipe writers use the same standards. I use the "spoon and level" method, which is what most people use, but some use a "scoop and level" method, which can result in a very different weight of flour—enough to throw off a small and sensitive recipe, especially cookies. To "spoon and level," use a scoop or spoon to lightly fill the measuring cup with flour, then use a straight-edge tool like a knife to level it smoothly. I keep a canister of flour on my counter, which makes it easier to measure properly without making a mess, and it keeps it handy too! I use unbleached all-purpose flour unless otherwise specified.

EQUIPMENT

I do admit to having a pretty well-stocked kitchen; after all, I have been cooking both professionally and recreationally for years—but in my everyday cooking, I rely on a fairly small group of tools and equipment that I can't do without. I encourage you to collect a few basics, if you don't already have them. Invest in the best quality you can afford and they will last for years! Having the right stuff at your fingertips will only make your cooking life easier and more pleasurable.

Baking Sheets

In professional parlance—half sheet pans. These roughly 11 by 17-inch pans with a raised, rolled edge are indispensable. They won't warp and pop out of shape in the oven (*grrr*) and are perfect for everything from baking cookies and galettes to roasting vegetables to just being placed underneath a potentially drippy baking dish full of lasagna. I use them constantly for everything. Ideally you should have at least two, and a few more if you like to bake cookies. If you can buy these from a restaurant supply store, they will be well-priced and lacking unnecessary bells and whistles like a textured surface. I am also a fan of quarter sheet pans, (about 9 by 13 inches) which are handy for so many things, such as toasting nuts, cooking a smaller piece of meat or fish, and roasting garlic.

Dutch Oven/Braising Pot

I have a few of these in different sizes, but a good medium one with a 5- to 6-quart capacity will work for most braises. Enameled cast iron is best, and they are usually marked with a number on the bottom that tells you how many centimeters it is in diameter. A size 26 will work for most braises. If you can't afford a new one, you'll find used ones easily in thrift shops and flea markets. Because of their nonreactive surface, you can cook, store, reheat, and serve all in the same pot. They also are good for simmering soups and for serving foods you want to stay warm as long as possible, like mashed potatoes.

Roasting Pans

Everyone should have one large (16 x 13-inch) heavy-duty roasting pan, even if you use it only once a year to roast a turkey. They also are good to roast two chickens at once, a leg of lamb, or pork shoulder. I also like to have a smaller one for a single chicken and myriad other things.

Baking Dishes

I have quite a few baking dishes in different sizes, materials, and depths, and I use them all the time. I have a shallow copper gratin that I have had for years, and I love it for everything from the Summer Corn Pudding on page 285, for roasting a chicken, roasting fruit for dessert, or making a fruit crisp (page 309). I also employ ceramic dishes in different sizes. This is another item that I urge people to invest in, as they are oven to table. Pyrex dishes are fine for cooking, but for serving, not so much. A beautiful or rustic dish will elevate your food so much more. You can find nice vintage ones at thrift stores and flea markets.

Skillets

I use heavy nonstick skillets for most of my cooking in all the basic sizes; 8-inch for breakfast, of course, but also for frying capers (see page 128) or sage leaves (page 28) or quickly toasting spices, for example. A 10-inch skillet is good for caramelizing onions or for making Flower Omelette Crepes (page 177). My 12-inch skillet gets the most use, because when I sauté, especially mushrooms, I never want to crowd the food. I have cast-iron skillets in various sizes, but for general purposes a 10-inch is a good all-purpose size. My favorite belonged to my grandmother, and others I have bought at yard sales.

Food Mill

There's no substitute for a food mill—one of the most old-fashioned tools in my kitchen. It's great when you don't want to worry about skins or seeds—say, when making tomato sauce with fresh tomatoes, applesauce with unpeeled apples, or raspberry sauce—all the skins and seeds will be left behind as a smooth puree is cranked out through one of three blades. It's also my tool of choice for making mashed potatoes (or gnocchi; page 189). A ricer is the next best choice for potatoes, but a food mill is much easier because it processes continuously—just keep adding potatoes as you turn the crank—and doesn't require as much elbow grease.

Food Processor

The food processor comes into play quite a bit in my recipes, so I hope you have one (or two), or a model that has a mini-insert for those jobs that would get lost in a full-size food processor bowl. I find those a little complicated to put together though, and prefer having a full-size machine and a mini version. Whether it's for starting a dough (page 351) or making creamy and smooth whipped ricotta or goat cheese to top a toast, Beet Hummus (page 61), or Chickpea Fritters (page 207), there really is nothing else that whizzes ingredients together the way a food processor does. I like the slicing blade for quickly shredding kale for my Famous Kale Salad (page 229) and the grating blade for large amounts of cheese or raw beets or carrots. The mini version, which is easy to tuck away in a drawer or cabinet when not in use, is good for small-scale recipes that would get lost in a bigger machine like Salsa Verde (page 34) or Roasted and Black Garlic Aioli (page 145), and does a good job of chopping without completely pulverizing ingredients like garlic or parsley when you're feeling lazy. Both machines have a nifty way of slowly drizzling oil into a mayonnaise or sauce, which not all users realize—in the big one it is usually the feed tube, and the mini has a little funnel in the lid that will release oil in a slow, steady stream. The mini is also excellent for chopping nuts without turning them into nut butter for Multi-Nut Shortbread (page 293).

Stand Mixer

If you like to bake and you don't have a stand mixer, this is something worth saving up for. While many recipes can be made with a hand mixer, or by hand, the vast majority of baking recipes you will come across, including the ones in this book, have been developed using a stand mixer, and the quality and success of your bakes will be better if you use one. Hand mixers are fine for whipping egg whites or foamy batters but aren't so good for creaming butter and sugar, where the stand mixer excels. Aside from that, there are many attachments you can get for a stand mixer that will save you money and space in the long run. It has a powerful motor, so why not use it for everything? In addition to the usual baking uses, I use my stand mixer to make ice cream and fresh pasta.

High-Speed Blender

The old blenders just don't cut it anymore. Since a Vitamix came into my life, I've had little use for the old-style ones. Other brands have rushed their versions to the market to compete with this workhorse. The powerful motor makes short work of blending almost anything into a perfectly velvety smooth puree. A high-speed blender makes the Roasted Strawberry–Basil Sherbet (page 353) as easy as blending a smoothie. I use mine to make creamy soups and, of course, smoothies all the time.

Bench Scraper

This tool is definitely one to have in your drawer. Aside from its traditional use for baking—it's there to help you lift a dough that's sticking, scrape your surface to clean it, mix and cut gnocchi (see page 189), and make Chocolate Curls (page 313)—it's also super handy for transferring piles of vegetables to the pot and about a million other things.

Offset Spatula

A small offset spatula is a non-negotiable item in my toolbox. I use it for both baking and cooking. It's perfect for smoothing the batter for a cake, swirling meringue, icing a cake or cupcakes, loosening a galette from the parchment, and transferring cookies to the cooling rack, but also for turning small and delicate foods like Chickpea Fritters (page 207) and other small and intricate cooking tasks.

Instant-Read Thermometer

The simplest version and the one I prefer is from OXO—I like the big digital readout on a screen that looks like a lollipop. It takes the guesswork out of cooking meat but is also useful when tempering chocolate or making yeast doughs.

Mandoline

Another non-negotiable item for me. My preference is the Kyocera with an adjustable ceramic blade because it's easy to use and easy to store, as it fits in a drawer. It's super handy for thinly slicing vegetables, like for my Shaved Vegetable Salad (page 227), and also for shaving radishes or fennel on top of salads and other dishes for a pretty finishing touch. It's also great for Parmigiano-Reggiano cheese. It's less than $20, so I don't feel bad if I need a new one every few years. The only problem with a mandoline is that it is very easy to cut yourself, and the guard that comes with it isn't very useful, so I highly recommend getting a pair of cut-resistant gloves to avoid this hazard! You can order both a mandoline and the gloves easily online.

A Note about Plastic

Like many of you, I have become more aware of my plastic use recently and am more mindful of the waste I create, both with packaging and in my cooking. This has led me to use less plastic, compost my food waste as much as possible, and use parts of vegetables I used to throw away. It's a work in progress. I may ask you to marinate something in a resealable plastic bag or store something in an airtight container, but by all means, you are welcome to use any alternative methods you have converted to. Keep using the high-quality plastic containers you have—they will last forever! Better in your drawer than in a landfill.

SAUCES, SPRINKLES, AND STUFF

OVEN-DRIED CHERRY TOMATOES

MAKES ABOUT 1 CUP

Little cherry tomatoes (see photo, page 24) add quick and easy pizzazz to almost any savory dish. I use them to top Tomato Toast with Labneh and Harissa (page 51) or to add texture, depth, and dimension to a dish that contains another form of cooked tomatoes, such as Fish in Crazy Water (page 139).

1 cup (½ pint) cherry tomatoes, cut in half
2 teaspoons olive oil
Scant ½ teaspoon salt
Freshly ground black pepper

1 Preheat the oven to 300°F. Line a baking sheet with parchment paper (not only to keep your pan clean but also to avoid any reaction between the metal pan and the acidic tomatoes).

2 Toss the tomatoes with the oil, salt, and pepper to taste right on the baking sheet. Spread them out evenly cut-sides up.

3 Bake for 50 to 60 minutes, until the tomatoes are wrinkly on the edges and just starting to brown on the bottom. Timing will vary based on the juiciness and size of the tomatoes. Let cool slightly, and use warm or cold.

TIMING TIP:

The tomatoes can be made up to 2 days ahead of time. Store in the refrigerator in a wide, flat airtight container, layered on top of one another. Bring back to room temperature before serving.

TIP:

If you find the job of halving cherry tomatoes tedious (I find it meditative), sandwich them between two lunch-size plates, and use a sharp knife to slice between the plates. It isn't a perfect method, because you can't control exactly where the cuts are on each individual tomato, but it works pretty well and takes seconds!

FRESH FAVA BEANS

MAKES 1 CUP

I adore fresh fava beans, and pounce on them when they show up in the spring. They are a lot of work though (worth it), for a fairly low yield, so I tend to use them as an accent or component of a dish rather than making them the main attraction. They make a nice addition to a Big Salade Niçoise (page 149), Meyer Lemon Gnocchi with Spring Vegetables (page 189), or sprinkled onto a piece of grilled bread with some lemony Whipped Ricotta (page 36) slathered on it and fresh herbs showered over top.

1½ pounds fresh fava beans in the pods
Salt

1 Shell the beans by pulling on the string that runs up one side of the pod. Bring a pot of generously salted water to a boil. Prepare an ice bath. Cook beans for 1 to 2 minutes; drain and rinse under cold water. Transfer to the ice bath. When cool, drain well.

2 Peel the skin on each bean and pop it out by gently squeezing. Some will split in half, which is fine. Chill until ready to use.

FRIED SAGE LEAVES

MAKES 24

I love fried sage leaves to garnish cold-weather dishes like the Creamy Baked Risotto with Butternut Squash and Fried Sage Leaves (page 167), but they look and taste great on top of almost anything that needs a little pick-me-up. Raw sage is too strong, and frying the leaves softens their rough edges and gives them a delightfully delicate crispness. They are easy to make and keep well for several days or more, sealed in an airtight container. It's easy to burn them, so heat the oil slowly and add the leaves all at once (which will keep the temperature down). The oil does not need to be screaming-hot, just hot enough for a test leaf to sizzle a little when you dip it in. Try them on top of a simple puree of potatoes or root vegetables, a toast of your own design, or on a pizza or salad. Don't use your best extra-virgin olive oil for this, and the sage-scented oil can be cooled and reused for cooking.

½ cup vegetable or pure olive oil

24 sage leaves, with about 1 inch of stem attached, and bone-dry

Salt

Place a paper towel–lined plate near the stove. Heat the oil in a small skillet over medium heat until hot enough for a sage leaf to sizzle when dipped in the oil, about 5 minutes. Carefully add all the sage leaves at once, and cook until they start to become spotted with dark green, about 1 minute. Remove with cooking tweezers, mesh spatula, or slotted spoon and drain on paper towels. They will turn a dark forest green and continue to crisp up after they've been removed from the oil. Sprinkle with salt.

CHERMOULA

MAKES ABOUT 1 CUP

A healthy dose of smoked paprika causes this Moroccan herb sauce to stop short of looking like a green sauce, but the flavor is bright and herbaceous and would be great spooned over any fish or shellfish (see Shrimp and Chickpeas with Chermoula, page 135).

¾ teaspoon coriander seeds

¾ teaspoon cumin seeds

2 garlic cloves, sliced

1 cup lightly packed fresh cilantro leaves and soft stems

1 cup lightly packed fresh Italian parsley leaves and soft stems

½ cup fresh mint leaves

Zest of 1 lemon (preferably organic)

1 teaspoon smoked paprika

¾ teaspoon salt

¼ to ½ teaspoon red pepper flakes

½ cup extra-virgin olive oil

¼ cup fresh lemon juice

1 Heat a small, dry skillet over medium-high heat. Add the coriander and cumin seeds and toast, shaking the pan frequently, for 1 minute. Let cool slightly and place in a food processor.

2 Add the garlic, cilantro, parsley, mint, lemon zest, paprika, salt, red pepper flakes, and oil and process until smooth. Just before using, stir in the lemon juice.

TIMING TIP:

You can make the chermoula up to 1 day ahead of time. Store in a glass jar or airtight container in the refrigerator.

ROASTED MEYER LEMONS

MAKES ABOUT 12 SLICES

This is a fantastic way to take advantage of the Meyer lemon's relative lack of acidity (compared to regular lemons). Cooking the lemons this way makes them totally edible, more like a vegetable than a garnish, as they appear in Shrimp and Chickpeas with Chermoula (page 137) or Kale and Prosciutto–Wrapped Chicken Breasts (page 123). You really can't sub regular lemons here; they are just too bitter in my humble opinion. The good news is that Meyer lemons have become commonplace in supermarkets, but, sadly, only from November until May. On another note, I've heard people complain about recipes that call for things to be sliced ⅝ inch thick, because it seems overly precise, but think of it this way—it's a little thicker than ¼ inch, and smaller than ½ inch, and that is the best way to describe it. No need to get the ruler out.

2 Meyer lemons, sliced ⅝ inch thick, seeds removed

1 tablespoon olive oil

½ teaspoon salt

¼ teaspoon sugar

1 tablespoon water

1 Preheat the oven to 400°F. Line a small baking sheet with parchment paper.

2 Bring a small saucepan of water to a boil. Drop in the lemon slices and cook for about 2 minutes. Drain. Transfer to the prepared baking sheet and toss with the oil, salt, and sugar. Spread the slices out over the sheet and sprinkle with the water.

3 Bake for 20 to 25 minutes, or until the lemons start to turn golden on the underside. Turn and bake for another 10 minutes, or until golden on the second side.

TIMING TIP:
The roasted lemons can be made up to 1 day ahead of time. Store in the refrigerator in an airtight container.

CHICKEN STOCK

MAKES 4 QUARTS

Aside from the basic ingredients listed below, there are many other ingredients you can add to chicken stock for more or different flavor, depending on what you have in your kitchen. Leek greens, mushroom stems, parsnips, or shallots are all good additions. You can also add a piece of turmeric root for a bright yellow stock, or ginger for a spicy broth to nurse a cold or to use as a base for an Asian-flavored soup. This recipe yields a bonus of plenty of silky poached chicken to use in recipes.

4 bone-in chicken breasts
   (3½ to 4 pounds)
2 stalks celery, cut in thirds
2 carrots, scrubbed and cut in thirds
1 large unpeeled yellow onion, quartered
2 garlic cloves, peeled
2 to 3 sprigs thyme
10 to 12 parsley stems
1 teaspoon black peppercorns
1 bay leaf
1 teaspoon salt

1 Place all of the ingredients in an 8-quart stockpot and add 18 cups filtered water. Bring to a boil over high heat. Lower the heat to maintain a bare simmer and skim any foam or scum that rises to the top. After 25 to 30 minutes, carefully remove the chicken breasts to a large bowl. When cool enough to handle, cut the meat from the bones and return the bones to the pot. Don't worry about being thorough here. It's OK if some meat remains on the bones, because it will continue flavoring the stock as it cooks. Let the chicken meat cool, then refrigerate for later use either in your finished soup or to add to salads, sandwiches, fried rice, and so on.

2 Continue simmering for a minimum of 30 minutes and as long as another 1½ hours. Let cool slightly in the pot.

3 Place a large sieve or colander over a large, deep bowl and set it in the sink. Slowly strain the liquid, being careful that the solids don't fall into the sieve all at once (it may be more than it can hold). Also make sure you are not pouring more than the bowl can hold—you may need a second bowl.

4 Let cool in the bowl for a bit, then ladle into storage containers (strain again as you do this, if needed). Let the containers sit on the countertop with the lids off until the liquid is at room temperature. Cover the containers and refrigerate. Once they are cold, you can freeze them for later use. They will keep refrigerated for up to 3 days and (at least) 6 months frozen.

HAZELNUT-PISTACHIO DUKKAH

MAKES ABOUT 1 CUP

Dukkah, where have you been all of my life? Truly, I don't know how I have survived so many years without this nutty, crunchy, seedy, spice-y sprinkle that has so many uses. Everyone should always have a jar of the stuff on hand at all times to sprinkle on top of soups, hummus (page 61), salads, and toast (page 41), or even knead into grissini dough (page 65). Change up the nuts or play with the proportions to suit your tastes or based on what you have on hand. If you don't feel like toasting and peeling hazelnuts or have trouble finding them, use almonds instead, but avoid pre-peeled roasted hazelnuts, as they just won't have that nutty fragrance and fresh taste that you get when you toast them yourself.

½ cup raw hazelnuts

2 tablespoons coriander seeds

1 tablespoon cumin seeds

2 tablespoons white sesame seeds

2 tablespoons black sesame seeds

½ cup raw pistachios

1 teaspoon flaky sea salt

Freshly ground black pepper

TIMING TIP:

Dukkah can be made completely ahead of time and stored in an airtight container for several weeks.

1 Preheat the oven to 350°F.

2 Spread the hazelnuts on a small baking sheet and toast in the oven for 10 to 12 minutes, until the skins are starting to flake off and the nuts smell and look toasty. Transfer to a bowl, cover with a folded dish towel, and set aside to cool. Rub off the skins (don't worry if they don't come off completely).

3 Heat a small, dry skillet over medium heat and add the coriander and cumin seeds. Toast until fragrant and slightly darkened, 4 to 5 minutes. Transfer to a plate and add the white and black sesame seeds to the same pan. Toast until the white seeds are golden brown, 3 to 4 minutes.

4 Combine the hazelnuts, pistachios, coriander and cumin seeds, and white and black sesame seeds in a mortar and pestle or a mini food processor and grind until everything is broken up but not finely ground—the idea is to leave some texture. Stir in the salt and pepper. Cool completely and store in an airtight container.

SALSA VERDE

MAKES 1 HEAPING CUP

There are many variations on this basic green sauce, not to be confused with the Mexican version, which shares only a name with the Italian version we have here. You can add other herbs if you have them on hand, especially, mint, oregano (sparingly), chives (go crazy!), tarragon (for some *je ne sais quoi*), or dill (why not?). Just stick to soft herbs, and leave out herbs like rosemary, sage, or thyme, which would be too strong here. You can add more oil if you want a thinner sauce. I like to wait to add the lemon juice until just before using to preserve its bright green color. I use it to dress the Fregola Salad (page 271), but it is good on almost everything! Try it over simple grilled fish or chicken, swirled into a hot or cold soup, or mixed into yogurt for a quick dip or sauce.

3 cups loosely packed fresh Italian parsley leaves (1 large bunch)

4 to 6 scallions, green and white parts, trimmed and roughly chopped

1 tablespoon capers, rinsed and chopped

3 anchovies or 1½ teaspoons anchovy paste

2 tablespoons white wine vinegar

½ teaspoon salt, plus more to taste

Freshly ground black pepper

¾ cup extra-virgin olive oil

1 lemon, preferably organic

1 Wash and dry the parsley well. Place it in a food processor along with the scallions, capers, and anchovies and pulse to chop. Add the vinegar and pulse again. Add the salt and season with pepper, then slowly stream in the oil through the hole in the lid until fairly smooth. Zest the lemon directly into the bowl and pulse to combine. Juice the lemon, set the lemon juice aside until ready to serve, then mix it in to taste.

2 Add more salt if needed, to taste.

TIMING TIP:

You can make the salsa verde up to 1 day ahead of time. Store in a glass jar or airtight container in the refrigerator.

WHIPPED GOAT CHEESE

MAKES ABOUT 1 CUP

Pureeing goat cheese until smooth and creamy makes it the perfect base for any number of ingredients to sit atop toast. It can be used interchangeably on any of the toast recipes with lemony Whipped Ricotta (page 36) if you want a stronger, or just different, flavor. It would provide a more pungent contrast to slightly sweet pickled rhubarb and grated raw beets. To change it up, whiz in some soft herbs at the end, like parsley, cilantro, chives, or tarragon. Or use it as a blank canvas to create your own toast art.

8 ounces soft goat cheese

6 to 8 tablespoons milk, as needed

1 tablespoon extra-virgin olive oil

Salt, to taste

Combine the goat cheese, 6 tablespoons milk, and oil in the bowl of a food processor and process until completely silky smooth. Add more milk, 1 tablespoon at a time, if needed to thin to a creamy, spreadable consistency. Season to taste with salt. Chill until needed.

TIMING TIP:

The whipped goat cheese can be made up to 2 days ahead of time. Store in the refrigerator in an airtight container.

WHIPPED RICOTTA

MAKES ABOUT 1 CUP

There is a very big difference between "fresh" ricotta cheese and the stuff that comes in tubs in the dairy aisle. In supermarkets, it will be sold in the cheese or deli section, or you may have to seek it out in a store that specializes in Italian products or cheese. It is worth seeking out.

8 ounces fresh whole-milk ricotta cheese

Zest and juice of 1 lemon (2 tablespoons juice)

$\frac{1}{8}$ teaspoon salt

Combine the ricotta cheese and lemon zest and juice in a food processor and process until completely smooth. Season to taste with salt. Chill until needed.

TIMING TIP:
The whipped ricotta can be made up to 2 days ahead of time. Store in the refrigerator in an airtight container.

BASIC COOKED CRANBERRY BEANS

MAKES 6 CUPS BEANS AND 3 CUPS BROTH

I love cranberry beans, also known as borlotti beans. I use them in soup (page 195), salad (page 233), or just on their own as a side or to throw into pasta or chili. Packed with their broth they freeze really well, and because they are a great base for any vegetable soup, I am always really excited when I find some in my freezer. I almost never soak my beans overnight—I find a quick soak works just as well.

1 pound dried cranberry beans
   (about 2½ cups)

8 cups water

4 large garlic cloves, peeled

½ small onion (don't trim the root,
   so it stays in one piece)

A few sprigs rosemary, thyme, or sage

1 bay leaf

1½ teaspoons salt

2 tablespoons olive oil (optional)

1 Combine the beans with abundant cold water in a large, deep saucepan. Either soak overnight or bring to a boil, let boil for 1 minute, turn off the heat, and let sit for at least 1 hour. Drain and rinse.

2 Combine the beans with the 8 cups water, the garlic, onion, herbs, bay leaf, salt, and oil (if using) in the same saucepan and bring to a boil. Reduce the heat to maintain a brisk simmer and cook, stirring occasionally, for 40 to 45 minutes, until tender. Start checking for doneness after 30 minutes. Cut through a bean—when it's done, the center no longer will look white and when you bite into it, it will be completely soft. Let the beans cool in their liquid—do not drain. If using for salad, they should still hold their shape but be nice and soft—it's a fine line. For soup, it's OK if they are a little undercooked, as they will cook again in the soup. Store the beans in their liquid for up to 3 days in the refrigerator and 3 to 6 months in the freezer.

SIMPLE STARTERS

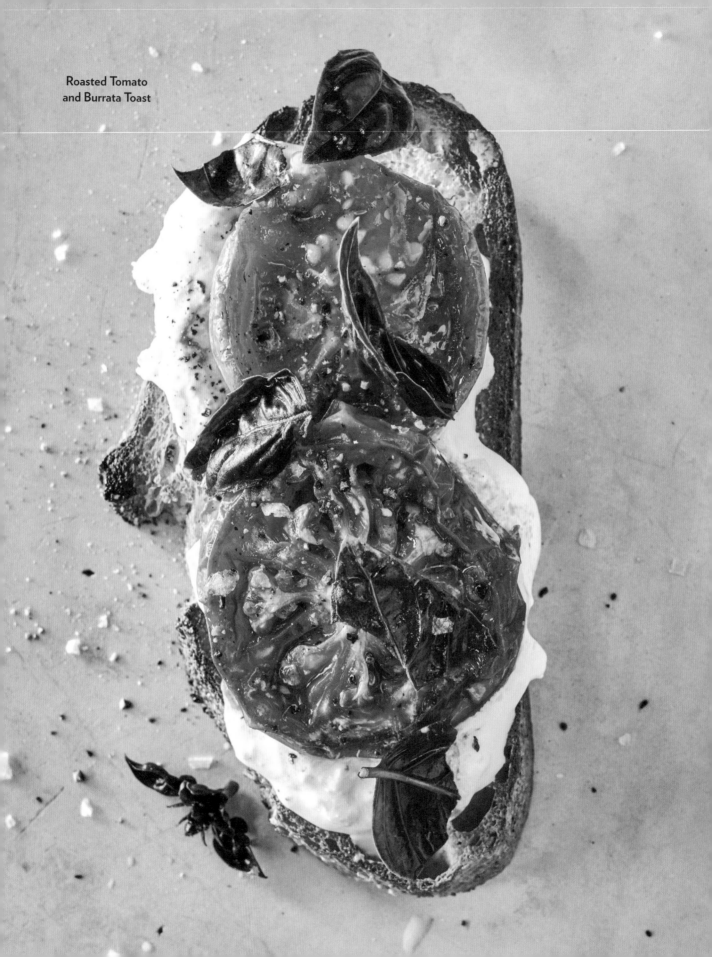

Roasted Tomato
and Burrata Toast

A TREATISE ON TOAST

How did toast become such a thing? We've been eating it all our lives, but with all of the exemplary bread one can buy now in just about any city or even small town, we have bread that really can stand on its own, and certainly as a base for any number of creative and tasty toppings. I guess it took avocado toast (thank you, Australia!) to make us realize that we could throw together a last-minute appetizer or snack with stuff we probably already have in the house. Call it bruschetta, crostini, tartine, or just call it toast. In our house, we try to keep some good bread in the freezer (already sliced) at all times, so I'm prepared for those moments when I need to whip something up on the spot. It doesn't take a lot of any one ingredient to make four big pieces of toast, which easily can be cut into smaller pieces for more dainty one- or two-bite morsels, so you just might find what you need at the bottom of your produce drawer and cheese bin. This isn't to say you should make appetizers with old vegetables, but you could in a pinch!

Here's the basic formula:

1 Slice some really good bread between ½ and ¾ inch thick and toast it, either in a toaster, under the broiler, one side at a time, or on a grill. Always aim for a crunchy outside and a bit of softness in the center.

2 Slather the bread with something soft and creamy, such as whipped goat cheese, bean puree or mash, ricotta, mashed avocado, mashed winter squash, hummus, babaganoush, or soft feta.

3 Top it with something warm, something cold, something crunchy, something meaty (if you have a soft topping, you won't need the creamy layer underneath to hold things on).

4 Garnish it—with herbs, nuts, dukkah (page 33), shaved radishes, fried sage, or any finishing touch that perks up the presentation and the flavor. Crunchy salt is always a good finish.

Kale Toast

Pea and Goat Cheese Puree Toast with Carrots and Radishes

Tomato Toast with Labneh and Harissa

Whipped Ricotta Toast with Pickled Rhubarb and Grated Beets

Melon Toast

Whipped Goat Cheese Toast with Peas, Shallots, and Bacon

Cassoulet Toast

Marinated Feta, Oyster Mushroom, and Corn Toast

CASSOULET TOAST

SERVES 4

When I set out to write this book, I thought I would include a cassoulet recipe. Then I decided that it was just too much of an undertaking. I figured if I didn't even want to take it on for recipe development, surely you wouldn't want to cook it. It is a project to be sure, and there are lots of good recipes out there already, but it is not for the faint of heart. But then I realized the essential flavors of cassoulet could be distilled into one hearty toast. It's greatly simplified, of course, and it isn't cassoulet, but it is very, very good! You could cut this into little bars as a pre-dinner bite or serve one toast per person alongside a crisp salad of bitter greens for lunch.

2 tablespoons olive oil, plus more
    for drizzling

1 small onion, thinly sliced

4 garlic cloves, peeled

Two 15.5-ounce cans butter beans,
    rinsed

½ cup canned chopped tomatoes

2 sprigs thyme

Salt and freshly ground black pepper

1 prepared confit duck leg (5 ounces)

1 cup plus 1 tablespoon water

4 thick slices airy country bread

Fresh Italian parsley leaves, chopped,
    for garnish

1 Heat a medium (10-inch) skillet over medium-high heat. Add 1 tablespoon of the oil, the onions, and 3 of the garlic cloves. Cook, stirring occasionally, for about 5 minutes, until the onions and garlic start to color. Reduce the heat to medium-low and continue cooking, stirring occasionally, for 25 minutes, or until caramelized.

2 Add the beans, tomatoes, thyme, the remaining 1 tablespoon oil, ¼ teaspoon salt, and 1 cup of the water. Turn the heat up to medium-high and bring to a simmer. Smash about one-eighth of the beans against the side of the pan with a fork to thicken the mixture. Cook until thickened, about 5 minutes.

3 Transfer to a bowl, discard the thyme, and smash the garlic cloves. Season with salt and pepper, stir well, and cover with foil to keep warm.

4 Preheat the broiler.

5 Rinse out the pan and return it to the stovetop. Add the confit duck leg skin-side down to the cold pan. Turn the heat to medium-low, add the remaining 1 tablespoon water, cover the pan, and cook for 10 minutes (when the skin softens, scrape it off the duck leg and continue cooking alongside it; this will become the crackling). Remove the lid, turn the duck leg, and continue cooking until the leg is warmed through and starting to crisp up, turning as needed.

6 Continue cooking the duck skin (as if it were a slice of bacon) until nice and crisp, keeping in mind that it will crisp more as it cools (as if it were a slice of bacon), about 3 minutes longer. Drain on a paper towel.

7 Toast the bread on both sides under the broiler until it is crisp on the outside and still soft inside. Rub each slice generously with the remaining garlic clove and top each slice with about ½ cup of the beans. Shred the duck meat and divide it evenly among the toasts. Season with salt and pepper, drizzle with more oil, if desired, and crumble the crackling over the top. Sprinkle with the parsley and serve.

TIMING TIPS:

- Up to 2 days ahead: Cook the bean mixture. Store in the fridge and rewarm when ready to serve.

- Up to 2 hours ahead: Cook the duck leg and prep the parsley.

- At the last minute: Toast the bread and assemble the toasts.

MARINATED FETA, OYSTER MUSHROOM, AND CORN TOAST

SERVES 4

I am completely smitten with Australia's Meredith Dairy's soft and creamy feta, which comes in a jar and is marinated in olive oil. If you can't find it, a soft goat cheese, Whipped Goat Cheese (page 35), or another creamy feta would work fine too.

1 tablespoon plus 1 teaspoon olive oil

8 ounces oyster mushrooms, trimmed and sliced

Salt and freshly ground black pepper

1 teaspoon unsalted butter

1 ear fresh corn, kernels cut from the cob

1 shallot, thinly sliced

4 slices good bread

Four 1-ounce cubes marinated feta cheese

Fresh tarragon leaves or Fried Sage Leaves (page 28)

Fennel fronds, optional

1 Heat a large (12-inch) skillet over high heat. Add 1 tablespoon of the oil and the mushrooms. Sear for about 2 minutes on each side, until softened and nicely browned. Season with salt and pepper and transfer to a plate.

2 Return the pan to the stovetop over medium-high heat. Add the remaining 1 teaspoon oil and the butter to the pan, then add the corn. Season with salt and pepper and cook, tossing, for 3 to 4 minutes, or until spotted with brown. Add the shallot and cook until wilted, another minute or two.

3 Toast or grill the bread, then smash a feta cube onto each slice, spreading it out to cover the toast. Top with the mushrooms and the corn mixture. Sprinkle with the tarragon and fennel, grind some pepper over the top, and serve.

TIMING TIPS:

• Up to 1 day ahead: Cut the corn off the cob.

• Up to 2 hours ahead: Cook the corn mixture.

• At the last minute: Sear the mushrooms, toast the bread, and assemble the toasts.

PEA AND GOAT CHEESE PUREE TOAST WITH CARROTS AND RADISHES

SERVES 4

This toast is a fresh take on peas and carrots, perfect in spring and early summer. I like it on baguette, as it doesn't overwhelm the delicacy of the toppings.

2 ounces soft goat cheese, softened

½ cup cooked fresh or thawed frozen peas

4 to 6 fresh mint leaves

Heavy cream or milk, as needed

Kosher salt and freshly ground black pepper

Fresh lemon juice

8 diagonal slices good baguette

1 to 2 small carrots, scrubbed or peeled

2 to 3 small radishes, such as breakfast radishes

Flaky sea salt

1 In a mini food processor, combine the goat cheese, peas, and mint. Pulse to puree, then drizzle in the cream as needed to loosen to a smooth, spreadable consistency. Season with salt, pepper, and lemon juice.

2 Toast the bread slices and spread each with some of the puree.

3 Use a mandoline to slice the carrots and radishes paper-thin over the toast. Sprinkle with flaky salt.

TIMING TIPS:

- Up to 1 day ahead: Make the goat cheese puree; bring it back to room temperature before serving.

- At the last minute: Toast the bread and assemble the toasts.

WHIPPED GOAT CHEESE TOAST WITH PEAS, SHALLOTS, AND BACON

SERVES 4 (OR MORE IF CUT INTO BARS)

Though the pea topping can be made an hour ahead of time, it's nice to warm it up again just before serving.

3 slices thick-cut bacon (3 to 4 ounces) cut into ½-inch crosswise strips

2 small shallots, cut into rings (about ⅓ cup)

1 cup shelled or frozen peas

Salt and freshly ground black pepper

4 slices crusty bread

½ cup Whipped Goat Cheese (page 35)

Fresh tarragon or basil leaves

1 Start the bacon in a cold small skillet and cook over medium heat until crisp, about 10 minutes. Scoop out and drain on a paper towel. Pour off all but 1 tablespoon of the bacon fat. Add the shallots and cook until softened, about 4 minutes. Add the peas and cook for 1 to 2 minutes, until heated through. Season with salt and pepper.

2 Toast the bread slices and spread with the whipped goat cheese. Top with the pea mixture and sprinkle with the herbs. Crack more pepper over the top.

TIMING TIPS:

- Up to 1 hour ahead: Make the pea mixture.

- Up to 2 days ahead of time: Make the whipped goat cheese.

- At the last minute: Toast the bread and assemble the toasts.

WHIPPED RICOTTA TOAST WITH PICKLED RHUBARB AND GRATED BEETS

SERVES 6

I like a light and airy bread for this delicate toast—nothing too grainy or dense. Ciabatta or something similar will work well.

2 stalks fresh rhubarb

¼ cup red wine vinegar

¼ cup sugar

1 teaspoon salt

½ cup water

½ cup Whipped Ricotta (page 36)

Six ½-inch-thick slices good bread, toasted or grilled

1 raw beet, trimmed, peeled, and grated

1 Thinly slice the rhubarb on a slight bias. Combine the vinegar, sugar, salt, and water in a small saucepan. Bring to a boil, then reduce the heat and simmer for a minute or two, until the sugar is dissolved. Add the rhubarb, return to a simmer, then transfer to a bowl to cool.

2 Spread 2 tablespoons of the whipped ricotta on each piece of toast. Drain the pickled rhubarb (reserving the liquid for another use) and divide among the toasts. Top with the grated beets and serve immediately.

TIMING TIPS:

- Up to 3 days ahead: Make the pickled rhubarb.
- Up to 2 days ahead: Make the whipped ricotta.
- Up to 1 day ahead: Grate the beets.
- At the last minute: Toast the bread and assemble the toasts.

MELON TOAST

SERVES 4

Given its mild flavor and sunny disposition, this toast is particularly good for breakfast or brunch, but is just fine as a dinner starter too. Oven-crisped prosciutto would work in place of the bacon.

4 thick slices chewy country bread

4 slices thick-cut bacon

½ cup fresh ricotta cheese

¼ to ½ peeled and seeded cantaloupe

Handful of fresh mint leaves

Flaky sea salt

Honey

Toast or grill the bread. Start the bacon in a cold medium skillet and cook over medium heat until crisp, about 10 minutes. Drain, then crumble into large pieces. Spread each slice of toast with one-quarter of the ricotta cheese. Slice the melon as thinly as possible with a vegetable peeler, knife, or mandoline and arrange on top. Sprinkle with the bacon, mint, and salt and drizzle with honey.

TIMING TIPS:

- Up to 1 hour ahead: Cook the bacon.

- At the last minute: Toast the bread and assemble the toasts.

TOMATO TOAST WITH LABNEH AND HARISSA

SERVES 4

This is a really simple one—you just have to think ahead one hour (or one day) to make the tomatoes. I like using fresh mini San Marzanos for this and a slightly sweet, dense sesame-crusted loaf.

4 slices good bread, preferably with sesame seeds

¾ cup labneh or plain Greek yogurt, any fat content

Harissa, to taste

Olive oil, to taste

1 recipe Oven-Dried Cherry Tomatoes (page 26)

Fresh mint leaves

Flaky sea salt

Toast or grill the bread and spread each slice with 2 to 3 tablespoons labneh. If your harissa is a thick paste, thin it out with oil and drizzle the harissa over the labneh. Top with the tomatoes and mint leaves and sprinkle with flaky salt.

TIMING TIPS:

- Up to 1 day ahead: Make the oven-dried cherry tomatoes.

- At the last minute: Toast the bread and assemble the toasts.

KALE TOAST

SERVES 6

Have you noticed that I love kale? I really do, and I use it a lot in my cooking, especially in the long winter, because it always seems to be in season somewhere. This simple toast is really all about that pure kale taste and emerald green color.

1 bunch Tuscan kale (about 1 pound)

1¾ teaspoons salt

3 garlic cloves, peeled

½ cup plus 1 teaspoon extra-virgin olive oil

6 thick slices ciabatta or similar airy, chewy bread

1 Preheat the oven to 325°F.

2 Choose 6 nice small kale leaves and set them aside. Strip the stems from the remaining leaves. Bring a large pot of water to a boil and add 1 teaspoon of the salt. Blanch the kale and garlic until the kale is wilted and bright green, about 1 minute. Drain and rinse with cold water. Put the garlic cloves in a food processor and squeeze all the water out of the kale. Transfer to the food processor along with ½ cup of the oil and ½ teaspoon salt.

3 Rub the reserved kale leaves lightly with the remaining 1 teaspoon oil and sprinkle with the remaining ¼ teaspoon salt. Put them on a small baking sheet and bake, turning occasionally, for 10 to 15 minutes, until crisp and barely browned. Time will vary depending on the thickness of the leaves, and the leaves will crisp a bit more as they cool. Toast or grill the bread. Warm the kale puree and spoon it over the toast slices. Top each with a kale leaf.

TIMING TIPS:

• Up to 2 days ahead: Make the kale puree.

• Up to 1 day ahead: Make the crisp kale leaves.

• At the last minute: Toast the bread and assemble the toasts.

ROASTED TOMATO AND BURRATA TOAST

SERVES 4

Although you certainly could use local seasonal tomatoes for this (choose small ones, like plum tomatoes), I have found the commercially produced brown tomatoes that you can find in just about any supermarket yield fantastic results every time, and they are available any time of year.

4 small brown tomatoes (such as Kumato or Brunetta), cut in half crosswise

¼ teaspoon salt, plus more for sprinkling

Freshly ground black pepper

Olive oil

1 large garlic clove, slivered

4 slices crusty bread

8 ounces burrata cheese

Fresh basil leaves, preferably opal

1   Preheat the oven to 300°F. Line a baking sheet with parchment paper.

2   Sprinkle the tomatoes with the salt, season with pepper, and drizzle with oil. Sprinkle with the garlic. Spread out over the prepared baking sheet and roast for 1 hour and 30 minutes to 1 hour and 45 minutes, until shriveled but still juicy. Let cool slightly, then slip off the skins.

3   Toast or grill the bread. Tear the cheese into pieces and top the bread with it. Top each piece of bread with 2 tomato slices. Drizzle with more oil and sprinkle with salt and pepper. Tear the basil leaves over the top.

TIMING TIPS:

- Up to 1 day ahead: Roast the tomatoes; warm slightly before serving.

- At the last minute: Toast the bread and assemble the toasts.

SMOKY CHEDDAR CRACKERS

MAKES 30 TO 35 CRACKERS

I've always been a sucker for a cheesy, salty, buttery cracker, and to me few things are better with chilled wine and cocktails. What I love about a recipe like this one is that you can make the logs ahead of time and keep them in the fridge or freezer until you need them. I like to bake them as close to party time as possible, not only so they are still a little warm and very fresh when eaten, but also so the incredible smell is still lingering in the air when guests come walking through the door. To facilitate that, cut them up, get them ready for the oven, and store the baking sheets in the fridge.

1 cup smoked almonds

¾ cup all-purpose flour

¼ teaspoon salt

¼ teaspoon cayenne pepper

½ teaspoon ground turmeric

¼ teaspoon freshly ground black pepper

1½ teaspoons smoked paprika

3 tablespoons cold unsalted butter, cubed

4 ounces sharpest yellow cheddar cheese, grated (about 1¾ cups)

⅓ cup plain Greek yogurt, any fat content

1 large egg white, lightly beaten

TIMING TIPS:

- Up to 2 weeks ahead: Make the logs and store in the freezer (or store for up to 3 days in the fridge).

- 1 day ahead: Transfer the logs to the fridge to thaw.

- Up to 4 hours ahead: Slice the crackers and lay out on baking sheets (or bake right away).

- Up to 1 hour ahead: Bake the crackers.

1 In a food processor, pulse the almonds until fairly finely ground but with some larger pieces. Reserve half of the nuts, leaving the remaining nuts in the food processor. Add the flour, salt, cayenne, turmeric, pepper, paprika, butter, and cheese. Pulse until combined. Add the yogurt and pulse until the dough comes together.

2 Transfer to a sheet of wax or parchment paper, divide into two equal pieces, and roll each into a log about 1½ inches in diameter and 5 inches long. Brush with the egg white and roll in the reserved almonds, pressing to adhere. Wrap in plastic wrap and chill until firm, at least 3 hours (or as long as 3 days ahead of time).

3 Preheat the oven to 375°F. Line a baking sheet with parchment paper.

4 Cut the logs into ¼-inch-thick slices and arrange on the prepared baking sheet a few inches apart (they won't spread). You can press any nuts that fall off onto the surface of the crackers. Bake for 15 to 17 minutes, until golden brown and firm in the center. Transfer to a cooling rack. Serve warm or at room temperature.

CASTELVETRANO NIBBLE

SERVES 6

This is more an idea than a recipe, and one you will surely be able to memorize. It's a lovely and pretty way to mix up the Spanish-ish flavors of green olives, Marcona almonds, and manchego cheese (see photo, page 38). My friend Elizabeth Fiore served this to me a few years ago before a dinner, and I thought how simple and yet how good it was, so now I am sharing it with you. Watch it disappear!

1 cup Castelvetrano olives, sliced off the pits and patted dry (about ¾ cup)

¾ cup salted Marcona almonds

4 ounces manchego cheese, cut into ½- to ¾-inch cubes

Place the olives, almonds, and cheese in a serving bowl. Toss to combine.

TIMING TIP:
The mixture can be made a few hours ahead of time; chill until 30 minutes before serving.

SMOKY EGGPLANT DIP

SERVES 6

I make this dip all summer long, when eggplants are plentiful and inexpensive (see Mezze Feast, page 204). I have a gas grill outside my kitchen door, and I use it often for things like this. If I had to start a fire to cook three eggplants, I'm pretty sure I wouldn't do it as often (but if you've already started a fire for something else, it's a great time to cook them). That said, you don't need a grill at all. Second best is cooking right on the gas burner of your stove. If you don't have *that*, you can use your broiler. The idea is to blacken the heck out of them however you cook them so that when you peel off all that black skin, a smoky flavor remains.

3 small Italian eggplants, about 1 pound each

1 to 2 garlic cloves, grated

½ cup plain Greek yogurt (any fat content) or labneh

2 tablespoons tahini

2 to 3 tablespoons fresh lemon juice, or to taste

¼ cup fresh Italian parsley leaves

¾ teaspoon salt, or to taste

Pinch of cayenne pepper

TO GARNISH (USE ANY OR ALL):

Olive oil

Sumac

Fresh Italian parsley leaves

Chopped oil-cured olives

Halved or quartered cherry tomatoes

1 Heat a grill to high.

2 Prick the eggplants all over with a fork so some steam can escape while they're cooking. Roast the eggplants, whole, on the grill, giving them a quarter turn every 4 to 5 minutes. Grill until the skin is charred and the flesh is soft and creamy, 20 to 25 minutes. Remove from the heat and place in a bowl until cool enough to handle but as hot as you can stand it. Pour off the excess liquid. Peel the skin off the eggplants, transferring the flesh to a sieve over a bowl as you work. Mix the garlic into the hot eggplant. (Combining the garlic with the eggplant while it is hot will help to soften the garlic's blow.)

3 Transfer half of the eggplant to a food processor and add the yogurt, tahini, lemon juice, parsley, salt, and cayenne to taste. Pulse until well combined. Add the remaining eggplant and pulse just a few times, until coarsely chopped, so there is some texture. Adjust the seasonings. Transfer to a shallow bowl and add your choice of garnishes.

TIMING TIPS:

- Up to 2 days ahead: Roast the eggplant and peel; season with the garlic while hot. Refrigerate.

- Up to 1 day ahead: Make the dip (but it is better made the same day as serving; return to room temperature and adjust seasonings if made the day before).

- At the last minute: Plate and garnish the dip.

BAKED RICOTTA

SERVES 6 TO 8

Imagine a cross between ricotta cheesecake (but savory) and a cheese soufflé, and you will have this dead-easy little cake that looks way more impressive than it ought to. It can be a blank canvas for whatever you want to serve with it or on it, given the amenable sweet flavor of ricotta. Please seek out a good, fresh ricotta from a good cheese shop or cheese department, not the stuff that comes in plastic tubs in the dairy aisle. This makes a fair amount, but I don't suggest cutting it down (though you could!) because the leftovers are good too. It's lovely warm from the oven, but it can be enjoyed for days from the fridge. It's firm and sliceable when cold and can be eaten just like that or rewarmed. Serve with toasted bread and sweet or savory condiments, such as fig jam or Calabrian chili paste.

Softened unsalted butter, for the baking dish

16 ounces fresh ricotta cheese

1 ounce grated Parmigiano-Reggiano cheese (1 fluffy cup), plus more for the top

1 heaping teaspoon chopped fresh thyme

½ teaspoon salt

Freshly ground black pepper

2 large eggs, lightly beaten

1 Preheat the oven to 400°F.

2 Butter a 2-cup soufflé dish or straight-sided baking dish and make a parchment collar by cutting off a piece of parchment paper that is long enough to wrap around the dish with a good overlap. Fold it so that it extends 2 inches above the rim of the dish and tie it on just under the rim with butcher's twine. This will contain the expanding mixture as it bakes.

3 In a medium bowl, combine the ricotta cheese, Parmigiano cheese, and thyme and stir with a fork. Add the salt and season with pepper, then stir in the eggs.

4 Transfer to the prepared dish and bake for 50 to 60 minutes, until puffed, risen, and browned on top. Remove the parchment collar and either serve right from the dish or unmold onto a plate.

TIMING TIPS:

- Up to 1 day ahead: Make the ricotta mixture, put it into the dish, and refrigerate.

- 1 hour ahead: Bake the ricotta.

BEET HUMMUS

MAKES 4 CUPS

The striking color of this beet hummus makes it a conversation piece at every party I serve it at. Serve with Dukkah Grissini (page 65) or some grilled flatbreads (I like Stonefire Naan), or Whole Grain Cumin Crackerbread (page 73). Use it as a dip for crudités, a shmear inside a grain bowl, a base for a toast or tartine, or a sandwich spread.

Two 15.5-ounce cans chickpeas

3 medium beets (about 14 ounces), scrubbed, trimmed, peeled, and quartered

1 tablespoon olive oil

3 large garlic cloves, peeled

¼ cup tahini

Juice of 2 lemons (about ¼ cup), plus more to taste

¾ teaspoon ground cumin

½ teaspoon coarse salt, plus more to taste

Extra-virgin olive oil

Hazelnut-Pistachio Dukkah (page 33)

Watermelon radish or other radish (optional)

Flatbreads or crudités

1 Preheat the oven to 425°F. Line a large baking sheet with foil.

2 Drain the chickpeas, reserve the liquid, and rinse thoroughly. Spread the chickpeas over the prepared baking sheet and top with the beets, plain olive oil, and 2 of the garlic cloves. Wrap loosely (but seal tightly) with the foil and roast until the beets are tender when pierced with the tip of a knife, 30 to 45 minutes.

3 Transfer the chickpeas, beets, and garlic to a food processor and process until smooth. Add the tahini, the remaining garlic clove, the lemon juice, cumin, and salt. Process until smooth, adding enough of the reserved chickpea liquid to thin it to a smooth, creamy consistency. Add a little more than you think you'll need, as it will thicken a bit as it cools. You probably will need about ½ cup. If you run out of cooking liquid, you can use plain water.

4 Adjust the lemon juice and salt to taste and refrigerate if not serving within a few hours. Thin with more bean liquid or water if needed, drizzle with extra-virgin olive oil, and serve with the dukkah, radishes (if using), and flatbreads or crudités.

TIMING TIPS:

- Up to 3 days ahead: Make the hummus; refrigerate.

- 1 hour ahead: Bring the hummus to room temperature and grill the flatbread.

- At the last minute: Garnish the hummus.

GRILLED PEAS IN THE POD, EDAMAME STYLE

SERVES 4

I can't resist fresh shell peas when they start appearing in the market, but I don't always have the time or the patience to shell them. This starter couldn't be any easier to make, and my guests enjoy getting messy eating them. If you don't have a grill platter, fold a large piece of heavy-duty foil in half and fold up the edges to make a little rim. Poke some holes in it using the tip of a sharp knife.

1 quart unshelled English peas
2 teaspoons olive oil
1 lemon, preferably organic
Flaky sea salt

1 Prepare a grill for direct grilling over high heat. Preheat a grill platter, basket, or wok.

2 Wash the peas well, pat dry, and toss with the oil.

3 Toss the peas onto the grill platter and cook, tossing occasionally, until lightly charred all over, about 10 minutes. Transfer to a serving platter and zest the lemon over the top. Sprinkle with salt and serve.

TIMING TIP:
Up to 1 hour ahead: Grill the peas.

DUKKAH GRISSINI

MAKES ABOUT 3 DOZEN

It's funny how good cooking ideas come to you when you have certain ingredients in the house, which is why I keep my pantry so well stocked—I want to make sure I have what I need when inspiration strikes. I had this dukkah around, and I thought—hey, that would be really good in grissini (crispy Italian breadsticks), and guess what? It really was! I thought of putting it on the outside, but I knew that it would burn and lose all its flavor, so I incorporated it into the dough. In addition to rolling, you can lift the grissini by both ends to help stretch it longer. The dukkah, if made according to the recipe on page 33, will be a bit chunky. Finely grind it in a spice grinder or food processor before using it in this recipe.

1 cup warm water

3 tablespoons extra-virgin olive oil, plus more for brushing

1 teaspoon sugar

1 teaspoon active dry yeast

2¼ cups all-purpose flour, plus more for rolling

¼ cup Hazelnut-Pistachio Dukkah (page 33), finely ground

½ teaspoon kosher salt

Flaky sea salt

NOTE:

These are easy and fun to make, but contrary to what your instincts might tell you, you must use little to no flour when you are rolling them out on the counter. Too much flour and they will just slide around and they will be hard to shape.

TIMING TIP:

The grissini can be made up to 2 days ahead. Store in an airtight container once cooled. Re-crisp in a warm oven if needed.

1 Preheat the oven to 425°F. Line two 13 x 18-inch baking sheets with parchment paper.

2 Combine the water, oil, sugar, and yeast in a liquid measuring cup, mixing it with a fork. Let stand until creamy, 3 to 5 minutes.

3 In the bowl of an electric mixer fitted with the paddle attachment, mix the flour, dukkah, and kosher salt on low speed to combine. Slowly pour in the liquid. Turn the dough out onto a work surface and knead until smooth, about 5 minutes, using only as much flour as needed to keep it from being too sticky. Using a bench scraper (page 21) would be helpful here.

4 Form into a ball, lightly dust with flour, cover with plastic wrap, and let it rest on the counter for 15 minutes. Cut one-quarter of the dough using a bench scraper, lightly flour it, and re-cover the remaining dough. Pat the dough into a rough rectangle, and cut into 10 more or less equal pieces, weighing about ½ ounce each. Roll between your hands at first to get a snake shape, about 6 inches long, started. Set on a work surface, and using little to no flour, roll from the center out, using your palms or fingers until the pieces are the same length as the baking sheet and the diameter of a pencil and place 10 grissini on the prepared baking sheet. Repeat with the remaining dough, baking in batches of 10.

5 Brush with oil, sprinkle with flaky salt, and bake for 10 to 12 minutes, until golden brown and crisp. Check frequently near the end of baking time and remove any that are getting too brown. If not serving the same day, make sure you bake them until crisp all the way through.

BLISTERED SHISHITOS WITH AVOCADO CREMA

SERVES 4 TO 6

This is one of my favorite simple starters to serve all summer long. It's not too filling but somehow substantial, making it the perfect thing to take the edge off the appetite while dinner is happening. I added a creamy avocado puree for the peppers to sit on and to swipe through, which gives it another dimension.

½ ripe avocado

3 tablespoons 2% plain Greek yogurt

1½ tablespoons fresh lime juice, or to taste

¼ teaspoon salt

Pinch of cayenne pepper

1 pint shishito peppers

Olive oil

Flaky sea salt

Aleppo pepper

1 Combine the avocado, yogurt, lime juice, salt, and cayenne in a mini food processor. Process until perfectly smooth.

2 Heat a grill or cast-iron skillet over high heat until hot.

3 Toss the peppers with the oil (just enough to coat lightly), and grill or sear, turning occasionally, until blistered all over, about 2 to 3 minutes per side.

4 Spread the avocado crema on a small platter and tumble the peppers over top. Sprinkle with salt and Aleppo pepper and serve.

TIMING TIPS:

- Up to 2 hours ahead: Make the avocado crema; store in the fridge in a deep airtight container with plastic wrap pressed onto the surface to prevent browning.

- Up to 1 hour ahead, but preferably at the last minute: Blister the shishitos, scrape any browned avocado crema off the top, and arrange on the platter.

BURRATA WITH PICKLED CHERRIES, SUMAC, AND BASIL

SERVES 6 TO 8

So many ways to eat burrata—and so little time! I love the acidity of the cherries and the tartness of the sumac with the creamy cheese. The sumac and purple basil are optional, but the colors make a beautiful presentation if you have them.

1 teaspoon whole black peppercorns

6 tablespoons red wine vinegar

¼ cup water

2 tablespoons sugar

½ teaspoon salt

1 sprig thyme

8 ounces (about 20) sweet cherries, pitted and cut in half

1 8-ounce ball burrata cheese

1 tablespoon ground sumac

Extra-virgin olive oil

½ cup fresh basil leaves, preferably opal

Good crusty bread, such as ciabatta

1 Tie the peppercorns in a small piece of cheesecloth or put them inside a metal tea ball. Combine the vinegar, water, sugar, salt, and thyme in a small saucepan. Bring to a boil, then reduce the heat and simmer until the sugar has dissolved. Add the cherries and cook just until they're heated through, about 2 minutes. Transfer to a glass or metal container and let cool. Cover and chill until ready to serve.

2 Place the cheese on a serving plate. Sprinkle with the sumac, letting some of it fall onto the plate. Scoop out some cherries with a slotted spoon, and spoon the cherries around the cheese. Drizzle with oil and serve with basil leaves and bread on the side.

> **TIMING TIP:**
> The cherries can be made up to 1 week ahead of time.

AVOCADO TAHINI DIP

SERVES 6 TO 8

We almost always include raw vegetables in our nibbles spreads (which my husband is mostly in charge of setting out), and this creamy dip makes crudités a little more exciting and indulgent. If you are prepping the vegetables in advance, store them in a container of lightly salted water in the fridge to crisp them up and add a little extra flavor.

2 avocados, quartered and cut into large chunks

¼ cup tahini

½ cup 2% plain Greek yogurt

3 tablespoons fresh lemon juice

1 small garlic clove, grated

¾ teaspoon salt

Few dashes of green hot sauce

½ teaspoon ground cumin

Small handful of fresh cilantro leaves (optional)

1 tablespoon toasted sesame seeds

1 tablespoon olive oil

Sliced raw fennel, carrots, or other seasonal vegetables

1 Place the avocado, tahini, yogurt, lemon juice, garlic, salt, hot sauce, and cumin in the bowl of a food processor. Pulse to combine, then process until completely smooth. Add the cilantro, if using, and pulse until finely chopped. Transfer to a serving bowl.

2 Scatter the toasted sesame seeds over the top and drizzle with the oil. Serve with sliced raw seasonal vegetables.

TIMING TIP:

Up to 3 hours ahead: Make the dip; store in the fridge with plastic wrap pressed onto the surface to prevent browning.

WHOLE GRAIN CUMIN CRACKERBREAD

MAKES 12

These big, amorphously beautiful crackers are easy to whip up, and will up your nibbles game by a lot. They are of course better than anything you can buy, and will keep well for a couple of days. You could change up the seeds to suit your taste, adding sesame or poppy in addition to or instead of the cumin. I especially like to scoop up Smoky Eggplant Dip (page 57) or Beet Hummus (page 61) with these.

FOR THE CRACKERS:

1½ cups whole-wheat flour

1½ cups all-purpose flour

2 teaspoons sugar

2 teaspoons salt

1 cup water

¼ cup extra-virgin olive oil

FOR THE EGG WASH AND TO TOP THE CRACKERS:

1 large egg yolk

2 tablespoons heavy cream or milk

2 to 3 teaspoons cumin seeds

2 to 3 teapsoons flaky sea salt

TIMING TIP:

The crackers can be made up to 3 days ahead and stored in an airtight container until serving.

1 Preheat the oven to 425°F. Line a baking sheet with parchment paper.

2 To make the crackers: Mix the whole-wheat and all-purpose flours, the sugar, and salt in a medium bowl. Combine the water and oil in a liquid measuring cup and drizzle into the dry ingredients in a steady stream, using a fork to mix as you go. When they are thoroughly combined, knead a few times on the countertop, until nice and smooth. Return to the bowl, cover with plastic wrap, and let rest for 15 minutes.

3 Divide the dough in half, keeping the half you're not working with covered and dividing the working piece in half again. Cut each half into 3 pieces, so you have 6 pieces total. Roll each piece into ⅛-inch-thick oblongs, about the width of your baking sheet (about 9½ by 3 inches). As you roll, transfer to the prepared baking sheet, fitting 3 per sheet.

4 To make the egg wash and top the crackers: Beat the yolk and cream together until thin and brushable. Use a pastry brush to very lightly brush each cracker. Immediately sprinkle with cumin seeds and salt.

5 Bake for 12 to 15 minutes, rotating and reversing the pans, until crisp and nut-brown but not burnt. Repeat, baking in batches, until all the dough is used. Let cool. They will become crispier as they cool.

CHARCOAL CRACKERS

MAKES ABOUT 24 STICKS OR 24 CRACKERS,
OR A COMBINATION OF BOTH

I was inspired, as I often am, by beautiful serving objects. In this case by this gorgeous blackened wood end grain board I own to create a black-and-white cheese board. Of course it had to have black crackers. Black foods are having a moment, and I usually am not one to slavishly follow a trend, but I couldn't resist on this one, as they create such a striking look. I really don't suggest ingesting large amounts of charcoal powder (as its "cleansing" effect extends to inadvertently absorbing any necessary medications you might be taking) as you might if drinking a black smoothie or eating a black ice cream cone, but it takes such a small amount to turn these crackers black that it shouldn't do anyone any harm. In fact, charcoal "biscuits" have been around in England for many years. Charcoal is easy to find online; just make sure you are ordering "food-grade" activated charcoal powder.

2 cups all-purpose flour

1 tablespoon activated charcoal powder

½ teaspoon kosher salt

1½ teaspoons baking powder

3 tablespoons cold unsalted butter, cut into pieces

½ to ¾ cup cold water

1 egg white, lightly beaten with a little water to thin

Poppy seeds or black sesame seeds, if making rounds

Flaky sea salt

TIMING TIP:

The crackers can be made up to 3 days ahead of time and stored in an airtight container until serving.

1 Preheat the oven to 350°F. Line a baking sheet with parchment paper.

2 Combine the flour, charcoal powder, kosher salt, and baking powder in the bowl of a food processor and pulse to combine. Add the butter and pulse until it resembles coarse meal. With the machine running, slowly stream in the water, stopping when the dough comes together in a mass.

3 Transfer the dough to a lightly floured surface and roll into a slightly thicker than ⅛-inch-thick, 12 x 12-inch square. For sticks, cut lengthwise into ¼-inch-thick strips. Roll back and forth between your hands a few times, then on the work surface to round and lengthen them. Place on the prepared baking sheet the long way. Alternatively, cut into rounds using a 2-inch cookie cutter and prick several times with a fork. Brush with the egg white and sprinkle with poppy seeds and flaky salt.

4 Bake for 18 to 20 minutes, until the crackers are firm and dry (they will continue to crisp as they cool). Cool completely, then store in an airtight container. Serve with bloomy rind and ash-covered goat cheeses, as well as other white cheeses, black grapes, and black figs for a black-and-white cheese board.

BOWL OF RED (TEXAS CHILI)

SERVES 6 TO 8

Any chili purist will tell you that chili does not contain beans or tomatoes. "That's soup," they might say. Soup is good too, but this here is chili: chunks of beef stewed with pureed chiles, hence the name. You could use pork shoulder in place of the beef if you prefer, but you might want to make it ahead so you can skim the hardened fat from the top. In any case, the beauty of this braised dish, like all braised dishes, is that it will only get better if made ahead of time, making it a perfect get-ahead dish. All you have to do when it's party time is heat it up slowly (in the same Dutch oven you cooked it in) and put out an array of garnishes for guests to make their own bowls. (See photo, page 2.)

2 ounces dried chiles, such as New Mexico, pasilla, guajillo, or ancho (about 6; use one or any combination)

2 dried árbol chiles

3 pounds beef chuck, cut into 1- to 2-inch pieces

Salt and freshly ground black pepper

3 tablespoons vegetable oil

1 medium onion, finely chopped

2 garlic cloves, chopped

1 tablespoon ground cumin

2 teaspoons dried oregano

One 12-ounce bottle dark beer

2 tablespoons masa harina

FOR SERVING:

Sliced scallions

Corn nuts

Grated sharp cheddar cheese

Sour cream

Lime wedges

Cilantro sprigs

Thinly sliced radishes

1 Break up the chiles and leave most of the seeds and stems behind. Place in a blender jar and pour 2 cups of boiling water over them. Let stand until the chiles are pliable and the liquid has cooled.

2 Meanwhile, pat the beef dry with paper towels and season well with salt and pepper. Heat 1 tablespoon of the oil in a large heavy skillet over high heat. Add half of the beef and cook until well browned on all sides, about 6 minutes. Transfer to a Dutch oven. Repeat with 1 tablespoon of the remaining oil and the remaining meat. Transfer to the Dutch oven.

3 Heat the remaining 1 tablespoon oil in the skillet and lower the heat to medium-low. Add the onion and garlic and cook until translucent, 8 to 10 minutes. Add the cumin, oregano, and 1 teaspoon salt.

recipe continues

I like to use a mix of chiles for the most complex flavor, and for balanced heat. Making a chile puree is simple once you know how, and forms the flavorful base for this chili and many sauces and soups. It's easy to break up the brittle and leathery chiles, leaving the stems and seeds behind.

4 Meanwhile, blend the chiles until smooth.

5 Add the beer to the skillet and bring to a boil, scraping the bottom of the pan. Add the chile puree and rinse the blender with 1 cup water. Add the liquid to the skillet.

6 Transfer the contents of the skillet to the Dutch oven and bring to a boil. Reduce the heat, cover, and simmer, stirring occasionally, for 2½ hours, or until the meat is tender. Remove the lid, increase the heat to high, and cook for 5 minutes to reduce it slightly. Move some of the meat to the side, stir the masa harina into the liquid, and simmer for a few more minutes to thicken. Season with salt. Serve immediately, or let cool and refrigerate until ready to serve. The flavor will improve as it sits.

BAKED PICI
WITH SAUSAGE RAGÙ

SERVES 8 TO 10

If you ever played with Play-Doh, you can make pici, the thick and chewy hand-rolled spaghetti from Siena. You have a couple of options when making this recipe. Although the pici are easy and fun to make, you might not always have the time or the inclination to do it. You can substitute any other pasta shape here, but broken bucatini will come the closest to handmade pici. You can serve the pasta right away after adding it to the sauce, but to serve it later, or the next day, you can turn it into an incredible baked pasta dish.

FOR THE PICI:

2 cups semolina flour, plus more
    for dusting

2 cups all-purpose flour

Pinch of salt

1 tablespoon extra-virgin olive oil

1¼ cups water

FOR THE SAUCE:

½ ounce dried porcini mushrooms

2 tablespoons extra-virgin olive oil

1 large or 2 small red onions,
    finely chopped

1 large or 2 small carrots, finely chopped

1 stalk celery, finely chopped

2 large sprigs thyme

3 or 4 garlic cloves, minced

1 pound sweet Italian sausage,
    removed from casings

½ cup dry red wine (or white if that's
    what you have open)

One 26-ounce box or can chopped or
    crushed tomatoes

¼ cup coarsely chopped fresh basil

Red pepper flakes

Salt and freshly ground black pepper

1 To make the pici: Combine the semolina flour, all-purpose flour, and salt in the bowl of a stand mixer fitted with the paddle attachment. Mix thoroughly on low speed. Combine the oil and water in a liquid measuring cup. With the mixer running on low speed, slowly add the water mixture until the dough comes together in one smooth mass. If there are still dry crumbly bits on the bottom of the bowl, add water 1 tablespoon at a time until it comes together. You want a fairly stiff dough that isn't sticky at all. Change to the dough hook and beat for a few minutes longer, until it looks smooth and pliable. Remove from the bowl and knead about 20 times on the counter, until nice and smooth. Avoid adding more flour unless it's sticky—you shouldn't need it. Place in a bowl, tightly cover with plastic wrap, and leave at room temperature to rest for 1 hour.

2 While the dough is resting, make the sauce: Place the mushrooms in a 1-cup liquid measuring cup. Pour boiling water over the mushrooms, filling the cup. Let stand until softened, about 15 minutes. Lift the mushrooms from the liquid and chop them. Set aside, reserving the liquid.

3 Heat a large, straight-sided skillet over medium heat. Add the oil, onion, carrot, celery, and thyme and stir to combine. Raise the heat if needed to get a good sizzle going, but be careful not to burn it. Adjust the heat as needed. Cook, stirring frequently, until golden brown and very soft, about 20 minutes. Add the garlic and mushrooms and cook until the garlic is golden and fragrant, about 5 minutes.

recipe and ingredients continue

TO FINISH:

1 cup heavy cream

½ cup panko breadcrumbs

2 tablespoons unsalted butter, melted

1 ounce (1 fluffy cup) grated
   Parmigiano-Reggiano cheese

¼ cup coarsely chopped fresh Italian
   parsley (optional)

4 Add the sausage and cook, stirring and breaking it up with a spoon, until browned, about 10 minutes. Add the wine and cook until absorbed, 2 to 3 minutes. Add the porcini liquid, the tomatoes, basil, and red pepper flakes (the sausage adds plenty of salt to this dish, so hold off until the end to add any additional salt). Bring to a boil, reduce the heat to maintain to a bare simmer, and cook for 45 minutes, or until thickened. Season with salt and pepper. Set aside.

5 While the sauce is cooking, start rolling the pasta: Cut the dough ball in half and cut one half into 4 pieces. Keep everything except one piece tightly covered under plastic wrap. Line a baking sheet with a clean dish towel and sprinkle with semolina flour. Roll a piece of dough into a long rectangle about 2 inches wide and about ¼ inch thick. Using a knife or bench scraper, cut off ¼-inch strips of dough. Using your hands, roll into little snake-like pieces that taper at the ends and are slightly thicker so that it's not too thick in the middle. They should be 4 to 5 inches long. It's better if you don't use flour—unless it's sticking, flour will make it harder to roll. Marble is the ideal surface. Transfer to a baking sheet. Continue in this way until all the dough has been rolled out (now is the time to enlist some help or turn on your favorite podcast), layering and sprinkling with more semolina as you go.

6 Bring a large pot of water to a rolling boil. Salt it generously and add the pasta. Return to a boil and cook, stirring, just until all the pasta floats to the top, 2 to 3 minutes. Scoop out 1 cup pasta water and drain the pasta. Add the pasta to the sauce and stir well to coat. If it seems at all dry, add some of the pasta water. Transfer to a 3-quart baking dish. At this point, you can cool and refrigerate and bake the next day.

7 Preheat the oven to 375°F. Remove the baking dish from the refrigerator at least 30 minutes before baking.

8 To finish, pour the cream evenly over the pasta. Combine the breadcrumbs and butter in a small bowl and add the cheese. Sprinkle over the top and bake for 35 to 45 minutes, until golden brown on top and bubbling around the edges. Garnish with the parsley (if using) and serve immediately.

TIMING TIPS:

- Up to 3 days ahead: Make the ragù and refrigerate.

- Up to 2 days ahead: Roll the pasta and refrigerate, tightly covered and well dusted with semolina.

- Up to 1 day ahead: Cook the pasta and combine with the sauce; transfer to a baking dish. Cover and refrigerate.

VIETNAMESE PORK TENDERLOIN

SERVES 4 TO 6

This simple grilled pork goes extremely well with the watermelon salad on page 225.

Two 1-pound pork tenderloins

Salt and freshly ground black pepper

¼ cup low-sodium soy sauce

2 tablespoons fish sauce

2 tablespoons sugar

½ teaspoon sriracha

2 small shallots, thinly sliced

1 Season the pork with salt and pepper. Whisk the soy sauce, fish sauce, sugar, sriracha, and shallots in a shallow baking dish. Add the pork and turn to coat. Cover and chill for at least 1 hour, and as long as overnight, turning halfway through.

2 Heat a grill to medium-high. Remove the pork from the marinade, scraping off excess, and grill on all sides, about 20 minutes, or until it reaches an internal temperature of 140°F. Let rest for 10 minutes before slicing.

TIMING TIPS:

• Up to 2 days ahead: Make the marinade and refrigerate.

• Up to 1 day ahead: Marinate the pork and refrigerate.

• Up to 2 hours ahead: Grill the pork; it is good at room temperature.

PORCHETTA CHOPS

SERVES 4

These take a few minutes to "dress," but once you do, they can be left to marinate in the fridge for up to a day until you're ready to cook them, making them perfect for an after-work dinner party or just a special family dinner. They also can be thrown on a medium-hot grill and cooked for 15 to 20 minutes, turning a few times. Once you've zested the orange, you might want to peel it, section it, and add it to the salad.

Four 1½-inch-thick center-cut, bone-in pork chops (about 3 pounds)

1¼ teaspoons salt

Freshly ground black pepper

6 teaspoons olive oil

4 garlic cloves, grated on a Microplane

Zest of 1 orange

1 large fennel bulb, fronds removed and reserved

2 tablespoons fresh rosemary leaves

16 fresh sage leaves

8 paper-thin slices pancetta (about 3 ounces)

1 tablespoon fresh lemon juice

1½ ounces shaved Parmigiano-Reggiano cheese

1 Season the chops on both sides with 1 teaspoon of the salt and plenty of pepper. Rub with 2 teaspoons of the oil, the garlic, and orange zest. Sprinkle both sides of the chops with some of the fennel fronds, rosemary, and 2 sage leaves on each side. Arrange 1 slice of pancetta on each side of each chop and tie it on securely using 2 pieces of crisscrossing butcher's twine. Chill until ready to cook.

2 Preheat the oven to 375°F. Bring pork to room temperature for 30 minutes.

3 Heat a large (12-inch) skillet with an ovenproof handle over medium-high heat. Add 2 teaspoons of the remaining oil, then add the chops. Cook until deeply browned on the first side, 8 to 10 minutes, then turn and cook for 5 minutes on the second side. Transfer to the oven and cook for 5 to 10 minutes longer, until they reach an internal temperature of 130°F. Let rest for 5 minutes before serving. Remove the strings.

4 Quarter the fennel bulb lengthwise and thinly slice it on a mandoline. Toss with the lemon juice, the remaining 2 teaspoons oil, and the remaining ¼ teaspoon salt. Top with the shaved cheese. Grind black pepper over top. Serve the salad alongside the chops.

TIP:

Most small cuts of meat, like chops, are cooked using what I call 8-5-5 timing. Eight minutes on the first side in a pan, 5 minutes on the second side, and then 5 minutes in a hot oven. You might need a few minutes more or less, but this is a good rule of thumb.

TIMING TIPS:

• Up to 1 day ahead: Prepare the chops and let them marinate in the refrigerator.

• Up to a few hours ahead: Trim the fennel bulbs.

• At the last minute: Cook the pork chops and make the salad.

PORK RACK ROAST WITH GRAINY MUSTARD AND ROSEMARY

SERVES 6

Pork loin is a great cut to serve a lot of people (and on the cheap too!), but it is so easy to overcook. That's why I love a bone-in pork loin—the bones keep the meat moist and juicy. You might have to special order one from your butcher (or ask for it at the butcher counter in your supermarket), but fortunately for me, this is a cut my regular supermarket always has in the case. To ensure a really juicy and flavorful roast, I brine it too, which of course requires a little forethought, but it's easy. You could skip the brine if you're not a planner, but if you want the oohs and aahs, I highly recommend it. While the roast is resting, carve it off the bones, cut up the bones, and return them to the oven to crisp so everyone gets a nice crispy bone to gnaw on.

FOR THE BRINE:

¼ cup light brown sugar

¼ cup salt

3 large garlic cloves, smashed

2 bay leaves

3 small sprigs rosemary

1 tablespoon juniper berries

1 teaspoon whole black peppercorns

2 cups water

FOR THE ROAST:

One 5- to 6-pound bone-in pork loin roast (7 bones)

Freshly ground black pepper

1 tablespoon olive oil

¼ cup grainy mustard

½ cup roughly chopped fresh rosemary

2 tablespoons dried herbes de Provence

1 To make the brine: Combine the sugar, salt, garlic, bay leaves, rosemary, juniper berries, peppercorns, and water in a small saucepan. Bring to a boil over high heat. Remove from the heat, transfer to a bowl, add 3 cups of ice, and stir to cool the brine completely. Place the roast in a large (2-gallon) resealable plastic bag. Place the bag in a wide bowl and carefully pour the brine into the bag. Seal the bag and refrigerate for at least 8 hours and as long as 12 hours, turning every few hours.

2 When you are ready to cook the meat, preheat the oven to 375°F.

3 Drain the brine and pick off any peppercorns and juniper berries. Pat dry and place in a small roasting pan. Season with plenty of pepper on all sides and rub with the oil and mustard. Pat on the rosemary and herbes de Provence. Arrange the roast bone-side down on the pan and roast for 1 to 1½ hours, until it reads 145°F on an instant-read thermometer. Remove from the oven, transfer to a carving board, and let rest for 10 minutes.

recipe continues

4 Turn the oven to broil. Trim the roast from the bones, cutting them into individual ribs, and broil the ribs until crisp, 8 to 10 minutes.

5 Slice the roast and serve with the bones.

> **TIMING TIPS:**
>
> • Up to 1 day ahead: Brine the pork; refrigerate.
>
> • Up to 6 hours ahead: Drain the roast, coat with the rub, and refrigerate again.
>
> • About 2 hours ahead: Cook the roast.

GRILLED BOHEMIAN STEAK WITH GARLIC SCAPES

SERVES 6

Depending on where you live, and what kind of mood your butcher is in, you might find this cut going by any number of names. They might not all be exactly the same cut, but the results will be similar—a flavorful, juicy, beefy-tasting steak that's quick to cook and easy to slice. The so-called Bohemian steak is the flap of the porterhouse, so just ask for that. Bavette is similar if not the same, and failing that, use skirt steak, hanger steak, or flank steak—any of them will work well! Garlic scapes are the bright-green curly flower stems that grow from the tops of hardneck garlic. Farmers lop them off to help the garlic grow, and you'll find them in your local farmer's market. What I love about garlic scapes, which are plentiful from late spring through the middle of summer, is that they can be used in so many different ways. Finely minced, they can be used to start any sauté, as you would with garlic or onion, or they can be pulverized to make a flavorful butter to melt onto steaks, and they are delicious as a whole vegetable, grilled for just a few minutes until charred. Leftover charred scapes can be chopped up and added to eggs, salads, or pesto; whizzed into a vinaigrette or marinade; or mixed into just about anything. Leftover scape butter can be used to start any sauté, to make garlic bread, or to melt into pasta, among many other uses.

FOR THE SCAPE BUTTER:

6 garlic scapes

½ cup (1 stick) unsalted butter, softened

½ teaspoon flaky sea salt

FOR THE STEAKS:

2 pounds Bohemian steak, skirt steak, or flank steak

Salt and freshly ground black pepper

1 bunch garlic scapes

Olive oil

1 Make the scape butter: Cut the scapes into 1- to 2-inch pieces, trimming off the very bottom and the pointed tops. Add the scapes to the bowl of a mini food processor and pulse until very finely chopped. Add the butter and salt and continue pulsing until well combined. Scrape onto the bottom third of a piece of parchment paper, fold the parchment over the blob of butter, and use the rim of the short side of a baking sheet to form a log; hold down the bottom part of the parchment but not the top part. It naturally will form a log as you gently push with the baking sheet. Twist the ends and chill until firm.

2 Prepare the steak: Season the steak liberally with salt and pepper. Rub with enough oil to coat lightly. Trim just the bottoms of the bunch of scapes, leaving the pointed tops. Toss with enough oil to lightly coat and sprinkle with salt and pepper.

recipe continues

3 Heat a grill to medium-high and grill the steaks for 3 to 4 minutes on each side, until nicely charred. Let rest for 5 minutes off the heat. Throw the scapes on the grill for the last 2 to 3 minutes of cooking and grill, turning, until lightly charred all over. Add 1 tablespoon of scape butter to the top of each steak and slice the steaks across the grain. Serve with the grilled garlic scapes.

TIMING TIPS:

- Up to 2 weeks ahead: Make the scape butter and refrigerate; freeze if making it more than 3 days ahead.

- Up to 2 hours ahead: Season the steak and trim the garlic scapes.

- At the last minute: Grill the steak and scapes.

ITALIAN-ISH RIBS

SERVES 6 TO 8

Ribs don't have to be reserved for summer barbecues—these ribs are inspired by Italian flavors and can be done completely in the oven, but if you have an outdoor smoker, that's a great way to cook them too. Ribs are pretty forgiving, and I am giving you several options for cooking and finishing them. I have had a wood pellet smoker for the last few years, and it is the perfect way to cook ribs outdoors, but you also can set up a basic kettle grill as a smoker using indirect heat, made especially easy with briquette holders that keep the charcoal off to the sides. Serve with Not Actually Baked Cranberry Beans (page 282).

FOR THE RIBS:

10 to 12 garlic cloves (about 1 head)

½ cup loosely packed fresh rosemary leaves

½ cup loosely packed fresh sage leaves

½ cup loosely packed fresh Italian parsley leaves

5 tablespoons olive oil

2 tablespoons light brown sugar

1 teaspoon ground coriander

1 teaspoon red pepper flakes

3 tablespoons fennel seeds

2 tablespoons smoked paprika

2 tablespoons plus 1 teaspoon salt

Freshly ground black pepper

2 racks pork spare ribs (about 4 pounds each)

1 To make the marinade: Place the garlic in a mini food processor and pulse until finely chopped. Add the rosemary, sage, parsley, and oil and pulse until the herbs are well chopped. Add the brown sugar, coriander, red pepper flakes, fennel seeds, smoked paprika, and 1 teaspoon of the salt and season with pepper.

2 Peel the membrane off of the underside of the rib racks—start by peeling a little off and then grabbing it with a paper towel; it should come off in big pieces. Season the ribs evenly with the remaining 2 tablespoons salt and lots of pepper. Rub both sides with the marinade. Let sit for 1 hour at room temperature or refrigerate overnight. Remove from the fridge about 1 hour before cooking.

3 To make the sauce: Heat a small (8-inch) skillet over medium-high heat and melt the butter in the oil. Add the onion and cook, stirring occasionally, until golden brown, 6 to 8 minutes. Combine the red wine, vinegar, and water in a measuring cup and deglaze the pan with the mixture, stirring and letting it reduce to a glaze. Add the honey, tomato sauce, salt, and red pepper flakes and bring to a simmer. Cook for 20 minutes, adding water if needed if it gets too thick, until it looks like a brushable glaze.

4 Depending on how you're going to be cooking the ribs, preheat the oven to 275°F or prepare your smoker and set it to 275°F.

recipe and ingredients continue

FOR THE SAUCE:

1 teaspoon unsalted butter

1 teaspoon olive oil

1 small onion, peeled and grated on the
    large holes of a box grater

¼ cup red wine

2 tablespoons balsamic or red wine
    vinegar

¼ cup water

2 tablespoons honey

1 cup tomato sauce

¼ teaspoon salt

Big pinch of red pepper flakes

5 If cooking in the oven, line a baking sheet with heavy-duty foil and fit a flat cooling rack inside the sheet (you probably will need two depending on the size of the racks). Place the ribs on top of the rack(s). If you don't have an appropriate rack, don't worry about it—just put the racks straight onto the foil. Roast for 3 to 4 hours, until the meat easily yields to a pressing finger or a small paring knife slides in easily when poked and the meat shreds a little. During the last 30 minutes of cooking—when the ribs feel done or almost done (an extra 30 minutes won't overcook them)—brush both sides of the racks with the sauce and return to the oven.

6 If cooking in a smoker, lay the ribs directly on the rack of the smoker. Cook for 2 hours, spraying occasionally with water or a mixture of water and cider vinegar (this will help keep them moist). At this point, they should be deeply burnished and fairly tender. If not, continue cooking until they are. Brush with the sauce, wrap each rack tightly in foil, and continue cooking for 1 to 2 hours, until the ribs flop over when picked up in the center with tongs. If making ahead, this step can be completed in the oven. If they still are stiff, cook them a bit longer. Let rest in the foil for 30 minutes. Unwrap the ribs and run them under the broiler briefly to tighten the sauce.

7 If the ribs were cooked in the oven, they can be served as is, or they can be finished on the grill. Heat a grill to medium. Place a piece of heavy-duty foil right on the grill. Place the racks on the foil and cook for about 5 minutes on each side, until caramelized.

TIMING TIPS:

- Up to 2 days ahead: Make the rub and refrigerate. Make the sauce.

- Up to 2 days ahead: Marinate the ribs with the rub and refrigerate.

- Up to 1 day ahead: Cook the ribs and refrigerate, especially if cooking in the oven and finishing on the grill. Either way, the cooked ribs will reheat beautifully wrapped in foil and heated in a 300°F oven.

KOREAN SHORT RIBS WITH KIMCHI AND ASIAN PEAR SALAD

SERVES 8

If you haven't bought short ribs before, you might be confused about the cuts—what you want are English-cut ribs, which will look like a big single bone with the meat running on top of it, as opposed to what's usually referred to as flanken, where you'll see three or four oval-shaped crosscut bones at the side of the cut. The meat nearly always falls completely off the bone, but if you want to keep it together for presentation purposes, just tie it in two spots with kitchen string. It does look nice, and maybe it cooks better too? The great thing about braises is that you can cook them way ahead of time—even freeze them for a few weeks—which means you can cook a mean dinner with very little last-minute fuss.

FOR THE SHORT RIBS:

6 pounds English-cut short ribs (8 pieces)

1 teaspoon salt

Freshly ground black pepper

2 tablespoons grapeseed or other neutral vegetable oil

1 onion, thinly sliced

4 tablespoons mirin

3 large garlic cloves, minced

2 tablespoons grated fresh ginger

1 Asian pear or crisp apple, grated (on the big holes of a box grater)

4 black garlic cloves (optional)

2 tablespoons low-sodium soy sauce

3 tablespoons gochujang

4 cups unsalted beef stock

1 tablespoon veal demi-glace concentrate (see page 16; optional)

2 cups short-grain brown rice, cooked in 3½ cups water, for serving

4 scallions (white and green parts), trimmed and thinly sliced

2 tablespoons black sesame seeds

1 Preheat the oven to 300°F.

2 To make the short ribs: Season the ribs with the salt and pepper and tie each rib with two pieces of kitchen twine.

3 Heat a 6-quart Dutch oven and a large (12-inch) nonstick skillet over medium-high heat. Divide the oil between the two pans. Add half of the short ribs to each pan bone-side up and sear until deeply browned, 7 to 10 minutes. Turn and continue to brown on all sides, another 8 to 10 minutes. Transfer the ribs to a baking sheet and pour out and discard all but 1 tablespoon of the fat from the Dutch oven. Pour all the fat out of the skillet.

4 Add the onions to the Dutch oven, reduce the heat to medium, and cook until soft and golden, 8 to 10 minutes. Deglaze the skillet with 2 tablespoons of the mirin. Add to the onions along with the remaining 2 tablespoons mirin. Add the garlic and ginger and cook until fragrant, 2 to 3 minutes. Add the grated pear, black garlic (if using), soy sauce, and gochujang to the pot and stir to combine. Arrange the ribs in a single layer, bones up (if possible), and add the stock and veal demi-glace (if using). Add 1 cup water if needed to cover the ribs. Bring to a boil over

recipe and ingredients continue

FOR THE SALAD:

1 Asian pear or crisp apple

1 cup cabbage kimchi, shredded

1 watermelon radish, ¼ daikon radish,
    or 6 to 8 red radishes, thinly sliced

high heat, cover, and place in the oven. After 1½ hours, remove from the oven and gently rearrange and turn the ribs. Return to the oven, checking every 30 minutes and removing the ribs as soon as they are tender. If you are making the ribs ahead of time, undercook them slightly, as they will cook a little as they cool and again when you reheat them.

5 Carefully remove the ribs and place them in a container. Cover the surface of the meat with plastic wrap to keep them from drying out. Let cool and refrigerate. Pour the liquid into a tall container. Let cool and refrigerate.

6 The next day, remove and discard the hardened fat from the liquid (if cooking right away, skim as much fat as you can from the top of the braising liquid). Pour into a Dutch oven and bring to a boil over medium-high heat. Lower the heat to medium and cook until slightly thickened, 7 to 10 minutes. Return the meat to the sauce, reduce the heat to low, and cook until the meat is heated through, about 15 minutes (you also can hold it in a 250° oven at this point).

7 To make the salad: Core the Asian pear and thinly shave it on a mandoline into a serving bowl. Toss with the kimchi, using a little of the kimchi liquid to coat. Thinly shave the radish and toss with the pear and kimchi.

8 To serve: Plate the ribs, along with a ladle of sauce, over brown rice, with the salad on top. Sprinkle with scallions and sesame seeds and serve.

TIMING TIPS:

- Up to 2 weeks ahead: Make the short ribs; freeze the meat and sauce separately. (Defrost in the fridge 1 day before serving.) If not freezing, make up to 3 days ahead and store in the fridge.

- Up to 2 hours ahead: Remove the ribs and sauce from the fridge; make the rice.

- Up to 1 hour ahead: Reheat the ribs on the stovetop and keep warm until serving time.

- Up to 30 minutes ahead: Crisp the rice.

- At the last minute: Make the salad.

FRENCH BEEF STEW

SERVES 8

Yes, in French, it's Boeuf Bourguignon, and I've had a lot of practice making it, both in real life and in my professional life. When I was the culinary consultant and food stylist on the film *Julie & Julia*, it was the dish I made the most often, so I got pretty good at making it and pretty good at making it look good too (once I had to make it look bad, which was hard). What I've discovered over time is that I really love the sauce and don't need to eat that much meat to be really satisfied, so I stretch this to feed more people by making room for a lot more vegetables than the classic. I also like jazzing it up with a more exotic array of mushrooms if I can get my hands on them, especially the mighty, meaty maitake, which drinks up the sauce luxuriously, but if not, I still like using a meatier mushroom than the classic button mushroom, and supermarket portobellos do just fine. I also like cutting the meat into larger pieces, so I suggest you buy one large whole chuck roast and cut it into 8 pieces for cooking. After it's braised and tender, it can be pulled apart into smaller pieces for serving, which again allows the more tender and open surface of the meat to absorb more of the flavor of the sauce. There's just one more thing I need to tell you—try to find some demi-glace concentrate to use here (see page 16), as it goes a long way in enriching and improving both the flavor and color of the sauce. Serve over Oven-Baked Polenta (page 273), mashed potatoes, buttered egg noodles, or with lots of crusty bread.

3 pounds beef chuck, cut into eight 2-inch-thick pieces 4 to 5 inches across

Salt and freshly ground black pepper

1 tablespoon unsalted butter

2 tablespoons olive oil

4 garlic cloves, very finely chopped

1 small onion, finely chopped

1 tablespoon tomato paste

2 tablespoons all-purpose flour

One 750-ml bottle dry red wine

2 cups water or unsalted beef stock

1 tablespoon demi-glace concentrate (optional; see page 16)

2 bay leaves

1 large sprig thyme

1 Preheat the oven to 325°F.

2 Season the beef with 1 teaspoon salt and a light coating of pepper. Heat a large (7-quart) Dutch oven over high heat. Add the butter and oil and brown the meat (in batches if necessary so it's in an uncrowded single layer) on all sides, turning every 3 to 4 minutes, for 10 minutes per batch. Turn more often as needed, and lower heat to prevent scorching as meat heats up. Transfer to a plate as you finish. Turn off heat to let pot cool a little, then return to medium-low heat. Add the garlic and onion and cook until softened, 10 to 12 minutes. Add the tomato paste and brown it on the bottom of the pan for 2 to 3 minutes. Return all the meat and the accumulated juices to the pan.

3 Add the flour and stir it in. Add the wine, water, demi-glace (if using), the bay leaves, and thyme and scrape the bottom of

recipe and ingredients continue

6 to 8 ounces slab bacon, cut into
½ by 1-inch pieces

1 pound small cippolini or white pearl
onions, peeled

2 bunches baby carrots (or small,
thin carrots)

1 tablespoon olive oil

8 ounces cremini, quartered and/or
portobello mushrooms, cut into 1-inch
pieces

8 ounces maitake or oyster mushrooms,
trimmed and sliced

3 tablespoons chopped fresh Italian
parsley

the pot with a wooden spoon to loosen any browned bits. Add
1 teaspoon salt, ¾ teaspoon pepper, and bring to a boil.

4   Cover the pot and transfer to the oven. After 1½ hours,
rearrange the meat and return to the oven with the lid askew
(this will allow the sauce to evaporate and thicken). Cook for
another 1 to 1½ hours, for a total of 2½ to 3 hours, until the meat
is very tender and the sauce has some body. It will continue
to cook as it cools and again when it's reheated. At this point,
remove from oven and cool slightly. Using two forks, shred the
meat into smaller serving pieces. Discard bay leaf and thyme
stems. If serving right away, keep warm over low heat, covered.

5   About an hour before serving, preheat the oven to 425°F.

6   Spread the bacon out on a rimmed baking sheet and place
it in the oven. After the bacon has begun to render and is
beginning to brown on the edges, about 8 minutes, pour off the
rendered fat, stir the bacon and add the onions and carrots
to the pan. Season very lightly with salt and pepper and roast
for 20 to 25 minutes minutes, stirring hallway through until
vegetables are tender and golden brown and bacon is crisp. On
a separate baking sheet, toss both mushrooms with the oil and
season lightly with salt and pepper. Place in the oven and bake
for 30 to 35 minutes, stirring occasionally, until golden and crispy.

7   To serve, stir some of the vegetables and bacon into the stew,
and adjust seasonings. Scatter the rest of the vegetables on top,
and sprinkle with the parsley.

TIP:

To peel cippolini or pearl onions, plunge
into boiling water for 1 minute. Drain and
rinse with cold water. They will be much
easier to peel.

TIMING TIPS:

- Up to 2 weeks ahead: Braise the meat, cool, and freeze.
  If not freezing, make up to 3 days ahead and store in the
  fridge.

- Up to 1 day ahead: Peel the cippolini onions.

- Up to 4 hours ahead: Prep the remaining vegetables;
  chop the parsley.

- Up to 1 hour ahead: Reheat the meat; roast the vegetables.

- At the last minute: Stir in the vegetables; sprinkle with
  the parsley.

OSSO BUCO SUGO WITH ORANGE GREMOLATA

SERVES 6 TO 8

This braise should be in everyone's back pocket—it is beyond delicious, and absolutely foolproof to make. Veal shanks are pretty pricey, so serving one per person is not only costly, but honestly, more meat than most people really want to eat in one sitting. With this recipe, you get all of the deep rich flavors of this classic braise in a sauce that serves as many people with half as much meat and that can be served mixed with pappardelle or over polenta. If you want to make this way ahead of time and freeze it, it reheats beautifully, and no one will ever know. Even if you don't freeze it, as with all braises, it's even better made at least one day ahead, making this very, very quick to get on to the table for guests.

1 ounce (about 1 cup) dried porcini mushrooms

3 pounds veal shank, 2 inches thick (about 3 pieces)

Salt and freshly ground black pepper

2 tablespoons olive oil

1 large onion, finely chopped

3 garlic cloves, minced

1 large carrot, diced (about ½ cup)

1 tablespoon coarsely chopped fresh rosemary

2 tablespoons tomato paste

1 cup dry red wine

1 sprig fresh thyme

1 bay leaf

1 strip orange peel

2 cups (one 17- or 18-ounce package or jar) crushed tomatoes

2 cups water or unsalted chicken or beef stock

1 tablespoon demi-glace concentrate (optional; see page 16)

Red pepper flakes

1 pound pappardelle, cooked

Grated Parmigiano-Reggiano cheese

Orange Gremolata (recipe follows)

1 Place the mushrooms in a 1-cup liquid measuring cup. Pour boiling water over the mushrooms, filling the cup. Let stand until softened, about 15 minutes. Lift the mushrooms from the liquid and chop. Set aside, reserving the liquid.

2 Season the veal shanks with 1½ teaspoons salt and 1 teaspoon pepper. Heat 1 tablespoon of the oil in a medium (4-quart) Dutch oven over medium-high heat and brown the shanks well on all sides, about 20 minutes total. Transfer to a plate.

3 Add the remaining 1 tablespoon oil, the onion, garlic, carrot, and rosemary to the Dutch oven. Reduce the heat to medium and cook, stirring often, until golden and soft, 8 to 10 minutes. Reduce the heat if it threatens to burn. Lift the porcini from the water, reserving the water. Squeeze dry and finely chop the porcini. Add to the onion mixture and cook for 3 to 4 minutes more. Add the tomato paste and cook until lightly browned, 1 to 2 minutes.

4 Add the wine and stir to deglaze, scraping up any browned bits from the bottom of the pan with a wooden spoon. Let it reduce until almost all the liquid is gone. Add the porcini liquid, the thyme, bay leaf, and orange peel. Add the tomatoes, the porcini liquid, water (pour it into the package or jar to rinse it out), and demi-glace (if using). Add 1 teaspoon salt and a healthy

recipe continues

When finishing a pasta dish, it is always best to undercook the pasta a little and add the pasta to the hot sauce, rather than the other way around. Heating everything together allows the pasta to absorb the flavors of the sauce and gets everything piping hot. Always reserve a little pasta water in case it's needed to loosen the sauce.

pinch of red pepper flakes. Turn the heat to high and bring to a boil. Return the meat to the pan (along with any accumulated juices), decrease the heat to low, cover, and simmer (make sure it stays at a bare simmer) until the meat is very tender and falling off the bone, 2½ to 3 hours. Let the shanks cool in the sauce for 30 minutes. Remove the shanks from the sauce and put them on a plate to cool slightly. Remove and discard the orange peel and thyme stems. Remove the meat from the bones, shredding it slightly as you go. Return it to the sauce, along with the marrow from the bones. Simmer the sauce for a bit if it needs thickening. Season with salt, pepper, and red pepper flakes. When ready to serve, toss the pasta with the sauce. Serve with the cheese and gremolata.

TIMING TIPS:

- Up to 2 weeks ahead: Make the shanks, cool, and freeze. If not freezing, make up to 3 days ahead and refrigerate.

- 1 day ahead: Defrost the sugo in the fridge.

- Up to 2 hours ahead: Make the gremolata.

- 1 hour ahead: Reheat the sugo.

- At the last minute: Cook the pasta and combine with the sugo.

ORANGE GREMOLATA

⅓ cup chopped fresh Italian parsley

3 large garlic cloves, finely minced

Zest of 1 large orange

In a medium bowl, combine the parsley, garlic, and orange zest.

SLOW-ROASTED LAMB SHOULDER WITH POMEGRANATE MOLASSES

SERVES 4 TO 6

Lamb shoulder is a great cut to make for a small crowd. The meat is very rich, so a little goes a long way, but you can cook two at once using the same method if you have more people to feed. I like to serve it with light and crunchy sides like Freekeh Salad with Pickled Onions, Feta, and Herbs (page 272). Like a pork shoulder, it is slow cooked until very tender, so it is impossible to overcook and easy to reheat. You might have to special order this cut; it should have just a blade bone in the center.

1 semi-boneless lamb shoulder
   (6 to 7 pounds)

1 tablespoon salt

Freshly ground black pepper

2 tablespoons olive oil

2 teaspoons ground cumin

⅓ cup fresh rosemary leaves

Juice of 1 lemon

4 large garlic cloves, sliced

1 large onion, sliced ¼ inch thick

1 cup white wine

¼ cup pomegranate molasses

1   Season the lamb with salt and pepper and rub it with the oil. Rub on the cumin, rosemary, lemon juice, and garlic. Put it all in a resealable plastic bag, refrigerate, and let marinate overnight.

2   Preheat the oven to 325°F. Line a 9 x 13-inch roasting pan with foil.

3   Remove the lamb from refrigerator 30 minutes before roasting. Scatter the onions over the bottom of the prepared roasting pan. Place the lamb in the pan, pour in the wine, cover tightly with foil, and roast for 2½ to 3 hours, until the meat yields when pressed. Pour off most of the liquid. Pour the pomegranate molasses over the top. Continue cooking uncovered for about 1 hour, basting frequently, until extremely tender and glazed.

TIMING TIPS:

- Up to 2 days ahead: Marinate the lamb and refrigerate.

- At least 4 hours ahead: Start cooking the meat.

- 1 hour ahead: Gently rewarm the meat, covered, if it's cooled.

CENTERPIECES

POULTRY

ROSEY HARISSA CHICKEN

SERVES 4

There are so many things I want to tell you about this chicken. First of all, an overnight soak in kefir renders the flesh juicy and tender, and the harissa deeply flavors the meat and the sauce—oh, the sauce—that is one of the highlights here. The sliced chicken should be served in the very flavorful sauce that is created by letting everything in the pan start to dry out and caramelize, and then deglazing, again and again, and then enriching with the roasted lemon and soft roasted garlic. Roses are often used in Middle Eastern cooking, and when New York Shuk came out with its Rosey Harissa seasoning, which is a dry version of harissa, it inspired me to take this recipe a step further. Of course you can skip the Rosey Harissa, but then you won't have such a good excuse (as I did) to sprinkle dried rose petals all over your chicken. There are many excellent brands of harissa (see page 14) available now, and they vary greatly in heat. When you taste the final sauce, you can decide if it needs more harissa stirred in at the very end.

1½ tablespoons plus 1 teaspoon salt

2 teaspoons freshly ground black pepper

One 4- to 5-pound chicken

¾ cup kefir

¼ cup fresh lemon juice

4 garlic cloves, grated on a Microplane

1 tablespoon fresh thyme leaves or 1 teaspoon dried thyme

3 tablespoons harissa, plus more to taste

2 large or 4 small shallots, cut in half with skin on (about 4 ounces)

1 head garlic

½ lemon

3 to 4 sprigs fresh thyme

1½ tablespoons New York Shuk–brand Rosey Harissa or paprika

Dried edible rose petals or rose buds (optional)

1 Combine 1½ tablespoons of the salt and the pepper in a small bowl. Place the chicken in a wide, shallow work bowl and season it inside and out with the mixture. Separate the skin from the breast.

2 In a separate bowl, combine the kefir, lemon juice, grated garlic, the remaining 1 teaspoon salt, the thyme leaves, and plain harissa. Place the chicken in a 1-gallon resealable plastic bag. Pour the mixture over the chicken and use a rubber spatula to help coat the chicken all over, inside and out, with the mixture. Push some of the marinade under the skin. Squeeze as much of the air out of the bag as possible. Refrigerate for at least 8 hours and up to 24 hours, turning occasionally.

3 Preheat the oven to 400°F.

4 Scatter the shallots in a small roasting pan or other heavy 9 by 13-inch pan. Remove the chicken from the marinade and let the excess coating drip off, leaving a thin coating, and put it in the pan. Cut off the top third of the garlic head. Put the large part facedown in the pan and the small part in the cavity. Put the lemon half cut-side down in the pan. Sprinkle the thyme sprigs on top. Add ¼ cup water to the pan.

recipe continues

5 Roast the chicken for 45 minutes, then reduce the oven temperature to 350°F.

6 Sprinkle the chicken with the Rosey Harissa and start basting with whatever juices have collected in the pan and in the cavity. Roast, basting every 15 minutes or so and adding ¼ cup water if the pan looks dry, until the leg feels very loose when jiggled, 1 hour and 30 minutes to 1 hour and 45 minutes. The idea is to let it dry a little so the flavors and juices caramelize but do not burn. Always add ¼ cup water before it starts to burn.

7 Transfer the chicken to a carving board to rest. Squeeze the lemon and garlic into the pan juices and mash the shallots with a fork. Strain the juices through a mesh sieve, pressing hard on the solids to extract all the juice. Spoon off some of the grease, if needed. Whisk in extra harissa if you want extra heat.

8 Pour the jus on a platter. Carve the chicken and arrange it on the platter to soak up the sauce but maintain the crispy skin. Crush the rose petals over the top of the chicken, if using.

BAKED TURKEY-SPINACH MEATBALLS

PROJECT

SERVES 6 TO 8

While it definitely takes a little time to put this dish together, the beauty is that it is completely together ahead of time. It can be made up to two days in advance, so all that's left to do before serving dinner is turn on the oven and make Oven-Baked Polenta (page 273) and a salad, like the Simple but Exceptional Green Salad (page 238). And just about everybody likes meatballs, making this a perfectly cozy dish for a chilly evening. Feel free to use any ground meat here—I've come to like the lightness of turkey, and the pancetta adds fat and flavor, but beef, pork, or veal, or any combination is fine too.

FOR THE MEATBALLS:

8 ounces baby spinach

1¼ teaspoons plus a pinch of salt

1 cup fresh white breadcrumbs (made from 3 slices crustless white sandwich bread)

2 large eggs, lightly beaten

1 garlic clove, grated on a Microplane

1 medium yellow onion, very finely chopped

1 ounce (1 fluffy cup) grated Parmigiano-Reggiano cheese

1 tablespoon finely chopped fresh rosemary

½ cup finely chopped fresh Italian parsley

Big pinch of crushed red pepper flakes, or to taste

1 teaspoon dried oregano

¼ cup pre-diced or sliced pancetta, finely minced

2 pounds 93% lean ground turkey

4 tablespoons olive oil

1 To make the meatballs: Pour 1 inch of water into a large saucepan. Add the spinach and a pinch of salt, cover, and cook over medium-high heat. After 2 to 3 minutes, toss with tongs and replace the cover. Repeat as needed until the spinach is completely wilted, about 5 minutes. Drain and rinse with cold water. Squeeze as much water out as you can with your hands, and then squeeze really dry with a clean tea towel (you can line it with a paper towel to keep the tea towel cleaner) by twisting the ends. Finely chop the spinach.

2 Line a baking sheet with parchment paper. In a large bowl, combine the spinach, breadcrumbs, eggs, garlic, onion, Parmigiano cheese, rosemary, parsley, red pepper flakes, oregano, the remaining 1¼ teaspoons salt, and the pancetta. Mix well using a large fork. Add the turkey and mix really, really well using your hands. If this makes you squeamish, wear plastic gloves or use a stand mixer with the paddle attached to combine the breadcrumb mixture with the meat (just don't overmix, and put the bowl and paddle in the dishwasher afterward).

3 Form into about twenty-eight 2- to 2½-ounce meatballs, putting them on the parchment-lined baking sheet as you form them. Heat 2 large (12-inch) skillets over medium-high heat and add 2 tablespoons of the oil to each. Divide the meatballs between the pans and cook until browned on all sides, turning as they brown, for a total of 10 to 12 minutes (or you can cook in consecutive batches if you have only one pan).

recipe and ingredients continue

FOR THE SAUCE:

4 garlic cloves, thinly sliced

½ cup red wine

Half of a 26.5-ounce box or 28-ounce can strained tomatoes (reserve remaining tomatoes for a later use)

Half of a 26.5-ounce box or 28-ounce can chopped tomatoes (reserve remaining tomatoes for a later use)

6 large fresh basil leaves, torn

1 teaspoon dried oregano

¼ teaspoon red pepper flakes, or to taste

½ teaspoon salt

Freshly ground black pepper

TO FINISH:

8 ounces fresh mozzarella cheese

1 ounce (1 fluffy cup) grated Parmigiano-Reggiano cheese

Fresh basil leaves, torn

4 Transfer the meatballs to a large, deep baking dish or shallow Dutch oven with a lid. Blot the grease from one of the skillets and deglaze with the wine. Cook over high heat, scraping up all the browned bits and letting the wine reduce by half, 1 to 2 minutes. Set aside.

5 Preheat the oven to 350°F.

6 To make the sauce: Add the garlic to the empty pan and cook over medium heat until the garlic is golden, 5 to 6 minutes. Add the wine from the other pan and reduce the wine until it is almost evaporated. Add the tomatoes, basil, oregano, red pepper flakes, salt, and pepper to taste and bring to a simmer. Simmer for 10 minutes, then ladle the sauce over the meatballs. Cover the baking dish (if it doesn't have a lid, crimp tightly with heavy-duty foil), set it on a parchment paper– or foil-lined baking sheet (you'll thank me later for this), and bake for 1 hour.

7 Remove from the oven and turn the heat up to 425°F.

8 To finish, tear or chop the mozzarella cheese and layer it over the top, sprinkle with the Parmigiano cheese, and return to the oven, uncovered, until the cheese is melted and spotted with brown and the sauce is thickened, about 12 minutes. Run under the broiler if you want to get it more browned on top.

9 Sprinkle with torn basil leaves and serve immediately with polenta (page 273) or, of course, pasta.

TIMING TIPS:

- Up to 3 days ahead: Make the meat mixture for the meatballs and refrigerate.

- Up to 2 days ahead: Form the meatballs; cover, and refrigerate until ready to cook.

- Up to 1 day ahead: Cook the meatballs and make the sauce. If making ahead, remove from the oven after baking the meatballs in the sauce for 1 hour.

- 2 hours ahead: Remove the meatballs from the fridge to warm up a bit.

- 1 hour ahead: Return to a 350°F oven until heated through, then add the cheeses and continue with the last step of the recipe.

MODERN CHICKEN AND DUMPLINGS

SERVES 8

I never went in for traditional chicken and dumplings, and it was not something that was served in my house growing up. But there is something so undeniably cozy and comforting about this dish that I just had to give it an update. Mushrooms, including dry porcinis, add a depth of flavor to the broth, and I did away with the peas that always turn gray after the too-long cooking time. Coarse cornmeal and tarragon added to the dumpling dough provide texture and flavor. This dish is perfectly suited for the theme of this book, because while there is some work involved, it can be done almost completely ahead of time. The stew, which is the main part of the dish, can and should be done a day or even two ahead of time. When it's time to serve, all you have to do is heat it up on the stovetop, drop in the dumpling dough, wait about half an hour, and dinner is served!

FOR THE BROTH AND STEW:

2 large bone-in chicken breasts (about 2 pounds)

4 large bone-in chicken thighs (about 2 pounds)

1 stalk celery, cut in thirds

6 carrots, 1 cut in thirds, 5 sliced into 1-inch coins (about 12 ounces)

1 small onion, skin on and cut in half

2 garlic cloves, peeled

1 bay leaf

1 sprig tarragon

2 sprigs thyme

2 leeks, green tops separated from white and light green bottoms, well washed

1 large fennel bulb, stalks separated from bulb

1 teaspoon whole black peppercorns

2½ teaspoons salt, or to taste

1 ounce dried porcini mushrooms

4 tablespoons (½ stick) unsalted butter

8 ounces shiitake mushrooms, stemmed and sliced ½ inch thick

1 To make the broth: Place the chicken breasts and thighs, celery, 1 carrot (the one cut in thirds), the onion, garlic, bay leaf, tarragon sprig, thyme sprigs, leek greens, fennel tops, peppercorns, ½ teaspoon of the salt, and 10 cups water in a large (at least 6-quart) Dutch oven. It will be very full. Cover and bring to a boil over high heat. Skim off any foam that rises to the top. Reduce the heat to maintain a simmer, partially cover, and simmer for 20 minutes. Remove the chicken to a plate to cool, then pull the meat from the bones. Return the bones to the broth and continue cooking for 40 minutes. Strain the broth, discarding the solids, and, if desired, skim off excess fat using a fat separator. Reserve the broth and rinse out the Dutch oven.

2 To prep the vegetables: Place the porcini mushrooms in a 2-cup liquid measuring cup, fill it with boiling water, and let sit until the mushrooms are soft, about 8 minutes. Finely chop the porcinis and reserve the liquid. Slice the fennel bulb into 2-inch pieces. Cut the leeks (white and light green parts) in half lengthwise, then slice into ½-inch-thick pieces. Set aside.

3 Set the Dutch oven over high heat and melt 2 tablespoons of the butter in it. Add the shiitake and cremini mushrooms

recipe and ingredients continue

8 ounces cremini mushrooms, trimmed and quartered

Freshly ground black pepper

2 tablespoons all-purpose flour

1 tablespoon chopped fresh tarragon

FOR THE DUMPLINGS:

1 cup all-purpose flour

1 cup coarse cornmeal

2 teaspoons baking powder

¾ teaspoon salt

1 tablespoon chopped fresh Italian parsley

1 teaspoon coarsely chopped fresh tarragon

3 tablespoons unsalted butter, melted

¾ cup plus 2 tablespoons whole milk

and cook, stirring, until well browned, 8 to 10 minutes. Add the chopped porcini mushrooms and ½ teaspoon salt and season with pepper. Transfer to a plate.

4 Melt the remaining 2 tablespoons butter in the Dutch oven over medium-high heat, add the fennel and leeks, and cook for 5 to 7 minutes, until translucent. Add the sliced carrots and flour. Reduce the heat to low and cook, stirring frequently, for 5 minutes more. Return the mushrooms and chicken meat to the pot and add the chopped tarragon. Carefully pour in the mushroom liquid, taking care to leave any sand or grit behind in the bottom of the cup. Add 6 cups of the warm stock, reserving the rest for another use. Raise the heat to high and bring to a boil, then reduce the heat to maintain a gentle simmer. Add the remaining 1½ teaspoons salt (or more if needed) and season with pepper.

5 To make the dumplings: In a medium bowl, mix together the flour, cornmeal, baking powder, salt, parsley, and tarragon with a fork. Add the melted butter and milk and stir with the fork to combine. Drop the dough into the pot with the chicken by the soup-spoonful to make 8 dumplings. Cover and cook for 25 minutes without removing the lid. Dumplings will be puffy and cooked through. Ladle some of the stew into bowls, and top each serving with a dumpling.

TIMING TIPS:

- Up to 2 days ahead: Make the broth and poach the chicken; prep the vegetables.

- Up to 1 day ahead: Finish making the stew. Let cool completely, cover, and refrigerate.

- About 1 hour ahead: Reheat the stew until hot, mix the dumpling dough, and finish the recipe.

ZA'ATAR CHICKEN THIGHS WITH GRILLED PEACH AND CRISPY COUSCOUS SALAD

SERVES 4 TO 6

I've shifted my pantry in recent years, as so many others have, to embrace Middle Eastern and North African flavors. Harissa, preserved lemons, za'atar, and sumac are in regular rotation in my kitchen. I highly recommend adding these ingredients (and more!—see page 14) to your larder if you haven't already, to open up a whole new world of possibilities. Za'atar, which varies regionally, but is usually made up of varying proportions of finely ground dry thyme (or wild thyme), sesame seeds, sumac, and salt, is often used as a finishing touch on hummus or sprinkled in oil for dipping bread, but I found it does something magical to chicken when sprinkled on rather generously and then grilled (or roasted). You could sub in chicken breasts here, but the extra fat in chicken thighs makes this extra crispy and hard to overcook.

FOR THE CHICKEN:

8 bone-in, skin-on chicken thighs (about 2 pounds)

2 teaspoons salt, plus more as needed

Freshly ground black pepper

Juice of 2 lemons

¼ cup olive oil

4 garlic cloves, thinly sliced

1 tablespoon harissa

1 teaspoon very finely chopped preserved lemon or New York Shuk preserved lemon puree, optional

2 tablespoons za'atar

2 tablespoons fresh thyme leaves

2 teaspoons garlic powder

1 To marinate the chicken: Season the chicken with the salt and plenty of pepper. Combine the lemon juice, oil, garlic, harissa, and preserved lemon (if using) in a small bowl. Put the chicken in a resealable plastic bag (or a bowl if you prefer not to use a bag) and pour the marinade over it. Make sure the chicken is well coated on all sides. Refrigerate for at least 30 minutes or up to 24 hours, turning occasionally.

2 To make the couscous: Combine the couscous and water in a small saucepan. Bring to a boil over medium-high heat, reduce the heat to low, cover, and simmer for 10 to 12 minutes, or until all the water is absorbed. Remove from the heat, and spread out on a dinner plate to cool. Heat a large (12-inch) skillet over high heat. Add 1 tablespoon of the oil and the couscous. Season lightly with salt. Cook, stirring at first, and then cooking undisturbed, pressing down lightly with a spatula, until browned and crunchy on one side only, about 5 minutes. Transfer to a mixing bowl.

recipe and ingredients continue

FOR THE SALAD:

¾ cup Israeli (pearl) couscous,
    preferably whole-wheat

1 cup water

¼ cup extra-virgin olive oil

2 tablespoons fresh lemon juice

1 teaspoon harissa, or more to taste

1 teaspoon honey

Salt and freshly ground black pepper

2 ripe but firm peaches, cut into
    8 wedges each

1 Kirby or Persian cucumber, cut in half
    lengthwise and thinly sliced
    (or ⅓ hothouse cucumber)

½ cup fresh mint leaves, some torn and
    some left whole, plus more
    for garnish

3 To make the dressing: In a small bowl, whisk together the lemon juice, harissa, and honey and season with salt and pepper. Slowly whisk in 2 tablespoons of the remaining oil.

4 To cook the chicken: Remove the chicken from the marinade, letting the excess drip off, and lay out on a baking sheet (I like to line with parchment, which makes it easier to wash for the cooked chicken) and coat with the za'atar, fresh thyme, and garlic powder. Heat a grill to medium heat and, using a perforated grill platter if you have one, cook the chicken thighs for about 10 minutes on the flesh side, until nicely browned, then turn and cook for 5 to 7 minutes on the skin side until the skin is crisp but not burnt. Turn back to the flesh side, turn grill down to the lowest setting, or move to a cooler part of the grill, and cook 6 to 8 more minutes until very tender.

5 While you're cooking the chicken, cook the peaches too. If you don't have a grill platter, place a piece of heavy-duty foil with some holes poked in it on one side of the grill (otherwise, use part of the platter the chicken is cooking on). Flatten it as much as possible using a spatula or tongs. Toss the peaches in the remaining 1 tablespoon oil and spread out on the prepared surface. Grill for 2 to 3 minutes on each side, until lightly browned. Transfer to the mixing bowl and combine with the couscous, cucumber, and mint leaves. Dress with enough of the dressing to moisten everything and season with salt and pepper. Pass any extra dressing on the side.

TIP:

Using a grill platter, an inexpensive accessory you can buy at a good hardware store or online, makes grilling small and delicate foods like peach slices, string beans, asparagus, mushrooms, etc., not only possible, but easy. It's also really helpful for fish fillets or this chicken, because it eliminates sticking, especially once it's well-seasoned.

TIMING TIPS:

- 1 day ahead: Marinate the chicken; cook the couscous and store it in the fridge.

- 2 hours ahead: Crisp the couscous and make the dressing. Prep the rest of the ingredients for the salad.

- About 1 hour ahead: Grill the chicken and cook the peaches.

- At the last minute: Toss together all of the salad ingredients.

KALE AND PROSCIUTTO-WRAPPED CHICKEN BREASTS WITH ROASTED MEYER LEMONS

SERVES 4 TO 6

I've never heard of a vegetable with so many different names. Dinosaur kale. Lacinato kale. Black cabbage. Cavolo nero. Tuscan kale. They are all the same thing, and it has become so common that it is pretty easy to find just about anywhere, anytime of year, and it's a must for this recipe because of its flatness. If you can't find it, use Swiss chard instead. This recipe works best with larger leaves, and you will need only four of them for this recipe, so save the rest for a salad (page 229) or to throw into a soup (page 229), a frittata, or whatever!

1 bunch Tuscan kale

4 boneless, skinless chicken breasts

1 teaspoon salt

Freshly ground black pepper

2 ounces fontina cheese (or other good melter)

4 thin slices prosciutto (2 ounces)

3 teaspoons olive oil

Roasted Meyer Lemons (page 30)

TIMING TIP:
The chicken can be wrapped with the cheese, prosciutto, and kale up to 1 day ahead of time.

1 Choose 4 nice, large, unblemished kale leaves. Reserve the rest for another use. Carefully cut the thick stem out from each, leaving the top of the leaf intact. Season each chicken breast with the salt and some pepper. Cut the cheese into 4 equal rectangles and place one on the center of each breast. Wrap a slice of prosciutto around the center of each breast, enclosing the cheese. Wrap the kale around the center of each breast, enclosing the prosciutto and using toothpicks to secure it on the underside. Rub the wrapped chicken breasts with 1 teaspoon of the oil.

2 Heat a large nonstick skillet over medium-high heat. Add the remaining 2 teaspoons oil to the pan and add the chicken. Cook for 5 minutes until chicken and kale are lightly browned, turn, and cook for 5 minutes on the other side. Add 1 tablespoon water, cover, reduce the heat to low, and cook for 2 to 3 minutes, until the chicken is cooked through.

3 Remove the toothpicks, slice the chicken, and serve with the roasted lemons.

GRILLED DRUMS AND WINGS WITH PLUM BBQ SAUCE

SERVES 4 TO 6

Make a batch of this fruity, tangy BBQ sauce to use as a last-minute slather on any cut of chicken, like thighs or breasts, or even turkey burgers that you are cooking on the grill. It freezes well, so split the batch up into three containers of about 1 cup each, which is enough to glaze about 3 pounds of chicken. As for the chicken—after years of being a total food snob about garlic powder, I received some as a sample and decided to give it a try again. I found that it adds a deep savory flavor to grilled meats in a way that fresh garlic can't, especially with a short (or no) marinating time. Fresh garlic tends to burn, while garlic powder permeates the meat. I figured if chefs everywhere are dehydrating everything they can get their hands on and pulverizing it into a powder, what's wrong with garlic powder?

FOR THE SAUCE:

1 tablespoon yellow mustard seeds

4 large black plums (about 1½ pounds),
    cut into chunks

2 garlic cloves, grated

1 tablespoon grated fresh ginger
    (from a 1-ounce thumb)

⅓ cup honey

2 tablespoons balsamic glaze or vinegar

¼ cup water

1 hot red chile, sliced, or to taste
    (or sriracha to taste)

1 cup strained canned tomatoes
    (or tomato sauce)

½ teaspoon salt, or to taste

Freshly ground black pepper

1 To make the sauce: Heat a large, wide saucepan over medium heat. Add the mustard seeds and toast for 2 to 3 minutes. Add the plums, garlic, ginger, honey, balsamic glaze, and water. Bring to a boil, cover, and cook for 2 to 3 minutes, until the plums start to soften. Add the chile, tomatoes, and salt and season with pepper. Reduce the heat to medium-low and cook uncovered for 1 hour, until thick and glossy. As the plums soften, press them against the sides of the pan to break them down. Add more salt or chile as needed. Set aside 1 cup of sauce and reserve the rest for another use.

2 To make the chicken: Season the chicken drumsticks and wingettes with the salt, pepper, and garlic powder and rub with the mustard and oil.

FOR THE CHICKEN:

1½ pounds chicken drumsticks
   (6 pieces)

1½ pounds chicken wingettes

1½ teaspoons salt

Freshly ground black pepper

2 tablespoons garlic powder

2 tablespoons Dijon mustard

1 tablespoon olive oil

3 Heat a grill to medium-low. Cook the chicken for 8 to 10 minutes per side, moving the pieces around the grill, until nicely colored on all sides. Brush all the chicken pieces with the sauce and turn them over, then brush the sides facing up with sauce. Cook for 3 to 4 minutes and turn again. Keep brushing and turning until all of the pieces are nicely caramelized, making sure they don't burn, 10 to 15 minutes total. Serve warm or at room temperature.

TIMING TIPS:

• Up to 3 months ahead: Make the BBQ sauce and freeze; if not freezing, it can be made up to 4 days ahead.

• Up to 1 day ahead: Season the chicken and store in the fridge.

• Up to 3 hours ahead: Grill the chicken; serve at room temperature or reheat just before serving.

CHICKEN TONNATO

SERVES 6

I've always loved tonnato sauce; in fact, it's one of the few recipes I've included a new version of from my first book, *Recipes*. It seems like it's enjoying a bit of a revival lately, which I am not sorry about, because everyone should keep a jar of this tasty, creamy sauce in their fridge in the summer to turn leftover cold meats or even vegetables into a sumptuous meal. It may seem strange to some to make a sauce out of canned tuna to serve with meat, but don't knock it 'til you've tried it! Even my husband, who claims to hate canned tuna, is a big fan. Of course it is the perfect thing to serve, especially for lunch, when the weather is very hot. My most memorable moment that really sealed the deal between me and the original Italian version, *vitello tonnato*, came when we were trudging through Venice on the hottest, muggiest night imaginable to reach our pre-chosen dinner destination. When we arrived at the restaurant, naturally there was no AC, so we opted for the garden, which may have been hotter than inside. When I looked at the menu, I simply could not imagine eating anything warm (as much as I love pasta), so I ordered *vitello tonnato*, and it was perfect. It actually was refreshing, and between that and a chilled glass of white, I finally stopped sweating.

FOR THE CHICKEN:

3 cups water

1 cup dry white wine

1 teaspoon whole black peppercorns

1 shallot, unpeeled and quartered lengthwise

A few sprigs herbs, such as tarragon and/or thyme

1 teaspoon salt

4 boneless, skinless chicken breasts

FOR THE POTATOES:

1½ pounds baby potatoes

1½ teaspoons salt

1   To poach the chicken: Combine the water, wine, peppercorns, shallot, herbs, and salt in a large, wide saucepan. Bring to a boil, then reduce the heat and simmer for 10 to 15 minutes. Add the chicken breasts in a single layer. Add more water as needed to cover the chicken. Return to a boil, boil for 1 minute, then turn off the heat. Cover the pan and let sit for 10 minutes. Remove the chicken from the liquid, transfer to a plate, and cover with plastic wrap to keep it from drying out. Place in the refrigerator.

2   To boil the potatoes: Place the potatoes in a large saucepan and cover with cold water by 2 inches. Add salt and bring to a boil. Simmer for 12 to 15 minutes (larger potatoes might need more time), stirring occasionally, until tender when pierced with the tip of a paring knife. Let cool in the water for 15 minutes, then drain. Chill if not using right away. Before serving, cut larger potatoes in half.

recipe and ingredients continue

FOR THE SAUCE:

One 5-ounce can light tuna packed in oil, preferably Italian

2 tablespoons capers, rinsed

2 anchovies or 1 teaspoon anchovy paste

Juice of 1 lemon (about 2 tablespoons)

1 small or ½ large garlic clove, peeled

Salt and freshly ground black pepper

¼ cup mayonnaise

⅓ cup extra-virgin olive oil, plus more for drizzling

Small handful of fresh Italian parsley leaves

TO SERVE:

¼ cup vegetable oil

One 3.5-ounce jar (about 5 tablespoons) large capers, rinsed and patted very dry

1 bunch arugula

½ cup oil-cured black olives

1 pint halved Sungold or cherry tomatoes

2 tablespoons olive oil, or as desired

Salt

3 To make the sauce: Combine the tuna with the oil it is packed in, the capers, anchovies, lemon juice, garlic, a pinch of salt and pepper, and the mayonnaise in a mini food processor or blender. Process for a few seconds to combine. Continue to process while slowly drizzling in the oil through the hole in the lid. Add the parsley and process for a few more seconds to combine. Set aside. Cover and chill until needed.

4 To fry the capers: Pour oil into a small skillet and heat over medium-high heat. Add the capers (make sure they are really dry first so they don't spatter) and fry until the buds open and they are beginning to brown and crisp up, about 5 minutes. Scoop the capers out of the pan using a slotted spoon onto a paper towel to drain. Discard the oil when cool.

5 To assemble and serve: Thinly slice the chicken and arrange on a platter with the arugula, potatoes, olives, and tomatoes. Drizzle the sauce over the chicken and top with the fried capers. Drizzle oil over the arugula, potatoes, and tomatoes and season with salt.

TIMING TIPS:

- Up to 2 days ahead: Poach the chicken and make the tonnato sauce. Store in the fridge.

- Up to 1 hour ahead: Slice the chicken and wash the arugula.

- At the last minute: Assemble the platter.

GRILL-ROASTED CHICKENS WITH HERBES DE PROVENCE AND EXTRA LAVENDER
AKA HOUSE CHICKEN
SERVES 4 TO 6

My husband, Steve, and I have been making this chicken together for years now. It's one of our go-tos for summer entertaining, because, well, roast chicken. Everyone seems to love it, and it goes with everything. We buy local farm-raised chickens from a wonderful farm called Iacono in East Hampton. I swear these chickens are juicier and tastier than all others. Seek out an organic free-range chicken from your butcher or supermarket, because it really does make a difference! I season the chickens (sometimes a day ahead of time, but usually right before cooking), and Steve cooks them on the grill while I get the rest of the dinner together. It takes less than an hour and a half to cook, and it is almost entirely hands off. The resulting birds are a deep mahogany color, lightly smoked, and very juicy. Any leftovers are great in salads and sandwiches the next day. Eaten cold, the smoky flavor is more pronounced.

The best way to turn your kettle-style grill into an oven/smoker is to use briquette holders (an inexpensive accessory), which hold the charcoal well off to the side of your grill in a compact, slow-burning pile. If you don't have them, you can bank the coals steeply to either side of the grill, which will achieve a similar effect. Light one chimney full of coals and divide between the two briquette holders. Add a handful of soaked wood chips to the top of each briquette holder. Place the chickens in between the coals, side by side in the center of the grill so they are getting only indirect heat. Open the top and bottom dampers just a bit and cover the grill. Adjust the dampers (open for hotter, closed for cooler) as needed to maintain a temperature of about 300°F. The chickens will turn a beautiful mahogany color early on, so don't be alarmed or think they are done. They will take anywhere from 1 to 1½ hours, until the legs move easily when wiggled or an instant-read thermometer reads 165°F when inserted into the thigh joint. Resist the temptation to open the grill frequently. Don't even look until 1 hour has passed. This is the way we cook house chicken, but the recipe also can be used to season chickens cooked in a wood pellet smoker or even the oven.

recipe and ingredients continue

Two 3½-pound organic chickens

2 tablespoons olive oil

1 tablespoon salt

1 teaspoon freshly ground black pepper

1 lemon, cut in half

1 large head garlic, cut in half crosswise

Fresh sprigs thyme

1½ tablespoons dried herbes de Provence (see page 15)

⅓ cup fresh rosemary leaves, roughly chopped

1 tablespoon dried lavender (optional)

1 tablespoon Aleppo pepper or 2 teaspoons red pepper flakes

1 Rub the chickens with 1 tablespoon of the oil. Season with the salt and black pepper, inside and out. Put half a lemon, half a head of garlic, and some thyme sprigs in each cavity. Rub with the herbes de Provence, rosemary, and lavender (if using). Use the remaining 1 tablespoon oil to help get the herbs to stick, then sprinkle with the Aleppo pepper. Proceed with the recipe, or wrap and refrigerate for up to 1 day.

2 Prepare a charcoal grill for indirect cooking. Use the briquette holders or bank hot coals steeply to each side of the grill.

3 Place the chickens on the grill and cook, covered, for 1 hour and 15 minutes to 1½ hours. They are done when the legs move easily and they reach an internal temperature of 165°F. Let the chickens rest for 10 minutes before carving into serving pieces.

TIMING TIPS:

- Up to 1 day ahead: Season the chickens and refrigerate until needed.

- Up to 1 hour before cooking: Remove the chicken from the fridge to warm up a little.

- 2 hours before serving: Light the fire and cook the chickens.

SHRIMP AND CHICKPEAS WITH CHERMOULA

SERVES 4

For those times when you don't want to plan ahead, dishes like this one are just what you need. It is very quick to put together but impressive enough for guests (your family will be impressed too!). It's worth it to seek out Castelvetrano olives (they sell them in a jar in my supermarket)—not only are they a lovely shade of green, but they aren't quite as salty and piquant as some other types, making them an almost vegetable-like addition to a dish—their olive-y flavor really comes through.

1 tablespoon plus 2 teaspoons olive oil

1 medium red onion, sliced lengthwise ¼ inch thick

One 15-ounce can chickpeas, drained and rinsed

¼ teaspoon ground coriander

¼ teaspoon ground cumin

¼ teaspoon smoked paprika

¼ teaspoon salt

1 pound jumbo (16/20) shrimp, peeled and deveined, tails left on

½ cup pitted and cracked Castelvetrano olives

1 recipe Chermoula (page 29), about 1 cup

1 recipe Roasted Meyer Lemons (page 30)

Cooked couscous

¼ cup lightly packed fresh mint leaves, torn

¼ cup lightly packed fresh cilantro leaves, torn

1 Heat a large (12-inch) nonstick skillet over medium-high heat. Add 2 teaspoons of the oil and the onion and cook for 6 to 8 minutes, until softened. Add 1 teaspoon of the remaining oil, the chickpeas, coriander, cumin, paprika, and salt. Cook, stirring, for 5 minutes. Transfer to a plate.

2 Return the pan to the stovetop and heat the remaining 2 teaspoons oil over high heat. Add the shrimp and turn after 1 to 2 minutes, when they start to brown. Cook for 1 to 2 minutes on the other side, until browned and cooked through. Return the chickpea mixture to the pan and add the olives. Deglaze with ¼ cup water. Add 3 tablespoons of the chermoula and the roasted lemons and cook for 2 minutes. Serve over couscous and sprinkle with the mint and cilantro. Drizzle more chermoula over the top and pass the rest on the side.

TIMING TIPS:

- Up to 1 day ahead: Make the chermoula and roasted lemons; peel the shrimp; pit and crack the olives. Refrigerate until ready to use.

- About 1 hour ahead: Make the couscous; prep the mint and cilantro.

- At the last minute: Finish cooking the dish.

HALIBUT, CLAMS, AND SCALLOPS WITH CORN AND FREGOLA

SERVES 4 TO 6

This might not seem like your typical make-ahead dish, but if you know which steps to do ahead of time, it comes together beautifully at the last minute. You can change up the seafood to suit your taste and budget, but the clams are a constant. They provide the powerfully flavorful broth that the dish is built on. You can even skip the fish and scallops altogether and just add a lot more clams. To stretch this to serve more people, cut the fish into smaller portions and add another dish to your menu.

8 ounces medium-grain fregola (Sardinian pasta)

3 tablespoons extra-virgin olive oil

2 to 3 garlic cloves, thinly sliced

Red pepper flakes

2 dozen littleneck clams, scrubbed with a brush

8 ounces dry white wine

1 large shallot, minced

2 ears fresh corn, kernels cut from the cob

1 small zucchini, diced

Coarse salt and freshly ground black pepper

Four 6-ounce pieces skinless halibut

6 to 8 sea scallops, muscle removed, rinsed and patted dry

1 cup mixed fresh herbs, such as chervil, parsley, opal basil, and fennel fronds

Calabrian chile paste (optional)

1 Cook the fregola in abundant salted water until al dente, about 8 minues. Drain, rinse, and set aside.

2 Heat 1 tablespoon of the oil in a large (12-inch) skillet over medium heat. Add the garlic and a big pinch of red pepper flakes. Cook, stirring, until the garlic is toasted and golden, about 3 minutes. Add the clams, wine, and 1 cup water; bring to a boil, reduce heat to medium, and cover. Cook until all the clams have opened, transferring them to a bowl as they do, about 10 minutes. Discard any that do not open. Cover the bowl with plastic wrap (this will keep the clams from drying out) and refrigerate until needed if not using right away. Pour the liquid from the saucepan into a large spouted measuring cup and let stand for a few minutes for any sand to settle to the bottom.

3 Rinse the skillet, add 1 tablespoon of the remaining oil, and place over medium-high heat. Season the halibut fillets and scallops with salt and pepper. Add the halibut to the skillet and sear for 3 to 4 minutes on the top side, until golden brown. Repeat with the scallops. Transfer to a plate and set aside.

4 Rinse the skillet and heat the remaining 1 tablespoon oil over medium-high heat. Add the shallot and cook until softened, about 3 minutes. Add the corn and zucchini, season with salt and

recipe continues

pepper, and cook, stirring, until softened and golden brown,
6 to 8 minutes. Add the cooked fregola and half of the clam
broth (pour it off carefully, leving the sand and garlic behind),
bring to a simmer, and cook until the liquid is nearly absorbed,
about 5 minutes. Transfer to a large, shallow baking dish. Cover
with foil and keep warm in the oven.

5 Pour the remaining broth into the skillet and bring to a boil.
Reduce it slightly, then stir in chiles (if using). Add the fish,
scallops, and clams, reduce the heat to low, and cook, covered,
just until everything is heated through and the fish is cooked,
about 5 minutes.

6 Arrange the seafood, seared side up, atop the fregola mixture
and pour the remaining liquid over the top. Sprinkle with the
herbs and serve immediately with the chile paste, if using, on
the side.

TIMING TIPS:

- Up to 1 day ahead: Make the corn-fregola mixture all the
  way through and refrigerate. If making within 2 hours, set
  aside at room temperature.

- Up to 3 hours ahead: Make the clams, sear the fish and
  scallops, and refrigerate.

- Just before serving: Heat the fregola mixture in a shallow
  baking dish covered with foil in a 350°F oven until hot,
  about 30 minutes. Continue with step 5 to reheat the
  seafood.

FISH IN CRAZY WATER

SERVES 4

I get the urge to make this once tomato season starts, and it's a good thing to make when there are *too* many tomatoes in the garden, or maybe, just maybe, you got carried away at the farmer's market. It is a great, easy, super tasty, and beautiful way to cook just about any kind of fish fillet and even shrimp or other shellfish. It would be good with halibut or striped bass—really, any firm meaty white fish. You just will have to adjust the cooking time depending on the thickness of the fillets—about ten minutes per inch is the rule of thumb. Did I mention it's a great way to cook fish indoors without stinking up your house?

This is a perfect get-ahead recipe, because the broth can be done completely ahead of time—all you need to do at the last minute is drop the fish in and poach it for a few minutes. A friend asked me for this recipe while I was writing this book, and because she was cooking for eight and doesn't like to have anything bubbling on the stove when she invites guests into her open kitchen, she asked if it could be finished in the oven—yes, it can! You could double the broth, transfer it to a flat baking dish (make sure the broth is hot when you do this), add eight pieces of fish, cover tightly with foil, and cook in the oven until the fish is done. This dish is easy to plate, and not really a family-style dish, so I do suggest you plate it individually—and serve spoons and/or extra toasts on the side so you can sop up every drop of the flavorful "crazy water," aka *acqua pazza*.

FOR THE FISH:

1½ pounds ripe red tomatoes
   (any kind but cherry)

3 tablespoons extra-virgin olive oil

2 to 3 garlic cloves, thinly sliced

4 cups water

1 to 3 teaspoons minced fresh red chile
   (depending on their heat level and
   your preferred heat)

Salt

2 large sprigs Italian parsley

¼ cup roughly chopped oil-cured olives

Four 6-ounce red snapper fillets

¼ cup chopped fresh Italian parsley

1 cup loosely packed fresh basil leaves

1 To make the fish: Bring a large saucepan of water to a boil. Cut a small X on the bottom of each tomato. Drop them into the water a few at a time and leave them for a few seconds. When the tomatoes are ripe and in season, the skins will release almost immediately. Otherwise it may take a little longer. Transfer to a colander and rinse with cold water (there's no need to shock with ice water, as we'll be cooking them right away). Peel the skins off the tomatoes and cut them into rough chunks, not too small, so they retain some texture after cooking.

2 Heat a large, wide skillet big enough to hold all the fish flat over medium heat and add the oil. Add the garlic and cook until golden brown all over, turning as needed. Let the pan cool down a bit (so the tomatoes don't spatter) and add the tomatoes, water, chile, ½ teaspoon salt, and the parsley sprigs. Bring to a simmer and cook, covered, for 15 minutes. Uncover, add the olives, and cook until reduced by half, about 15 minutes.

recipe and ingredients continue

FOR THE TOAST:

8 slices ciabatta, or other airy bread

4 to 6 flat anchovies

½ cup (1 stick) unsalted butter, softened

TO SERVE:

1 batch Oven-Dried Cherry Tomatoes
  (page 26)

3 Meanwhile, make the toast: Preheat the broiler and line a baking sheet with foil.

4 Mash the anchovies in a small bowl using a fork and add the butter. Stir until well incorporated. Spread the butter on one side of the bread and spread the bread out on the prepared baking sheet. Toast in the broiler on both sides until golden brown and crunchy and darker on the edges. Remove from the broiler and keep warm. Roll leftover butter into a log (see instructions on page 91) and freeze until needed for other uses (see Note).

5 Remove and discard the parsley sprigs and add the fish skin-side up to the pan. Spoon some of the liquid over the top, cover, and cook over medium-low heat for 8 minutes, or until the fish is just done. Carefully transfer the fish fillets to each of 4 shallow bowls. Stir the chopped parsley into the broth and taste for salt. Sprinkle the cherry tomatoes over the fish, ladle some of the broth into each bowl, top with the basil leaves, and serve the toast on the side of each bowl.

TIMING TIPS:

- Up to 2 days ahead: Make the anchovy butter and oven-dried cherry tomatoes. Refrigerate until ready to use.

- Up to 1 day ahead: Make the tomato broth; chop the parsley. Refrigerate until ready to use.

- At the last minute: Heat up the broth and poach the fish; broil the toast.

NOTE:

Use leftover anchovy butter to finish pasta dishes, spread on an impromptu toast (like the burrata toast on page 53), or melt onto grilled steak, fish, or chicken.

WINTER GRAND AIOLI

SERVES 6

A grand aioli usually is a summer dish of a big bowl of homemade garlic mayonnaise surrounded by steamed vegetables and some kind of seafood, like cold shrimp or poached salmon. It's a lovely thing to serve in warm weather, but I like the idea of turning it into a cold-weather, eat-with-your-hands feast. The aioli itself is made more complex by using lots of roasted garlic, and black garlic if you can get your hands on some. It adds a bit of sweetness and a lot of umami to the aioli, which makes it really craveable. Here's how I like to do this: Make a lot of seasonal roasted vegetables, steam a few artichokes, buy a couple of whole cooked lobsters from my local seafood market, pan-roast a nice big piece of salmon simply seasoned with salt and pepper, set it all out ahead of time (room temperature is fine for all of this), and then after everyone sits down at the table, I deliver piping hot potatoes and a warm loaf of bread and let everyone have at it. Plates and forks are optional.

2 delicata squash

Olive oil

Salt and freshly ground black pepper

4 large beets, stems trimmed to
    2 inches, peeled, and cut in half

1 bunch thin carrots, stems trimmed
    to 2 inches and peeled

1 bunch Hakurei or other small turnips,
    stems trimmed to 2 inches, peeled,
    and cut in half

1½ pounds fresh skinless salmon

4 whole steamed artichokes (page 146)

Whole Roasted Cauliflower (page 147)

2 cooked lobsters (store-bought),
    cracked

Roasted and Black Garlic Aioli
    (page 145)

Crispy Semolina Potatoes (page 275)

1 loaf good, crusty bread

1 Preheat the oven to 425°F.

2 Cut the squash crosswise through the center and scoop out the seeds. Cut into ⅓-inch-thick rings. Coat lightly with oil and season with salt and pepper. Spread out on a baking sheet. Repeat with the beets, carrots, and turnips. You should be able to fit them onto two baking sheets. Roast, turning occasionally, for 30 to 45 minutes, until nicely browned and tender.

3 Meanwhile, cook the salmon. Season the salmon with salt and pepper and coat it with oil. Coat a medium nonstick skillet with a small amount of oil and heat over medium-high heat. Place the salmon top-side down in the pan and cook until browned, 3 to 5 minutes. Carefully turn and cook for 3 minutes on the second (skin) side. Transfer to the oven to cook through to your liking, about 5 minutes for medium.

recipe continues

4 Arrange the roasted vegetables, the artichokes, cauliflower, lobsters, and salmon on a large platter or a series of plates and platters. Scoop the aioli into one or two bowls. Serve the hot potatoes and bread on the side.

TIMING TIPS:

- Up to 1 day ahead: Make the aioli, prep the vegetables, and steam the artichokes. Refrigerate until ready to use.

- Up to 3 hours ahead: Roast the vegetables and par-cook the potatoes.

- Up to 2 hours ahead: Cook the salmon; leave at room temperature.

- 1 hour ahead: Arrange the vegetables and seafood on platters.

- Just before serving: Cook the potatoes and warm the bread.

ROASTED AND BLACK GARLIC AIOLI

MAKES ABOUT 1 CUP

As you probably already know, aioli is just a fancy name for garlic mayonnaise. A lot of people are afraid to make homemade mayonnaise because of the mistaken notion that it is difficult, or, worse, dangerous (on account of the raw eggs involved), but I am here to tell you that you can master this easily, and you will be rewarded richly for it. The Winter Grand Aioli (page 143) is all about celebrating this velvety sauce, though you can use it on sandwiches, salads, or steamed asparagus, or just about anything. This particular variation uses roasted garlic rather than raw garlic, which mellows out the flavor considerably, and is a bit easier to digest to boot. Black garlic (see page 14) lends another dimension of flavor, but if you can't get your hands on it, it's perfectly OK to leave it out. The aioli can be made by hand with a bowl and whisk, but I prefer a mini food processor. It comes out thick, rather than drippy, and the little funnel releases a steady stream of oil into the emulsion as it blends at just the right speed. I seek out local farm eggs, but if you are using supermarket eggs, look for ones that are pasteurized in the shell.

2 heads garlic

2 tablespoons extra-virgin olive oil

2 large egg yolks

4 black garlic cloves or 1 tablespoon black garlic molasses (optional)

4 teaspoons fresh lemon juice, or to taste

2 teaspoons water

½ teaspoon salt, or to taste

¾ cup neutral oil, such as safflower or canola

1 Preheat the oven to 400°F.

2 Place each head of garlic in the center of a square of aluminum foil. Drizzle with the oil, wrap loosely, and place in a small baking dish. Bake for 1 hour, or until very fragrant and completely soft to the touch and the skin is golden brown. Remove from the oven and let cool.

3 Use a serrated knife to saw off the top of the garlic heads. Cut as close to the top as you can while still exposing all of the separate compartments. Squeeze the garlic heads into the bowl of a mini food processor until all the soft roasted garlic comes oozing out (think of it as a tube of toothpaste).

4 Add the egg yolks, black garlic (if using), the lemon juice, water, and salt and process until very smooth. With the machine running, dribble in a drop or two of oil, then a drop or two more. Keep adding oil, very, very slowly at first, and then start dribbling it in in a slow, steady stream until all of the oil has been added.

5 Scrape into a bowl and adjust the seasonings with salt and lemon juice. Cover and refrigerate until ready to serve.

TIMING TIP:
The aioli can be made up to 2 days ahead. Store in an airtight container in the refrigerator.

WHOLE STEAMED ARTICHOKES

SERVES 4 OR MORE AS PART OF WINTER GRAND AIOLI

Whole artichokes are a perfect addition to the Winter Grand Aioli (page 143).

4 large artichokes

2 lemons

Salt

1 teaspoon black peppercorns

Sprig of fresh thyme (optional)

2 garlic cloves

2 tablespoons olive oil

1 Trim the artichokes; snap off the tough outer leaves. Using a sharp knife, cut off the top third of the artichoke. Snip the tips of the remaining leaves with scissors. Trim the base with a paring knife. Spread the leaves open so you can access the choke, scoop out the hairy choke with a melon baller as best you can (or forget it, and let people do it at the table). Squeeze some lemon into the center, and toss the lemon into a bowl of water with the artichoke while you repeat with the remaining artichokes.

2 Fill a pot large enough to fit the 4 artichokes comfortably with 2 inches of water. Add a big pinch of salt, the peppercorns, thyme (if using), garlic, and olive oil and bring to a simmer. Add the artichokes cut side down and cover the pot. Steam until tender, 25 to 30 minutes. The leaves should pull off easily, and a paring knife inserted into the heart should meet no resistance. Drain well, and serve warm or at room temperature.

TIMING TIP:
The artichokes can be made up to 2 days ahead of time.

WHOLE ROASTED CAULIFLOWER

SERVES 4 TO 6

Think of this recipe for roasted cauliflower as a blank canvas—you could serve it draped with tahini sauce (page 183) and sprinkled with pomegranate seeds and toasted pepitas, or with a dollop of thick yogurt or labneh on top and quick-pickled onions (page 272) and a sprinkle of sumac. Or keep it simple and serve it as part of the Winter Grand Aioli feast (page 143). Remember, it becomes soft enough to spoon into, so it's fun to plunk it on the table and let guests serve themselves.

1 small onion, sliced lengthwise

1 tablespoon olive oil

1 head cauliflower (preferably orange), trimmed

4 tablespoons (½ stick) unsalted butter, softened

Salt and freshly ground black pepper

½ cup chicken or vegetable stock

¼ cup Parmigiano-Reggiano cheese

1 Preheat the oven to 400°F.

2 Toss the onions with the oil in a small roasting pan or cast-iron skillet. Transfer to the oven and cook, stirring once or twice, until they start turning golden, about 25 minutes.

3 Coat the cauliflower with the butter and season generously with salt and pepper. Add to the roasting pan along with the chicken stock. Cover tightly with foil and bake for 30 minutes, or until just tender when pierced with the tip of a paring knife.

4 Remove the foil, increase the oven temperature to 425°F, and sprinkle the cauliflower with the cheese. Bake until golden brown on top, about 20 minutes. Transfer to a serving plate, spoon over the onions and any liquid in the pan, and serve.

BIG SALADE NIÇOISE

SERVES 6 TO 8

This salad is one of my summer go-tos when I invite people to lunch, which is one of my favorite low-stress ways to entertain. While it does take some time to prepare all of the separate components, they can be done largely ahead of time. Even the final platter can be arranged an hour or two ahead and popped back into the fridge until a little before serving time. Yes, you can use a good oil-packed tuna if you don't want to poach the tuna yourself, but poached tuna makes the whole thing a little more special. One thing I really love about this salad, or any composed salad, really, is the freedom of choice it allows my guests. People can take exactly what and how much they want and easily reach back in for seconds. Sometimes I arrange this as a mirror image on a large platter, so that I can put the salad down in the center of my long table and all the ingredients are within everyone's reach. Change up the ingredients according to what's available and in season—if you can't find fresh baby artichokes, it's OK to use ones from a jar, prepared ones from the produce section, or just leave them off altogether. Be creative, and assemble the freshest and best produce for this table-pleasing warm-weather meal.

FOR THE TUNA:

Two small, 1-inch-thick yellowfin tuna steaks (about 1½ pounds), left whole

Salt and freshly ground black pepper

2 cups olive oil

1 bay leaf

2 to 3 garlic cloves, smashed

A few sprigs thyme

2 strips orange zest

FOR THE DRESSING:

1 teaspoon anchovy paste or 2 mashed anchovies

1 tablespoon capers, rinsed and chopped

1 tablespoon Dijon mustard

3 tablespoons minced shallot (1 small)

Salt and freshly ground black pepper

3 tablespoons red wine vinegar

1 tablespoon fresh lemon juice

½ cup olive oil (reserved from poaching tuna)

1 To make the tuna: Season the tuna with salt and pepper. Place the olive oil, bay leaf, garlic cloves, thyme, and orange zest in a small saucepan large enough to hold the fish in one layer. Slowly heat the oil over low heat until the garlic starts to sizzle, about 5 minutes. Add the fish and cook for 8 to 10 minutes, turning once about halfway through. Remove the fish from the oil and let cool. If making ahead of time, return the fish to the oil when the oil has cooled. Chill until ready to serve.

2 To make the dressing: In a small bowl, whisk together the anchovy paste, capers, mustard, shallot, salt and pepper to taste, vinegar, and lemon juice. Let sit for a few minutes for the flavors to meld. Slowly whisk in the oil.

3 To make the salad: Place the potatoes in a steamer basket set inside a large, wide saucepan filled with a couple inches of water and steam over medium heat until tender when pierced with the tip of a sharp paring knife, about 15 minutes. When the potatoes are cool enough to handle, slice them, and immediately dress them with 3 tablespoons of the dressing. Season with salt and pepper. Set aside.

recipe and ingredients continue

FOR THE SALAD:

1 pound baby potatoes

Salt and freshly ground black pepper

4 large eggs

1 quart baby artichokes (around 12)

1 lemon, cut in half

1 pound string beans, trimmed

2 to 3 heads Little Gem, Bibb, or Sucrine lettuce, cut into quarters

2 cups cherry tomatoes, halved

1 cup Kalamata and/or oil-cured olives

1 cup shelled and cooked fava beans (see page 27), or any cooked or canned bean

Lemon wedges

4 Place the eggs in a small saucepan, cover with cold water, add a healthy pinch of salt, and bring to a boil over medium-high heat. Let the water boil for 1 minute, then turn off the heat. Let stand for 8 minutes, then remove eggs from the water and rinse with cold water. Place the eggs in a bowl of ice water and peel them. Set aside. Cut them in halves or quarters before serving.

5 If you are lucky enough to find fresh baby artichokes, peel all of the tough outer leaves off, pare the bottoms, and cut the pointy tops off. Cut in half lengthwise, rubbing with lemon as you work. Bring a medium saucepan of water to a boil, squeeze any remaining lemon juice from the lemon, and toss the lemon into the pot. Add 1 teaspoon salt and return water to a boil. Add the artichokes and use a pot lid slightly smaller than the pot to keep them submerged. Simmer until tender, 8 to 10 minutes. Drain and toss with a little of the dressing. Set aside.

6 Bring a large pot of water to a boil, add a healthy pinch of salt, then add the string beans. Cook until bright green and crisp-tender, 2 to 3 minutes. Drain and rinse with cold water, then place in a bowl of cold water until chilled. Drain and pat dry. Set aside.

7 Arrange the ingredients on a large platter in roughly this order: lettuce, potatoes, artichokes, string beans, tomatoes, olives, eggs, and fava beans. Flake the tuna into large pieces and arrange on top. Drizzle with the dressing and serve with lemon wedges and more dressing on the side.

TIMING TIPS:

- Up to 2 days ahead: Make the poached tuna and artichokes; refrigerate.

- Up to 1 day ahead: Cook the potatoes, make the dressing, and prep the green beans. Refrigerate until ready to use.

- Up to 4 hours ahead: Blanch the green beans and keep chilled; cook the eggs.

- Up to 2 hours ahead of time: Assemble the sald and keep chilled and covered until 30 minutes before serving.

SPICE-ROASTED SALMON WITH PICKLED MUSTARD SEEDS, CITRUS, AND HERBS

SERVES 4 TO 6

I like my salmon with a spicy rub and tangy, acidic accompaniments as a foil to the fatty richness of the fish. This dish is very easy and quick to make and beautiful to behold. It's self-saucing—making its own flavorful liquid as the mustard seeds, spices, cooking juices, and citrus mingle together. It's easily adaptable for a bigger crowd—just get a bigger piece of fish.

FOR THE PICKLED MUSTARD SEEDS:

½ cup yellow mustard seeds

1 cup water

¾ cup white wine vinegar or cider vinegar

¼ cup sugar

1½ teaspoons salt

FOR THE SALMON:

2 clementines, peeled and sectioned

2 blood oranges

1 Cara Cara orange (or ruby red grapefruit)

2 pounds skinless salmon fillet

2 teaspoons olive oil

2 teaspoons ground cumin

2 teaspoons ground coriander

2 teaspoons paprika

2 teaspoons salt

Freshly ground black pepper

1 cup lightly packed fresh herbs, such as parsley, dill, chervil, and mint

1 To make the pickled mustard seeds: Heat a small saucepan over high heat. Add the mustard seeds and toast until fragrant, about 3 minutes. Add the water, vinegar, sugar, and salt. Bring to a boil, then reduce the heat to maintain a simmer. Cook until the seeds are soft and plump and most of the liquid has been absorbed (it still should be spoonable), about 20 minutes. Transfer to a bowl to cool.

2 To make the salmon: Peel all of the citrus with a knife, removing all of the white pith. Cut crosswise into slices. If using grapefruit, cut out each section, leaving the membrane and pith behind.

3 Preheat the oven to 450°F. Line a large baking sheet with foil.

4 Place the salmon on the prepared baking sheet and rub with the oil. Mix together the cumin, coriander, paprika, salt, and pepper to taste and rub all over the salmon, making sure the top is well coated first. Roast for 12 to 15 minutes (depending on

recipe continues

You will have more pickled mustard seeds than you will need for this recipe, but they keep well in the fridge for months. Stir some into your vinaigrette, use as a condiment with pork or chicken, spread on your sandwiches, or dollop some on deviled eggs. Anywhere mustard might go, pickled mustard seeds can go!

thickness), for medium, or to desired doneness. Using two large spatulas, carefully transfer the fish to a serving platter, top with ¼ cup pickled mustard seeds, the citrus, and the herbs.

TIMING TIPS:

- Up to 1 week ahead: Make the pickled mustard seeds; refrigerate until ready to use.

- Up to 2 hours ahead: Prepare the citrus; leave at room temperature. Prep the herbs and refrigerate; coat the salmon with the spices and refrigerate.

- At the last minute: Cook the salmon and top with the pickled mustard seeds, citrus, and herbs.

CLAMS WITH CHORIZO AND SMOKED PAPRIKA

SERVES 4 TO 6 AS AN APPETIZER, 2 FOR DINNER

Clams are the ultimate quick and impressive dish. They're incredibly easy to cook, and they have such a powerfully good flavor. This dish comes together in no time, and is perfect for a "sitting around a table with a few beers" kind of dinner.

6 ounces fresh chorizo, removed from casing

3 garlic cloves, thinly sliced

1 teaspoon sweet smoked paprika

1 small red chile, sliced

24 littleneck clams, scrubbed

1 cup dry white wine

1 heaping cup cherry tomatoes, quartered

¼ cup fresh Italian parsley, chopped

Grilled crusty bread

1 Heat a 10-inch skillet over medium heat.

2 Add the chorizo to the pan and break it up with the back of a wooden spoon. Cook until the chorizo browns and shows no traces of pink, 4 to 6 minutes. Add the garlic and cook until golden, 2 minutes more. Add the paprika and chile and stir. Stir in the clams and add the wine. Cover the pan and cook until the liquid is simmering and the clams are starting to open, 5 to 6 minutes. Stir, then replace the lid and cook for 4 to 5 more minutes until all the clams have opened. Discard any that remain closed.

3 Add the tomatoes and stir. Cover and cook until the tomatoes are heated through but still hold their shape, 2 to 4 minutes. Remove the pan from the heat. Garnish with parsley and serve with grilled bread.

> **TIMING TIPS:**
> • Up to 1 hour ahead: Cook the chorizo, garlic, and spices.
> • At the last minute: Cook the clams; grill or toast the bread.

GRILLED SALMON WITH ZUCCHINI NOODLES AND GRILLED ROMANO BEANS

SERVES 2

This has become an easy go-to dinner for my husband and me in the summer, when life gets busy. It is quick, easy, healthful, and beautiful. While most of the recipes in this book are for larger groups, this one is just perfect for two. Romano beans, also called flat beans, really take to being thrown on the grill right next to the salmon as it cooks. If they are not in season, regular green beans or asparagus would work well too. I use a perforated grill platter (see page 121) to cook this, partly so the salmon doesn't stick, and also so the Romano beans don't fall through the grates, which would be tragic.

2 green zucchini, about 8 to 10 ounces each, cut on a spiralizer

Salt

Two 6- to 8-ounce salmon fillets, preferably wild

Freshly ground black pepper

1 tablespoon plus 2 teaspoons olive oil, plus more to coat the fish

1 pint Romano beans

2 garlic cloves, finely minced (about 1 tablespoon)

¼ cup slivered fresh basil, plus more for garnish

Red pepper flakes

10 Sungold tomatoes, cut in half

TIMING TIP:
This is a dish that comes together quickly at the last minute. However, you could make the zucchini noodles earlier in the day to save some time and last-minute mess.

1 Place the zucchini noodles in a colander set over a bowl and sprinkle with ½ teaspoon salt. Let sit for 15 to 20 minutes, tossing and occasionally lightly pressing, until a good amount of liquid has drained out. Blot with a paper towel to dry slightly.

2 Meanwhile, place the salmon on a plate, season with salt and pepper, and lightly coat with oil. Toss the Romano beans with 2 teaspoons oil and season with salt and pepper.

3 Heat the 1 tablespoon oil in a large (12-inch) skillet over medium heat. Add the garlic and cook until golden and fragrant, 2 to 3 minutes. Add the zucchini noodles and the slivered basil and cook for 3 to 4 minutes, until hot. Season with salt, pepper, and the red pepper flakes.

4 Heat a grill to high. Preheat an oiled grill platter. Place the fish skin-side down on the grill platter and cook for 2 to 3 minutes on each side, until cooked to desired doneness. Add the beans alongside the fish and cook, tossing once or twice, for 2 to 3 minutes, until lightly charred all over.

5 Reheat the noodles and toss in the basil and a pinch of red pepper flakes. Divide between 2 plates and top with the salmon. Strew the beans on top, scatter the tomatoes around the edges, and garnish with more basil.

GRILLED SWORDFISH WITH SPICY OLIVE RELISH

SERVES 4

Swordfish is back in my life after a long hiatus. For a time, it was mostly banned because of severe overfishing as a result of its popularity. But it's back (but cross-check your source with www.seafoodwatch.org), and it's one of the best fish to throw on the grill, along with tuna, which you easily could substitute here. Swordfish steaks tend to be large, and the entire crosscut is often sold, but they easily can be cut into two or more smaller pieces if you want to serve everyone a whole steak. More simply, grill larger pieces and slice before serving on top of the tomatoes and smothered with the olive relish. This looks great and allows the assertive flavors of the relish to soak in a bit to the somewhat bland fish. It also helps stretch the fish a lot further, especially if you are serving other dishes, like Fregola Salad (page 271), alongside (just skip the olives in that salad).

FOR THE RELISH:

1 cup pitted Kalamata olives, roughly chopped

Zest of 1 lemon

2 tablespoons fresh lemon juice

1 tablespoon chopped Calabrian chiles or Calabrian chile paste (or harissa)

¾ cup loosely packed soft herbs, such as basil, chives, parsley, or fennel fronds

1 stalk celery, thinly sliced

2 tablespoons olive oil

1 To make the relish; Combine the olives, lemon zest, lemon juice, chiles, herbs, celery, and olive oil in a small bowl and set aside.

2 To make the fish: Coat the swordfish with the oil, garlic, rosemary, salt, and pepper. Let marinate at room temperature for at least 15 minutes.

3 Heat a grill to high heat.

4 Place the swordfish steaks on the grill and cook for about 3 minutes per side, to desired doneness. Alternatively, sear the fish in a heavy skillet over medium-high for 3 minutes per side. Cooking time will vary depending on the thickness of the steaks; if they are thicker than 1 inch, increase the time accordingly.

recipe and ingredients continue

FOR THE FISH:

Four 6-ounce pieces swordfish,
    cut 1 inch thick, skin removed

1 tablespoon olive oil

1 large garlic clove, grated on a
    Microplane

1 tablespoon fresh rosemary leaves

Salt and freshly ground black pepper to
    taste

3 to 4 beefsteak or heirloom tomatoes

5 Slice the tomatoes and arrange them on a platter or divide among 4 serving plates. Arrange the steaks on top of the tomatoes (or slice the fish) and spoon the relish over the top. Serve warm or at room temperature.

TIMING TIPS:

- Up to 2 hours ahead: Make the olive relish; season the fish and refrigerate.

- Up to 1 hour ahead: Grill the fish—it's OK to serve this at room temperature.

- Just before serving: Slice the tomatoes and fish (if slicing) and top with the olive relish.

FRIED BLACK RICE WITH SHRIMP, SHIITAKES, AND SHISHITOS

SERVES 6

This dish was not intended to be alliterative; it just turned out that way. Fried rice is a pretty common dish in our house, as my husband is very good at cleaning out the fridge when he cooks, and I am more of a start-from-scratch kind of person. I am happy to cook the rice fresh for this, and I have a fondness not just for the taste and texture of black rice but for the color, which provides a striking backdrop for whatever you put in it and instantly elevates it above plain old white or brown rice. Luckily it's become a pretty common supermarket item, often labeled as "forbidden rice," but I don't forbid you, I encourage you to keep some in your pantry and use it often. Of course you can change up the ingredients to accommodate any tasty leftovers you may have and leave out anything you don't have or like. With an egg on top, it makes a full meal; if you want to serve this as a side, either add scrambled egg or leave the egg out altogether.

1 cup dry black rice (or 3 cups leftover cooked rice)

Salt

3 tablespoons neutral oil, such as canola, safflower, or grapeseed

8 large shiitake mushrooms, stems discarded and thickly sliced

4 thick scallions, whites and greens separated, sliced on a bias

¾ cup fresh corn kernels (cut from the cob)

8 to 10 shishito peppers, thickly sliced crosswise

1 small hot red chile, cut into thin rings

8 ounces medium shrimp, peeled and deveined, tails removed

1 to 2 tablespoons kimchi juice (optional)

6 large eggs, fried in butter (optional)

Freshly ground black pepper

1 Combine the dry rice with 1¾ cups water and a large pinch of salt in a small saucepan. Bring to a boil, stir, cover, and reduce the heat to maintain a steady simmer. Cook for 30 minutes, or until all the liquid is absorbed. Remove from the heat and let stand for 10 minutes. Fluff with a fork and transfer to a plate or small baking sheet to cool.

2 Heat a large, wide skillet or wok over high heat. Add 1 tablespoon of the oil and the mushrooms. Cook for 3 to 4 minutes, until nicely browned on both sides. Season lightly with salt. Transfer to a plate.

3 Let the pan cool a bit, then add the remaining 2 tablespoons oil and heat over medium-high heat. Add the white parts of scallions, the corn, shishitos, and red chile. Cook for 4 to 5 minutes, until everything begins to brown. Add the rice—and a little water if it is sticking—and cook, tossing, for 2 minutes.

recipe continues

Clear space in the pan and add the shrimp. Cook for 1 to 2 minutes on each side, then mix everything together, adding the scallion greens and reserved mushrooms. Add the kimchi juice (if using).

4 Divide among 6 plates and top each one with a fried egg, if desired. Crack pepper over the top and serve.

TIMING TIPS:

- Up to 1 day ahead: Cook the rice; refrigerate until ready to use.

- Up to 1 hour ahead: Prep the vegetables and make the fried rice.

- Just before serving: Reheat the rice and fry the eggs.

VEGETARIAN (OR NEARLY)

CREAMY BAKED RISOTTO WITH BUTTERNUT SQUASH AND FRIED SAGE LEAVES

SERVES 6 TO 8

Everyone loves a good, creamy risotto, but it's a little hard to pull off at the last minute with the nearly constant stirring required. I don't know about you, but I've got lots of other things to do twenty minutes before sitting down to eat! This version can be made well ahead of time—up to one day before you want to serve it, so all you have to do is pop it in the oven about a half hour before you're ready to serve, and you'll have a bubbling, creamy side dish that everyone will love. Serve it with chicken, pork, or turkey meatballs, or as a meatless main with a green salad (page 238) on the side.

4 to 5 cups low-sodium chicken or vegetable stock

4 cups diced butternut squash (from 1 medium squash)

1 tablespoon olive oil

3 tablespoons unsalted butter

2 medium shallots, minced (about ½ cup)

1 tablespoon chopped fresh rosemary or sage

1½ cups Arborio rice

½ cup dry white wine

Freshly grated nutmeg

1 teaspoon salt, plus more to taste

Freshly ground black pepper

1 cup grated Parmigiano-Reggiano cheese

3 ounces Taleggio or fontina cheese, grated

¼ cup panko breadcrumbs

Fried Sage Leaves (page 28)

1 Set a saucepan with the stock on the back burner of the stove and add the squash. Bring to a simmer over medium heat. Lower the heat and simmer, partially covered (so you don't cook off too much of the stock), until the squash is just tender, about 10 minutes. Keep warm over low heat.

2 Heat the oil and 1 tablespoon of the butter in a low, wide saucepan over medium-low heat and add the shallots and rosemary. Cook, stirring frequently, until the shallots are softened and golden, about 8 minutes. Turn up the heat to medium-high, add the rice, and cook, stirring, until the grains look slightly translucent, 2 to 3 minutes. Add the wine and cook until it's nearly absorbed. Add a ladleful of stock (it should be just enough to barely cover the surface of the rice) and using a slotted spoon, add a few spoonfuls of squash. Cook at a lively simmer, stirring very frequently, until it's nearly absorbed, about 2 to 3 minutes. Continue adding stock and squash in this way until the rice is very creamy but still al dente, 15 to 20 minutes total. You may not need all of the stock, but do add all of the squash, pressing some of it against the side of the pan as you go to add starch to the liquid. Add 1 tablespoon of the remaining butter, the nutmeg, and salt and season with pepper. Stir in ¾ cup of the Parmigiano cheese and the Taleggio cheese.

recipe continues

3 Transfer the risotto to a large bowl to cool slightly, stirring occasionally. Add enough extra stock to make the risotto a little soupy (you want it extra loose, as it will continue to absorb liquid). Transfer the mixture to a medium baking dish. Either set aside for up to 2 hours or cover and refrigerate until ready to use.

4 Preheat the oven to 375°F.

5 Melt the remaining 1 tablespoon butter, mix with the breadcrumbs and the remaining ¼ cup Parmigiano cheese, and sprinkle on top. Bake for 30 to 35 minutes, until bubbling and golden brown. Garnish with the fried sage leaves. Serve immediately.

TIMING TIPS:

- Up to 1 day ahead: Make the risotto and buttered breadcrumbs. Refrigerate until ready to use.

- About 1 hour ahead: Remove the risotto from the fridge to let it warm up.

- About 35 minutes before serving: Bake the risotto; make the fried sage leaves.

GRANDMA PIE WITH BROCCOLI RABE AND SAUSAGE

SERVES 8 TO 10

I first became acquainted with the Grandma Pie, a Long Island specialty, on one of my many trips back and forth between New York City and my place on the eastern end of Long Island. I love pizza, so I was always tempted to stop about halfway home for a slice. The pizza was pretty average at this particular place, but still, it was pizza. One day they had grandma pie, and it was better than average and exactly what I wanted—a nice neat car snack—not too saucy and crisp on the bottom. I continued to ask for it on subsequent trips, but they rarely had it! A big pan of pizza (or two) is a great way to feed a crowd, and happily. If you have vegetarians, it's easy to leave off the meat—you could substitute with well-roasted sliced shiitake mushrooms, which will lend a meatless note of umami.

FOR THE DOUGH:

1½ teaspoons active dry yeast

1½ cups warm water

1 teaspoon sugar

2 tablespoons olive oil, plus more
   for the bowl

3½ cups all-purpose flour, plus more
   for kneading

1½ teaspoons salt

1 To make the dough: In a large liquid measuring cup, dissolve the yeast in the warm water. Stir in the sugar and oil. Combine the flour and salt in the bowl of a stand mixer fitted with the paddle attachment. Mix briefly to combine, then slowly pour in the yeast mixture on low speed until well combined. Mix for about 5 minutes on medium speed, until smooth. Use a bowl scraper to ease the dough into a ball, and transfer to a smaller well-oiled bowl. Turn it a few times to make sure the dough and the sides of the bowl are all well-oiled. Cover tightly with plastic wrap, and refrigerate overnight, or see note below if you want to make right away.

2 To make the pizza: In a medium bowl, combine the tomatoes, garlic, oregano, basil, and salt and season with red pepper flakes. Set aside.

3 Heat a large (12-inch) nonstick skillet over medium-high heat. Add the sausage and cook until no longer pink, breaking it up with a wooden spoon as it cooks, 6 to 8 minutes. Remove from the pan and set aside. Meanwhile, wash the broccoli rabe. Drain the broccoli rabe (but not very well; you want it to be dripping

recipe continues

FOR THE PIZZA:

One 28-ounce can San Marzano
    tomatoes, drained and broken up
    (cores removed and liquid discarded
    or saved for another use)

2 to 3 garlic cloves, chopped
    (1 heaping tablespoon)

½ teaspoon dried oregano

6 fresh basil leaves

¾ teaspoon salt, plus more as needed

Red pepper flakes

10 ounces (4 links) hot Italian pork
    sausage, removed from casings
    (optional)

1 bunch broccoli rabe, thick stems
    removed

¼ cup olive oil

8 ounces fresh mozzarella cheese,
    sliced ¼ inch thick and torn

wet). Add it to the pan and increase the heat to high. Season lightly with salt and cover. Cook for 2 minutes, tossing once or twice. Remove with tongs to a plate and drain off any extra liquid.

4 About 1 hour before you want to assemble the pizza, remove the dough from the refrigerator.

5 Preheat the oven to 500°F. If you have a pizza stone, place it on the bottom rack of the oven and preheat it too.

6 Pour the oil into a 13 by 18-inch rimmed baking sheet and spread the dough in the pan. If it pulls back, cover with plastic wrap and let rest for 10 minutes. Spread the dough to fill the entire pan.

7 Sprinkle on the cheese, followed by the sauce, and then the broccoli rabe and sausage. Place on the pizza stone or bottom rack of the oven. Bake for 25 to 30 minutes, until crisp on the bottom and browned on the edges. Cut into squares and serve immediately.

TIMING TIPS:

- Up to 1 day ahead: Make the dough and refrigerate; brown the sausage and cook the broccoli rabe; prepare the tomatoes and store in the fridge.

- About 1 hour ahead: Prepare the pizza for the oven and bake.

NOTE:

Making pizza dough a day (or two) before you need it is not only convenient, but it also allows for a slow rise and a chance for fermentation, which equals flavor. If, however, last-minute inspiration for pizza strikes, you can skip the refrigeration step, and just let the dough rise until doubled at room temperature—it will take about 1 hour.

PINK PASTA

SERVES 6 TO 8

One of the best investments you can make is for a pretty oven-to-table dish (or two) so you can make a baked pasta recipe like this one (and myriad other oven-to-table baked things) look gorgeous. I love my copper pieces, and this one technically is a tarte Tatin dish, but I prefer it for baked pasta. The ingredients are so simple for this dish—they can be found in any supermarket—and it is quick to prepare, but the whole is so much greater than the sum of its parts. Like any of the baked pasta recipes in this book, you can serve it à la minute if you want. But baking it not only allows you to get ahead in style, it adds an irresistible crunchy top that your guests will fight over.

Unsalted butter, for the baking dish

2 tablespoons olive oil

2 medium red onions, sliced lengthwise into ¼-inch-thick wedges

2 large garlic cloves, thinly sliced

1 large head radicchio, cored and sliced into ½-inch-thick ribbons

Salt

8 ounces soft goat cheese

1½ cups heavy cream

1 pound short pasta, such as gemelli, strozzapreti, or penne

4 ounces thinly sliced prosciutto, torn into bite-size pieces (optional)

6 ounces fontina cheese, cut into ½-inch cubes

Generous gratings of nutmeg

10 to 12 grinds black pepper

1 fluffy cup grated Parmigiano-Reggiano cheese (1 ounce)

TIMING TIP:

The entire dish can be made and assembled 1 day ahead. Refrigerate until 1 hour before ready to bake.

1 Preheat the oven to 375°F. Butter a large (3-quart) baking dish and set aside.

2 Heat the oil in a large (12-inch) skillet over medium-high heat. Add the onions and cook until lightly browned and softened, 10 to 12 minutes total. After the first 7 minutes, add the garlic.

3 Add the radicchio and ½ teaspoon salt and cook until wilted, 3 to 4 minutes. Crumble in the goat cheese, add the cream, and bring to a simmer. Remove from the heat and set aside.

4 Cook the pasta in a pot of liberally salted water until shy of al dente. You want it a little firmer than usual, as it will continue to soften while baking. Scoop out 1 cup of the pasta water, drain pasta, and add the pasta and the water to the skillet with the vegetables, stirring.

5 Fold in the prosciutto (if using) and two-thirds of the fontina cheese. Toss well and season with nutmeg, salt, and pepper. Transfer to the prepared baking dish. Dot the top with the remaining fontina cheese and sprinkle with the Parmigiano cheese. Transfer to the oven and bake for 30 to 35 minutes, until golden brown on top and bubbling at the edges. Serve immediately. Alternatively, let the assembled dish cool, cover with foil, and refrigerate until ready to serve. Take out of the refrigerator about 1 hour before baking and bake 45 to 50 minutes.

SQUASH AND SQUASH BLOSSOM FRITTATA

SERVES 6

Squash blossoms, which are available all summer both in the Union Square Greenmarket, where I often shop, or at the various farm stands that I frequent in Long Island, really embellish this easy-to-make frittata in the most beautiful way, but it still is delicious without them. In fact, squash blossoms, truth be told, don't add all that much in terms of flavor, but they sure add a "wow" factor to anything they adorn.

1 tablespoon olive oil

4 small (baby) zucchini or 2 large zucchini (about 12 ounces total), cut into ¼-inch coins

Salt and freshly ground black pepper

1 bunch scallions (about 7 thin), white and green parts, trimmed and sliced

6 large eggs

¼ cup heavy cream or milk

12 fresh basil leaves, slivered

½ ounce (½ fluffy cup) grated Parmigiano-Reggiano cheese

¼ cup ricotta cheese

2 large squash blossoms, cleaned, petals separated (optional)

½ cup baby cherry tomatoes or Sungold tomatoes

1 tablespoon melted unsalted butter

1 Preheat the broiler.

2 Heat a medium (10-inch) nonstick skillet over medium-high heat. Add the oil and zucchini and season with salt and pepper. Cook, tossing, until golden and crisp-tender, about 6 minutes. Add the scallions and reduce the heat to medium-low. Beat the eggs well with the cream, ½ teaspoon salt, and some pepper. Stir in the basil and Parmigiano-Reggiano cheese. Use a spatula to pull back the edges to the center as they cook until almost set, 5 to 7 minutes. Dollop the ricotta cheese all over the top and arrange squash blossom petals (green sides up) and tomatoes on top. Brush the squash blossoms with the butter, then place under the broiler for 2 to 3 minutes, until golden brown. Crack pepper over the top and serve warm or at room temperature.

TIMING TIP:
This comes together quickly at the last minute.

TIP:

If the frittata seems like it might be stuck to the pan, cover the pan with a lid and let it sit for a few minutes off the heat. The steam that's created will help it release from the pan.

FLOWER OMELETTE CREPES

SERVES 6

You can use any kind of edible flower, including chive blossoms, violas, squash blossoms (just separate the flowers into petals), or soft herbs like parsley, chervil, chives, or tarragon to make these pretty crepe-like omelettes. It's key to have the flowers or herbs ready next to the stove as you make these, because you only have a short window to sprinkle them on before the egg sets. These are very easy to make, but like any crepe, it may take one or two until you get the timing and heat level right, so be prepared with an extra egg or two. It is also essential to have a really nonstick pan. I love that you can make them completely ahead of time (even a day ahead), pile them up on a plate as you would with crepes, and refrigerate until needed. You can fold them around cheese (any kind, including soft goat cheese and ricotta) and cooked vegetables (a few cooked asparagus or some spinach would be nice), warm them in the oven at 300°F just long enough for the cheese to melt, and voilà—omelettes for a crew and no sweat on your brow, and they look pretty too!

6 large eggs

Salt

Unsalted butter, as needed

Edible flowers and herbs

Humboldt Fog, soft goat cheese or any cheese of your choosing

Cooked vegetables, such as asparagus or spinach (optional)

TIMING TIPS:

- Up to 1 day ahead: Make the crepes and refrigerate.

- Up to 2 hours ahead: Fill the crepes.

- At the last minute: Pop the crepes in the oven to warm up.

1 Using a whisk, beat 1 egg with a big pinch of salt in a small bowl until thoroughly blended and smooth. Heat a medium (10-inch) nonstick skillet over medium-low heat until hot. Add a bit of butter (1 to 2 teaspoons), let it melt, and swirl it around to coat the pan evenly.

2 Add the egg, scraping every bit of it in with a rubber spatula, and swirl until it coats the entire surface of the pan and is just set, about 20 seconds. Quickly arrange some of the flowers and herbs on the surface. Cover and cook for 2 minutes, or until the egg is firmly set—you should be able to lift it at the edge without tearing. If not, cover and cook for a few seconds longer. Gently flip and cook on the other side for about 15 seconds. Transfer to a dinner plate and repeat. Pile up the crepes right on top of each other as you go. Let cool, wrap tightly in plastic wrap, and refrigerate.

3 When ready to serve, preheat the oven to 300°F.

4 Cut a small, flat piece of cheese (about 1 ounce) and place it near the edge of a crepe. Fold the crepe in half, and then in half again (at this point you could refrigerate until ready to serve). Place on a baking sheet and bake for about 10 minutes, just until they are warm and the cheese has melted. Serve immediately.

SUMMER VEGETABLE GALETTE

SERVES 8 TO 12

I recently served this at an all-girls dinner party for ten. I thought, "Well, not much of this will get eaten, because my friends aren't buttery pastry-eaters" but boy was I wrong. It was eaten, and raved about, with most people going back for seconds. It works beautifully as a side dish alongside any simple protein, and provides a substantial option for a vegetarian guest. I'd also happily serve this for lunch with just a green salad to go along with it.

It may seem like a lot of trouble to roast all of the vegetables first before tucking them into their blanket of flaky, buttery dough (rather than just using raw vegetables), but trust me, it makes a huge difference. Always in search of the easiest route to delicious, I tried just baking the vegetables in the crust, but, *meh*. I ended up with grayish eggplant, tepid-tasting zucchini, so-so tomatoes, and, well, you get the picture. Roasting everything first concentrates all the flavors and cooks out excess moisture, so you end up with a succulent flavor bomb of a tart that is hard to resist.

FOR THE CRUST:

2 cups all-purpose flour, plus more for rolling out the dough

½ teaspoon salt

1 teaspoon sugar

Big pinch of Aleppo or cayenne pepper

2 teaspoons fresh thyme leaves

¾ cup grated Parmigiano-Reggiano cheese (grated on the small round holes of a box grater)

14 tablespoons (1¾ sticks) cold unsalted butter

1 To make the crust: Combine the flour, salt, sugar, pepper, thyme, and Parmigiano cheese in the bowl of a food processor. Pulse to combine. Cut the butter into tablespoon-size pieces and toss into the bowl. Pulse until the butter is broken down into almond- to pea-size pieces. Transfer to a wide bowl and continue to break down the butter by combing your hands through the flour mixture and flattening the butter chunks between your fingertips (but work quickly to keep the butter cold). When there are no more large chunks of butter left, drizzle in ¼ cup ice water (I like to make ice water in a large measuring cup, and then measure out ¼ cup in a smaller measuring cup) while stirring with a fork to distribute it evenly. Press together with your hands. If it seems very dry and crumbly (a little crumbly is OK), dribble in a tiny bit more water. Knead once or twice, then form into a rough rectangle and wrap in plastic wrap. Press down, and use a bench scraper to form it into an even better rectangle, 1 to 1½ inches thick. Refrigerate for at least 1 hour or up to 2 days, or freeze for up to 1 month.

recipe and ingredients continue

FOR THE ROASTED VEGETABLES:

4 Kumato (brown) tomatoes or
     plum tomatoes, cut crosswise into
     3 thick slices

1 tablespoon olive oil

Salt and freshly ground black pepper

2 garlic cloves, thinly slivered

3 to 4 sprigs fresh thyme

1 pound Fairy Tale or Japanese eggplant

1 pound small zucchini, cut into
     ¾-inch-thick coins

1 medium red onion, sliced into
     ½-inch-thick wedges

FOR THE CHEESE FILLING:

10 ounces fresh ricotta cheese

4 ounces soft goat cheese

2 garlic cloves, grated on a Microplane

2 tablespoons shredded fresh basil

2 large eggs, lightly beaten

TO FINISH:

2 ounces aged goat cheese
     (soft goat cheese with a white rind)

½ cup halved Sungold or other cherry
     tomato

1 large egg yolk

2 tablespoons heavy cream or milk

¼ cup grated Parmigiano-Reggiano
     cheese (grated on the small round
     holes of a box grater)

Fresh basil, for garnish

2 To make the roasted vegetables: Preheat the oven to 300°F. Line a baking sheet with parchment paper.

3 On the prepared pan, toss the tomatoes with 1 teaspoon of the oil and season with salt and pepper. Spread out evenly, top with the garlic and the thyme sprigs, and bake for 1 hour and 15 minutes, or until shriveled on the edges and starting to brown. Set aside.

4 Turn the oven temperature up to 450°F.

5 If using Fairy Tale eggplant, cut them in half lengthwise. If using Japanese eggplant, cut into ½-inch-thick bias-cut slices. In a large bowl, toss the eggplant, zucchini, and red onion in the remaining 2 teaspoons oil and season with salt and pepper. Spread out on 2 baking sheets with the cut sides down. Roast for 15 to 18 minutes, without turning, until the zucchini are browned on one side, the eggplant is tender and browned, and the red onions are softened and lightly browned. Remove the vegetables to a plate as they are done. Take care not to overcook them, because they will be cooking some more in the galette. Let cool and reduce the oven temperature to 400°F.

6 To form the galette: Line an 11 x 18-inch baking sheet with parchment paper and have it nearby. On a lightly floured surface, roll out the dough, taking care to retain the roughly rectangular shape, about 13 by 20 inches. Continue rolling from the center out, flouring as needed. It's a good idea to flour the top with your hand, roll it up onto the rolling pin, and flip it over once or twice so it doesn't stick. Work quickly so the dough doesn't get too soft. Roll the dough onto the rolling pin and unroll it onto the prepared pan. The dough will hang off the edges a little, but that's OK. Pop it back into the refrigerator while you make the cheese filling.

7 To make the cheese filling: Combine the ricotta cheese, soft goat cheese, garlic, basil, eggs, ¼ teaspoon salt, and a few grinds of pepper. Stir well to combine. When the dough is firm and cold again, spread the cheese mixture over it, leaving a 2-inch border. If the vegetables aren't ready, chill again.

8 Assemble and bake the galette: Arrange the roasted tomatoes, zucchini, eggplant (with the browned sides up), and onions on top of the cheese, mixing them up however you please. Scatter the aged goat cheese and cherry tomatoes on top. Fold the dough over the edges of the tart, forming a 2-inch-wide border. Mix the egg yolk and cream with a fork and brush the exposed pastry with the egg wash. Sprinkle the Parmigiano cheese over the top, aiming for the pastry. Bake for 35 to 40 minutes, until the filling is bubbling, the pastry is deep golden brown, and your whole house smells amazing. Serve warm or at room temperature topped with a handful of basil leaves.

TIMING TIPS:

- Up to 1 month ahead: Make and freeze the dough; defrost in refrigerator 1 day before using.

- Up to 1 day ahead: Make the cheese filling and refrigerate.

- Up to 8 hours ahead: Roast the vegetables and assemble the galette.

- Up to 2 hours ahead: Bake the galette; reheat if desired.

ZA'ATAR TOFU BOWLS

SERVES 4

I like to serve these bowls for a Sunday lunch when I might be hosting a vegetarian, but it's a good time for any of us to eat something healthy and light to make up for whatever damage we did the night before. Speaking of the night before, I might use some accidentally-on-purpose leftover roasted vegetables, and even the rice or beans (always planning ahead!). Bowls *are* the modern way to eat leftovers, after all. Adding some freshly cooked or prepared elements or warming the vegetables doesn't make this feel like leftovers at all. Change up the vegetables according to what's in season, what you like, or what you may have in the house. Winter squash, cauliflower, shallots, fennel, and summer squash all are good options.

FOR THE ZA'ATAR TOFU:

One 14- to 16-ounce block medium-firm tofu, drained

2 tablespoons olive oil

1 tablespoon za'atar (see page 15)

1 teaspoon garlic powder

½ teaspoon salt

2 garlic cloves, slivered

FOR THE TAHINI SAUCE:

½ cup tahini

2 tablespoons white miso (I prefer the "less sodium" variety)

2 teaspoons low-sodium tamari

A few dashes of sriracha

2 teaspoons maple syrup

¼ cup plain Greek yogurt (any fat content)

2 tablespoons fresh lemon juice

1 To make the za'atar tofu: Cut the tofu lengthwise into 4 rectangular slabs and wrap them in a few layers of paper towel. Press down lightly and weight with something moderately heavy, like a few cans on top of a small cutting board, for 10 to 15 minutes to squeeze some of the water out.

2 Cut each rectangle of tofu into 3 squares, so you have 12 squares total, and place on a dinner plate. Rub with 1 tablespoon of the oil and dust with the za'atar, garlic powder, and salt. Turn to coat well. Heat a large (12-inch) skillet over medium-high heat until quite hot. Add 1 tablespoon oil, the fresh garlic, and the tofu. Cook until the tofu is browned and crisp on both sides, 3 to 4 minutes per side. If not serving right away, keep warm at the lowest setting your oven has—this also will crisp the tofu a little more.

3 To make the tahini sauce: Combine all of the ingredients in a small bowl and whisk together until smooth, adding ¼ cup warm water or more as needed, until it reaches a thick, creamy but pourable consistency. Set aside.

4 Preheat the oven to 425°F.

5 To roast the vegetables: Place the Broccolini, turnips, and carrots (in separate sections) on a large baking sheet. Coat

recipe continues

FOR THE BOWLS:

1 small bunch Broccolini, separated into stalks, tough stems removed

4 small Hakurei or 2 larger turnips, trimmed, peeled, and quartered

1 small bunch carrots, trimmed and peeled (½ inch of stem left on)

Olive oil

Salt and freshly ground black pepper

3 cups cooked black or brown rice

1½ cups white beans (any cooked or canned bean will work)

1 medium beet, peeled and grated

2 large radishes, cut into paper-thin slices

Sumac (optional)

lightly with oil and season with salt and pepper. Roast for 20 to 35 minutes, until golden brown and tender, removing any pieces that are done early.

6 To assemble the bowls: Divide the rice and beans among 4 bowls. Add the roasted vegetables and tofu. Garnish with the grated beet and radish slices. Serve the sauce on the side, sprinkled with sumac (if using) and a drizzle of oil.

TIMING TIPS:

- Up to 1 day ahead: Cook the beans and rice (the rice is better cooked fresh and served warm; re-steam briefly before serving if making ahead); trim and cut up the vegetables; make the tahini sauce. Refrigerate until ready to serve.

- Up to 1 hour ahead: Make the tofu; keep warm in oven or in pan (rewarm at the last minute). Roast the vegetables; grate the beets. Take the tahini out of the fridge to warm up.

- At the last minute: Assemble the bowls and garnishes and serve with the tahini sauce.

STRESS-LESS CHEESE SOUFFLÉ

SERVES 4

Making a soufflé isn't as tricky as you might think, given all the dire warnings (Don't you dare open the oven! Avoid loud noises!) that usually come with recipes for them. In fact, you can assemble a soufflé many hours ahead of time, as long as you put the soufflé mixture in the dish it will be baked in and stick it in the fridge (yes, really!). Also, let's manage our expectations of loftiness, and let's be OK with a slightly sunken soufflé. Your guests will think you are a real genius pulling this thing out of the oven and serving them scoops of piping-hot cheese heaven. Making it in a flat baking dish means it doesn't have so far to fall, and also creates a lot more surface area to brown, turning it into something a little different and more casual than the classic toque-like affair. You can add any herbs you like to this soufflé, or even finely chopped cooked spinach. I like to serve this for brunch, lunch, or a light supper with a Simple but Exceptional Green Salad (page 238). I still advise you to time this so you can serve it immediately upon removing from the oven for the best effect.

3 tablespoons unsalted butter, plus more for the dish (softened)

Grated Parmigiano-Reggiano cheese, for the dish

2 shallots, minced

¼ cup all-purpose flour

1 cup whole milk

1 heaping cup grated Gruyère cheese (about 3 ounces)

A few gratings of nutmeg

Big pinch of cayenne pepper

½ teaspoon salt

Freshly ground black pepper

4 large egg yolks, at room temperature

6 large egg whites, at room temperature

Pinch of cream of tartar

1 Generously butter a small (9 x 7-inch, 1-quart) baking dish and dust with Parmigiano-Reggiano cheese, tapping out any excess.

2 Heat the butter in a medium saucepan over medium-low heat. Add the shallots and cook until translucent, 4 to 6 minutes. Add the flour and cook, stirring constantly, for 2 to 3 minutes more. Slowly whisk in the milk. Bring to a boil over medium-high heat, lower the heat to maintain a simmer, and simmer for 5 minutes, stirring frequently; it will be very thick. Add the Gruyère cheese and stir until melted. Season with the nutmeg, cayenne, salt, and pepper to taste—it should be overseasoned at this point, as you will be diluting the flavor considerably with the eggs. Whisk in the egg yolks one at a time. Transfer to a large bowl and keep warm by covering with foil and keeping in a warm place.

recipe continues

3 In the bowl of a stand mixer (you also can do this by hand with a bowl and whisk or a hand mixer), beat the egg whites with the cream of tartar until stiff peaks form. Be careful not to overbeat—it still should look creamy and smooth, not crumbly and dry. Whisk about one-third of the whites into the cheese sauce to lighten the mixture, then fold the remaining whites in until well combined. Transfer to the prepared baking dish and chill until needed, unless you are baking right away.

4 Preheat the oven to 400°F.

5 Place the baking dish on a baking sheet and bake for 5 minutes. Reduce the oven temperature to 375°F and bake until puffed and golden and not too jiggly in the center, 15 to 20 minutes longer.

MEYER LEMON GNOCCHI WITH SPRING VEGETABLES

SERVES 6 TO 8

Gnocchi are the ultimate belly-filling, soul-satisfying comfort food, but you don't want to be standing around making gnocchi when guests are at your door. Not that they are only for guests—a two-year-old would find a lot to like too! There are a couple of ways to get ahead here. You could form the gnocchi and let them sit at room temperature for an hour or so before boiling. You could, of course, just continue with the recipe, brown, and serve, but to get ahead, coat with a little olive oil after cooking and draining, wrap tight, and refrigerate until needed. You also could spread them out on a parchment-lined baking sheet, freeze until hard, and transfer to a resealable plastic bag. Keep frozen until ready to cook—do not defrost! The only caveat for this method is that you must have abundant boiling water, and you should boil in smaller batches so that the water doesn't take too long to return to a boil. Just scoop them out with a slotted spoon and drain while you cook the rest. They will be a little more "furry" looking, but by the time they are browned, they will be just fine. The one thing you do not want to do is keep the uncooked gnocchi in the fridge for more than a few hours, as they will just get gummy and sticky.

This is just one (lighter and fresher) way to serve these pillowy gnocchi. They freeze well, so even if the recipe makes more than you need, you'll have them handy in the freezer when inspiration (or cravings) strike. They also can be served quickly and simply with brown butter, sage, and Parmigiano-Reggiano, or with your favorite tomato sauce with whatever veggie add-ins you want. They aren't at all difficult to make, but you will want a ricer or a food mill (my preference) to process the potatoes. A food mill is useful for many other things (applesauce, tomato sauce, fruit purees, etc.) and requires less elbow grease than a ricer, so I highly recommend making the small investment in this very old-fashioned but extremely useful kitchen tool.

FOR THE GNOCCHI:

4 large russet potatoes (about 3 pounds), unpeeled, scrubbed, left whole

1 tablespoon plus 2½ teaspoons salt, plus more for cooking the gnocchi

2 large eggs

Zest of 1 lemon, preferably Meyer

1½ cups all-purpose flour, plus more as needed

1 Place the potatoes and 1 tablespoon of the salt in a large saucepan and cover with cold water by 3 inches. Cover and bring to a boil over high heat. Reduce the heat to medium-high, uncover, and cook, turning the potatoes occasionally, until they meet no resistance when pierced with the tip of a sharp paring knife, 35 to 40 minutes. If the potatoes are large, it might take a few minutes longer.

recipe and ingredients continue

TO FINISH:

1 tablespoon plus 2 teaspoons butter

1 tablespoon plus 2 teaspoons olive oil

Salt and freshly ground black pepper

1 bunch (about 1 pound) asparagus, trimmed, and cut into 2-inch lengths

1 cup cooked fava beans (see page 27), or fresh or frozen (thawed) shelled peas

1 lemon, preferably Meyer

¼ cup soft fresh herbs, such as parsley, chives, chervil, and tarragon

---

TIMING TIPS:

- Up to 1 month ahead: Make the gnocchi and freeze on baking sheets; once hard, transfer to a resealable plastic bag.

- Up to 1 day ahead; Boil the gnocchi and drain thoroughly. Refrigerate until ready to use.

- At the last minute: Brown the gnocchi and finish the dish.

TIP:

If you don't have a food mill or a ricer, you can grate the potatoes on the large holes of a box grater. You also can use leftover mashed potatoes!

2 Drain in a colander and peel (just pull off the skin with your fingers) as soon as they are cool enough to handle—use a paper towel or clean kitchen towel to help you handle the heat. Pass the potatoes through a food mill fitted with the finest disk into a bowl, or use a ricer. Spread the potatoes out onto a couple of layers of paper towel and let cool until lukewarm. Remove the paper towels, form the potatoes into a mound, and make a well in the center. Break the eggs into the well and add the remaining 2½ teaspoons salt and the lemon zest. Use a fork to beat the eggs and gradually start incorporating the potatoes. Knead until smooth, using a bench scraper to help you work the dough. Sprinkle 1 cup of flour over the top and gently knead it in until it is all mixed together and forms a dough. Add the remaining ½ cup flour and knead until incorporated. Transfer to a lightly floured surface, lightly flour the dough, and knead 10 to 12 times to ensure that everything is well incorporated and the dough is soft and smooth. If it still feels at all sticky, add more flour by the tablespoonful until it doesn't. You want to add as little flour as possible so the gnocchi remain light and soft. Because of the variables in size and moisture levels in the potatoes, you will need to use your instincts a bit here. If you are unsure, cook a test gnocchi. The main point is to add enough flour so they stay together when cooked.

3 Divide the dough into 4 pieces. On a lightly floured surface, gently roll the dough into a thick rope about ¾ inch in diameter. If it gets too long to manage, cut it in half using the bench scraper or a knife. Cut into 1-inch pieces and transfer to a generously floured, parchment-lined baking sheet. Refrigerate until needed if cooking within a few hours, otherwise freeze them in single layers on the baking sheet. Once frozen, transfer to a container or resealable plastic bag until needed.

4 Bring a large pot of water to a boil. Add a small handful of salt. Carefully drop in half the gnocchi (if they have been frozen previously, go straight from the freezer to the water) and return to a boil. Cook for 2 to 3 minutes, until they float. Scoop them out with a strainer or slotted spoon and drain thoroughly. Coat lightly with oil and refrigerate if not using right away. Repeat with the remaining gnocchi.

5 When ready to serve, heat a large (12-inch) nonstick skillet over medium-high heat. Add 1 tablespoon oil and 1 tablespoon butter. Sprinkle with salt and pepper. Cook half the gnocchi, tossing occasionally, until deep golden brown on both sides, about 5 minutes. Transfer to a plate. Repeat. After all the gnocchi have been browned, add another 2 teaspoons oil and 2 teaspoons butter to the pan. Add the asparagus and cook for 3 minutes, or until just tender. Add the fava beans and cook until heated through, about 1 minute. Return the gnocchi to the skillet and toss to combine. Zest the lemon over the top, then cut the lemon in half and squeeze the juice of half a lemon over the top. Season with salt and pepper. Sprinkle on the herbs and serve immediately.

GIAMBOTTA

SERVES 4 TO 6

You know when you go to the farmer's market or farm stand (or get a CSA box) in the summer and you buy way too much of everything because it all looks so good, but then when you get it all home you're not quite sure what to do with it all? (That's me, all the time.) Or maybe you just want to celebrate summer through produce? Well, here's your answer. Giambotta, aka ciambotta, as your Italian grandmother made it, more closely resembles ratatouille than this vegetable stew, which aims to be way more colorful, less tomato-y, and a whole lot fresher tasting than the traditional summer veggie stew. So, here's the thing, you can use any variety of vegetables to make this, and the proportions don't really matter that much—just think of it as a cooked salad, follow the basic guide-lines, and you really can't go wrong—but I like to start with the vegetables that can stand up to a little more cooking to build the flavor for the stew, like shallots, leeks, fennel, corn, yellow wax beans, Romano beans, yellow squash, and then add the more delicate and vibrantly colored vegetables, like green beans, zucchini, radishes, and tomatoes and herbs toward the end so that the whole thing ends up looking gorgeous and has a contrast of flavors, textures, and colors. A parm rind would not be out of place stewing along with everything to add a little extra flavor to the broth. Serve it on its own as a vegetarian main course for lunch or dinner, perhaps with an egg on top, with some grilled halloumi, grated parm, or simple cranberry beans (page 37), or alongside any simple grilled meat or fish, along with crusty bread to mop up the juices.

¼ cup extra-virgin olive oil, plus more for drizzling

1 small onion, halved and thinly sliced

2 medium shallots, sliced crosswise (about 1 cup)

2 cups sliced leeks, white and light green parts (1 large)

2 garlic cloves, thinly sliced

Salt and freshly ground black pepper

1 cup fresh corn kernels (cut from the cob of 1 large or 2 small ears)

2 cups sliced fennel (2 to 3 baby, 1 medium, or ½ large)

1 cup Romano beans, cut into 2-inch lengths

1 Heat the oil in a large, wide, shallow pot over medium heat. Add the onion, shallot, leeks, and garlic, season with ½ teaspoon salt, and cook until softened, about 8 minutes. Add the corn and fennel and cook, stirring, for 4 to 5 minutes, until the fennel is softened and translucent. Add the Romano beans, wax beans, and yellow summer squash.

2 Season with ½ teaspoon salt and pepper, add 1 cup water, cover, and cook over medium-low heat for about 6 minutes, or until the vegetables have softened. Add the green beans, radishes, zucchini, and broccoli and another ½ cup to 1 cup water, depending on how soupy you want it.

recipe and ingredients continue

1½ cups wax beans, cut into 2-inch lengths

1 yellow summer squash, cut into ½-inch-thick half-moons (about 1½ cups)

1 small zucchini, cut into ½-inch-thick half-moons (about 1½ cups)

2 cups green beans, cut into 2-inch lengths

1 bunch radishes, cut in half lengthwise if large

1 to 2 cups tiny broccoli or Broccolini florets

1 pint cup cherry tomatoes (such as Sungolds)

½ cup fresh basil leaves, torn if large

½ cup fresh Italian parsley leaves

3 Cover again and cook for 5 minutes more, or until the green beans are bright green and crisp-tender. Add the tomatoes, and cook just until heated through, 1 minute. Season to taste with salt and pepper, drizzle with more oil, and sprinkle with the basil and parsley.

TIMING TIPS:

- Even though you could prep all the vegetables ahead of time, I like to prep this as I go, as the vegetables are added in succession. I just keep prepping as I add each vegetable.

- If cooking ahead by an hour or two, stop before adding the green beans, radishes, and broccoli. Reheat and add these ingredients at the last minute.

RIBOLLITA EN CROUTE

SERVES 8 TO 10

Yes, I know, I'm mixing metaphors (and languages) here. I also know that this is *not* the traditional way to make ribollita, which literally means "reboiled" in Italian. You take yesterday's minestrone, add some old stale bread to it, and boil it again, resulting in a thick and hearty soup that sticks to your ribs. This version does too, but I am not an Italian grandma with lots of day-old bread lying around, so I created this one, which is a bit more exciting to serve and eat with its crusty cheesy top that slowly dissolves into the soup. Exactly how much bread you will need depends on the size of your pot. This is best made in a larger pot and finished and served in a 7-quart oven-to-table enameled cast-iron pot. You want the soup to come pretty close to the top of the pot, and then cut or tear the bread so the slices slightly overlap and cover the entire top of the pot. Parmigiano-Reggiano rind and dried porcini add deep flavor to the broth, bringing the whole thing to the next level. I implore you to cook dry beans for this recipe, whether you use my recipe on page 37, or cook them in your Instant Pot. It is really not a very onerous task, and I promise you will be rewarded with superior flavor and texture. Canned white beans, which you could use if you absolutely must, can be a bit mushy, so I recommend adding them in the last five minutes of simmering time; make up the difference of the bean liquid with additional stock.

1 ounce (about 1 cup) dried porcini mushrooms

Boiling water, to cover the mushrooms

3 tablespoons extra-virgin olive oil

2 large yellow onions, chopped

4 to 5 garlic cloves, minced

6 carrots, diced

3 stalks celery, diced

1 medium head fennel, chopped

1 tablespoon chopped fresh rosemary

One 2-pound butternut squash, peeled, cut in half, seeded, then cut into ½-inch chunks

2 cups canned or boxed chopped tomatoes (one 17.6-ounce package)

3 cups Basic Cooked Cranberry Beans (page 37), plus 2 cups of their broth, or two 15.5-ounce cans Roman or cannellini beans, with their liquid

1 Preheat the oven to 375°F and line a baking sheet with parchment paper.

2 Place the mushrooms in a 1-cup liquid measuring cup. Pour boiling water over the mushrooms, filling the cup. Let stand until softened, about 15 minutes. Lift the mushrooms from the liquid and chop. Set aside, reserving the liquid.

3 In a large soup pot, heat the oil over medium heat. Add the onion, garlic, carrots, celery, fennel, rehydrated mushrooms, and rosemary and cook until the vegetables have softened, about 12 minutes. Add the squash, tomatoes, beans and their liquid, the reserved mushroom liquid (leaving any sand or grit behind at the bottom of the cup), and stock. Bring to a boil and add the bay leaf, Parmigiano-Reggiano rind, and salt and season with pepper. Partially cover, lower the heat to maintain a simmer, and simmer until the squash is tender, about 30 minutes.

recipe and ingredients continue

7 cups homemade or boxed low-sodium chicken stock or vegetable stock, plus more for drizzling

1 bay leaf

Parmigiano-Reggiano cheese rind (see page 14)

1 teaspoon salt, plus more to taste

Freshly ground black pepper

3 cups chopped Tuscan kale (stems removed; about ½ bunch)

Six ½-thick slices rustic country bread, about 1 pound

½ cup grated Parmigian-Reggiano cheese

4 Stir in the kale and taste for seasoning.

5 Transfer to a 7-quart Dutch oven, filling to within 1 inch of the top. Cut and tear the bread slices to fill up the entire surface of the soup, pressing down a little. Drizzle the bread with chicken stock to moisten slightly. Sprinkle the grated cheese all over the top. Place on the baking sheet and bake until the soup is bubbling and the bread is golden brown and crusty, about 25 minutes.

TIMING TIPS:

- Up to 2 days ahead: Make the soup base, but don't add the kale; refrigerate.

- 1 hour ahead: Reheat the soup and stir in the kale. Top with the bread and cheese and bake.

NOTE:

Although I always call for kale leaves to be stripped from the stems, save the stems to use as a vegetable unto itself. In the case of this soup, thinly slice them and toss them in when the vegetables are simmering. Try tossing them into salads for a little crunch or lightly sauté them and add to a pasta or egg dish.

If you have more soup than will fit in your Dutch oven, just leave some on the side to achieve the desired effect. It won't go to waste!

NOT-FRIED EGGPLANT PARM

SERVES 4 TO 6

There are a couple of reasons I prefer this to the traditional breaded and fried eggplant Parmigiana. First of all, I am way too lazy to do a standard breading procedure (flour, egg, breadcrumbs) most of the time. Second, I don't like to do a lot of frying at home because it's messy, and third, I try not to eat much fried food! I do really love eggplant Parm, though, and I was determined to find a way to improve upon baked versions I had done or tasted before that were a little watery and a little *meh*. Adding torn bread and fresh tomatoes adds the bread element back into the dish—the croutons get crispy on top while they absorb excess moisture from the eggplant and fresh tomatoes on the bottom—irresistible! Go for the biggest baking dish you have, or better yet, divide between two dishes so there is plenty of room in between the eggplant for the bread and fresh tomatoes. This dish is super-simple to put together, can be assembled ahead of time, and is a real crowd-pleaser.

4 tablespoons olive oil, plus more for greasing

4 small (8 to 12 ounces each) Italian or graffiti eggplants

½ teaspoon salt

Freshly ground black pepper

1 recipe Basic Tomato Sauce (recipe follows)

6 cups torn airy bread, such as ciabatta, hard crusts removed

2 cups fresh mini San Marzano, cherry, or grape tomatoes, cut in half

½ teaspoon red pepper flakes

½ cup grated Parmigiano-Reggiano cheese

8 ounces burrata cheese

Handful of fresh basil leaves, torn

1 Preheat the oven to 425°F. Grease a baking sheet with oil and set aside.

2 Cut the eggplants in half lengthwise (I like to leave the stems on not only for looks but to hold the flesh together). Score the cut sides lightly in a crisscross pattern, sprinkle with the salt and some pepper, and brush with 2 tablespoons of the oil. Arrange cut-side down on the prepared baking sheet and roast for 20 to 25 minutes, until soft and turning golden and creamy but not totally collapsing (remember, you'll be cooking them again).

3 Arrange the eggplant halves cut-side up in 2 large baking dishes, leaving plenty of space between them. Spread the tomato sauce on top of the eggplant and dribble it around the bottom of the dish too. Arrange the torn bread in between the eggplant, then do the same with the tomatoes. Drizzle with the remaining 2 tablespoons oil. Sprinkle with the red pepper flakes and Parmigiano cheese.

4 Reduce the oven temperature to 375°F and bake for 30 minutes. Remove from the oven. Tear the burrata and sprinkle

recipe continues

it all over the eggplant. Continue baking for 5 to 10 minutes more, until the cheese has melted and the bread is golden brown. Top with the basil leaves and serve immediately.

TIMING TIPS:

- Up to 3 days ahead: Make the tomato sauce; refrigerate.

- Up to 1 day ahead: Roast the eggplant; refrigerate.

- Up to 4 hours ahead: Assemble the dish; refrigerate. (If done only 1 hour ahead, you can leave at room temperature.)

- At the last minute: Bake the assembled eggplant dish.

BASIC TOMATO SAUCE

MAKES ABOUT 2 CUPS

1 tablespoon olive oil

1 small onion, diced

2 to 3 garlic cloves, thinly sliced

One 26- to 28-ounce can or box chopped tomatoes

1 cup water

¼ teaspoon salt

¼ teaspoon red pepper flakes

Freshly ground black pepper

2 or 3 fresh basil leaves, torn

Heat a large (12-inch) skillet over medium heat. Add the oil, followed by the onion and garlic. Cook, stirring occasionally, for 8 to 10 minutes, until light golden. Add the tomatoes and water (rinse out the can or box) and bring to a boil. Lower the heat to maintain a low, steady simmer. Add the salt, red pepper flakes, black pepper to taste, and the basil. Simmer for 25 to 30 minutes, until slightly thickened but still a little loose.

WINTER VEGETABLE LASAGNA

SERVES 10 TO 12 (AT LEAST!)

Everyone should have a good lasagna in their repertoire, and this vegetarian one is a safe but satisfying bet if you're serving a mixed crowd of meat-eaters and non-meat-eaters, like I usually am. I hate leaving vegetarians out, and most carnivores would have no objections to this comforting dish. You also could serve some grilled or pan-roasted sausage on the side to round out this menu. Like any lasagna, it takes some work to put it together, but like any of my projects, the joy of popping something into the oven that was assembled the day before makes up for any kitchen fatigue I might have been feeling, as the mess is a fast-fading memory. When I have done all of the prep needed to assemble this crowd-feeder, the last thing I want to do is start boiling lasagna noodles, so I opt for the no-boil kind, which are getting better and better, but be my guest if that is your preference—you would go about layering in the same way with the cooked noodles.

FOR THE SAUCE:

2 tablespoons olive oil

1 onion, finely chopped

4 garlic cloves, thinly sliced

1 stalk celery or ½ small fennel bulb, finely chopped

1 to 2 carrots, finely chopped

1 tablespoon chopped fresh rosemary

One 6-ounce can tomato paste

One 28-ounce can crushed tomatoes

1 teaspoon salt

Freshly ground black pepper

Pinch of red pepper flakes

Fresh basil (optional)

FOR THE RICOTTA FILLING:

2 heaping cups (about 20 ounces) fresh ricotta cheese

6 ounces whole-milk mozzarella cheese, grated

2 large eggs, lightly beaten

¼ cup chopped fresh Italian parsley

1 To make the sauce: Heat the oil in a large (12-inch) skillet over medium heat and add the onion and garlic. Cook until softened, 8 to 10 minutes. Add the celery, carrots, and rosemary and cook until vegetables have softened, another 5 to 7 minutes. Add the tomato paste and cook, stirring constantly, for 3 to 4 minutes, until lightly browned and sticking to the pan. Add the crushed tomatoes, fill the can with water, and add the water to the pan. Season with the salt and some pepper. Add the red pepper flakes and basil (if using). Bring to a boil, then reduce the heat to maintain a low simmer, partially cover, and cook, stirring occasionally, for 45 minutes to 1 hour, until slightly thickened.

2 Make the ricotta mixture: In a large bowl, combine the ricotta cheese, mozzarella cheese, eggs, parsley, Parmigiano cheese, and salt and season with pepper.

3 Preheat the oven to 425°F.

4 To make the vegetables: Combine the carrots, onions, 2 tablespoons of the oil, ½ teaspoon of the salt, and pepper to taste on a small baking sheet. Toss to coat and spread out over

recipe and ingredients continue

½ cup grated Parmigiano-Reggiano
cheese

½ teaspoon salt

Freshly ground black pepper

FOR THE VEGETABLES:

3 carrots, sliced ¼ inch thick on the bias
(about 1½ cups)

1 medium onion, sliced lengthwise about
¼ inch thick

6 tablespoons olive oil

1½ teaspoons plus a big pinch of salt

Freshly ground black pepper

2 small heads cauliflower of different
colors, or 1 large head cauliflower
(1 pound, 13 ounces), separated into
florets (about 6½ cups)

1 pound Portobello mushrooms, trimmed
and sliced

1 pound baby spinach

TO ASSEMBLE:

16 no-boil lasagna noodles (one 9-ounce
package)

10 ounces whole-milk mozzarella
cheese, torn into pieces

½ cup grated Parmigiano-Reggiano
cheese

⅓ cup grated Pecorino Romano cheese

Olive oil, for the foil

TIMING TIPS:

• Up to 2 days ahead: Make the
tomato sauce and roast the
vegetables simultaneously;
make the ricotta mixture;
cook the spinach.

• Up to 1 day ahead: Assemble the
lasagna; keep refrigerated.

• Up to a few hours ahead: Bake
the lasagna; keep warm.

the sheet. Roast, stirring occasionally, for 35 to 45 minutes, until
golden brown. Combine the cauliflower with 2 tablespoons oil,
½ teaspoon salt, and pepper to taste on a second small baking
sheet. Toss to coat and spread out over the sheet. Roast for
25 to 30 minutes, until golden brown. Combine the mushrooms
and the remaining 2 tablespoons oil, the remaining ½ teaspoon
salt, and pepper to taste on a third small baking sheet. Toss to
coat and spread out over the sheet. Roast for 25 minutes, or until
tender. When all the vegetables are done, combine them on one
of the baking sheets and let cool.

5 Place the spinach in a large pot with 1 inch of water in the
bottom. Sprinkle with the big pinch of salt, cover, and cook
over medium-high heat, tossing occasionally with tongs, until
completely wilted, about 10 minutes. Drain and rinse with cold
water. Squeeze out excess water and roughly chop. Set aside.

6 Assemble the lasagna: Spread 1 cup sauce in the bottom of
a deep 3-quart (9 x 13-inch) baking dish. Add a layer of slightly
overlapping noodles (4 to 6 pieces). Add 1 cup sauce, half of
the ricotta mixture, and half of the spinach. Add another layer of
noodles, 1 cup sauce, and half of the roasted vegetables. Add a
layer of noodles, 1 cup sauce, the remaining ricotta mixture, and
the remaining spinach. Add one more layer of noodles and the
remaining sauce. Top with half of the mozzarella cheese and the
remaining roasted vegetables. Scatter the remaining mozzarella
cheese and the Parmgiano-Reggiano cheese over the top. If you
like things spicy, sprinkle red pepper flakes over every layer.

7 Grease a large piece of foil, place on top, and crimp tightly
around the edges.

8 Reduce the oven temperature to 350°F. Line a baking sheet
with parchment paper or foil. Set the baking dish on the baking
sheet. Bake for 45 minutes (or 1 hour if cold). Remove the foil,
increase the oven temperature to 375°F, and continue baking
for 20 to 25 minutes, until the top is golden and the edges are
bubbling. Let cool for 15 minutes before slicing and serving.

MEZZE FEAST

SERVES 6 TO 8

I love a good feast, and my guests do too. It's a pretty easy way to feed a bunch of people in a very casual way. Each individual component is pretty simple, and you by no means need to make all of them, but make sure you have enough dishes to create a nice varied and colorful plate after people serve themselves. Feel free to add more vegetable or salad items according to what is in season.

Smoky Eggplant Dip (page 57)

Whole Grain Cumin Crackerbread (page 73)

Roasted Beets with Their Greens over Labneh (page 206)

Chickpea Fritters (page 207)

Cucumbers dressed with olive oil, salt, and sesame seeds

Tomato salad with olive oil, salt, and pepper

Mint leaves

TIMING TIPS:

- Up to 1 day ahead: Make the smoky eggplant dip (or at least roast the eggplant), crackerbread, and the chickpea fritter mixture. Trim the beets and wash and dry the greens.

- Up to 1 hour ahead: Dress the cucumbers and tomatoes; roast the beets.

- At the last minute: Make the chickpea fritters; serve immediately.

ROASTED BEETS WITH THEIR GREENS OVER LABNEH

SERVES 4 TO 6

This is a pretty simple dish, but the parts add up to something special. I prefer to roast beets peeled and quartered for this dish, because I like the caramelization you get by doing this. Look for beets with nice greens, and make sure to wash them really thoroughly, because they can be quite sandy. If your beets don't have nice greens, and you want to add a green element, use a small bunch of Swiss chard instead. You could sprinkle some crushed pistachios or Hazelnut-Pistachio Dukkah (page 33) over the top if you wanted to.

1 bunch small beets, greens trimmed and reserved

1 tablespoon olive oil, plus more for drizzling

Salt and freshly ground black pepper

1 cup labneh or plain Greek yogurt (any fat content)

Juice of ½ lemon

Flaky salt

1 Preheat the oven to 425°F.

2 Trim the beet stems to ½ inch. Scrub the beets well to remove any grit and sand, then peel with a vegetable peeler, making sure to peel well around the stem. Wash the greens well and tear into large pieces; set aside. Cut the beets in half or in quarters or even eighths if large. If very small, leave whole. Toss with the oil, season with salt and pepper, and spread out on a small baking sheet. Roast for 35 to 45 minutes, turning from time to time, until evenly browned on all sides and tender when pierced with the tip of a paring knife. Add the greens to the sheet, drizzle with oil and sprinkle with salt, toss to coat with your hands, and cook 3 to 5 minutes longer, until wilted. Toss the beets with the greens.

3 Spread the labneh on a small platter and top with the beets and greens. Drizzle with oil and squeeze the lemon half over top. Sprinkle with salt and pepper and serve warm or at room temperature.

CHICKPEA FRITTERS

MAKES 18

These easy-to-make pancakes are kind of falafel-ish but not at all traditional in any way. They make a vegetarian feast like this one satisfying even for meat-eaters.

Two 15-ounce cans chickpeas, drained, rinsed, and patted dry

½ cup loosely packed fresh Italian parsley leaves

½ cup loosely packed fresh cilantro leaves

½ cup sliced scallions, green and white parts (1 small bunch)

1 large garlic clove, thinly sliced

½ teaspoon ground cumin

½ teaspoon ground coriander

2 teaspoons green or red hot sauce, or to taste

1 tablespoon tahini

¼ cup all-purpose flour

1 teaspoon baking powder

1 large egg

½ teaspoon salt

Freshly ground black pepper

1 cup grated zucchini

4 tablespoons olive oil, plus more as needed

1 Combine half of the chickpeas, the parsley, cilantro, scallions, garlic, cumin, coriander, hot sauce, tahini, flour, baking powder, egg, salt, and pepper to taste in the bowl of a food processor. Pulse until everything is well combined but stopping short of a smooth paste. Add the remaining chickpeas and pulse, stopping when it's still a bit chunky. Transfer to a medium bowl and fold in the grated zucchini. If not cooking right away, chill until ready to cook (for up to 1 day).

2 Preheat the oven to 350°F.

3 Heat a large (12-inch) skillet with an ovenproof handle over medium-high heat until hot. Add 2 tablespoons of the oil. Scoop up a soupspoon-ful of the chickpea mixture and carefully place it in the oil. Gently press down with the back of the spoon into a patty. Repeat until the pan is full. Cook for 2 to 3 minutes, until browned and crusty on the bottom. Flip and cook for 2 to 3 minutes on the other side (you may need to add a bit more oil for the second side), until browned and crusty. It's really important to let the crust form, because that's what holds the patties together. Transfer to a baking sheet. Repeat with remaining chickpea mixture. Bake for 5 to 7 minutes, until heated through and slightly puffed. Serve immediately.

SALADS

SMASHED BEET AND WARM GOAT CHEESE SALAD
(ODE TO THE '80S)

SERVES 6

A lot of people will tell you that warm goat cheese is out of style, but I don't care much about styles. If it tastes good, I eat it. And warm goat cheese tastes good! It has never gone out of style in my book, and in this recipe, I bring it thoroughly up to date with smashed twice-cooked beets that get crispy on the edges (see photo, page 208).

2 bunches beets, in assorted colors, about 8 (about 1 pound, trimmed) trimmed and scrubbed

Salt

3 tablespoons olive oil

Freshly ground black pepper

8 ounces fresh goat cheese (not too creamy), cut into six ¾-inch thick discs

½ cup whole hazelnuts, toasted and ground (see Tip)

2 teaspoons fresh thyme leaves

5 ounces arugula (about 6 lightly packed cups)

2 tablespoons sherry vinegar

TIP:

To toast hazelnuts, spread the hazelnuts on a small baking sheet and toast in a 350°F oven for 10 to 12 minutes, until the skins are starting to flake off and the nuts smell and look toasty. Transfer to a bowl, cover with a folded dish towel, and set aside to cool. Rub off the skins (don't worry if they don't come off completely).

1 Preheat the oven to 425°F.

2 Put the beets in a small saucepan and cover with 2 to 3 inches of water. Add a big pinch of salt and bring to a boil. Reduce the heat to maintain a brisk simmer and cook until tender when pierced with the tip of a paring knife, 25 to 35 minutes. The timing will greatly depend on both the size and freshness of the beets. Let sit in the cooking water for 10 minutes. Drain off the hot liquid and fill the pot with several changes of cold water. Let sit until cool enough to handle. Put your hands under the water and slip the skins off the beets.

3 Smash the beets by placing them on a clean baking sheet and pressing down lightly with a glass or small plate. You are just trying to crack them open, but if some of them break up completely, it's fine. Drizzle the beets, still on the sheet, with 1 tablespoon of the oil and season with salt and pepper. Roast, turning once, for 30 to 35 minutes, until golden brown and crisp on the edges.

4 While the beets are cooking, put the cheese on a small plate and gently coat with 1 tablespoon of the oil, and sprinkle with salt, pepper, and herbs. Transfer to a clean plate and then coat on all sides with the nuts. Transfer to a small baking sheet and bake for 8 to 10 minutes, until golden brown.

5 Spread the arugula on a platter or on 6 individual plates and top with the beets and warm cheese. Drizzle with the vinegar, the remaining 1 tablespoon oil, and a sprinkle of salt and pepper.

GREEN BEAN SALAD WITH TAHINI AND QUINOA

SERVES 6 TO 8

This salad is a good one to make anytime you find nice slender green beans. It even makes a fresh and crunchy Thanksgiving side dish. If you find beans that are not so slender or tender, and you have the patience, halve each one lengthwise (it doesn't have to be perfect) before blanching, which will make them less chewy and also help the dressing to permeate them.

FOR THE PICKLED SHALLOTS:

½ cup red wine vinegar

1 tablespoon sugar

½ teaspoon salt

½ cup sliced (lengthwise) shallot, sliced lengthwise (1 large shallot)

FOR THE SALAD:

¼ teaspoon plus a big pinch of salt

1 pound green beans, stem end trimmed

¼ cup tahini

2 tablespoons fresh lemon juice (from 1 lemon)

3 tablespoons warm water

1 small garlic clove, grated on a Microplane

Pinch of cayenne pepper

2 tablespoons olive oil

½ cup cooked quinoa

¼ teaspoon salt

¼ teaspoon freshly ground black pepper

2 tablespoons slivered fresh mint, basil, dill, or parsley

1 tablespoon toasted sesame seeds

1 large radish, thinly sliced on a mandoline

1 To make the pickled shallots: Combine the vinegar, sugar, and salt in small saucepan and bring to a boil over medium heat. Reduce the heat and simmer until the sugar dissolves. Add the shallots, raise the heat again, and return to a boil. Transfer to a bowl to cool.

2 To make the salad: Bring a large pot of water to a boil and add a large pinch of salt. Have a bowl of ice water ready. Add the green beans and blanch for 1 to 2 minutes, until bright green and crisp-tender. Drain and transfer to the ice water; leave until thoroughly cool. Drain and pat dry and place in a large bowl.

3 Whisk together the tahini, lemon juice, water, garlic, salt, cayenne, and oil in small bowl.

4 Add the tahini dressing, quinoa, salt, pepper, mint, and sesame seeds to the green beans and toss. Drain the shallots and sprinkle on top and finish with the radish.

TIMING TIPS:

- Up to 1 day ahead: Trim the green beans. Make the dressing and pickled shallots. Cook the quinoa. Refrigerate until ready to use.
- Up to 4 hours ahead: Blanch and chill the green beans.
- Just before serving: Assemble the salad.

KALE AUX LARDONS WITH SOFT-STEAMED EGGS

SERVES 4

This is an updated version of the bistro classic *frisée aux lardons* but employing the more modern darling of the sturdy greens world, kale. Don't let anyone tell you that kale is "so last year." There's a reason there are so many kale salads out there in the world and several in this book. Kale holds up for hours once dressed, making it absolutely perfect for my style of casual entertaining, and it is almost universally liked. If you can find a tender, leafy kale like red Russian or any other young and tender kale, use it; otherwise shred larger leaves into thin ribbons. It's a substantial and satisfying salad to add to a buffet or family-style meal with other dishes, or it can stand alone for lunch or brunch. You also could serve this salad with an egg on each plate.

3 tablespoons extra-virgin olive oil

2 slices whole grain bread, cut into 2- to 3-inch long batons

6 ounces (about two ¼-inch-thick slices) slab bacon, cut into ¼-inch-thick pieces

1 small shallot, minced

½ cup low-sodium chicken stock

2 tablespoons red wine vinegar

1 tablespoon grainy mustard

Salt and freshly ground black pepper

½ bunch (6 ounces) tender leafy kale (such as red Russian), stems removed and leaves torn (about 4 cups total)

4 large eggs, cold

1 In a medium skillet, heat 2 tablespoons of the oil over medium-high heat. Add the bread batons and cook, tossing frequently, until well browned and crisp, 10 to 12 minutes. Transfer to a plate and set aside.

2 In the same pan, cook the bacon over medium-low heat for 13 to 15 minutes, until crisp but still soft and juicy. Use a slotted spoon to transfer to a paper towel and set aside to drain.

3 Pour all but 1 tablespoon fat from the pan. Add the shallot to the pan and cook for 5 minutes, or until softened and translucent. Add the chicken stock and reduce by half, about 5 minutes. Whisk in the vinegar and mustard and bring to a boil. Whisk in the remaining 1 tablespoon oil and season with salt and pepper. Keep warm.

recipe continues

- Up to 1 day ahead: Wash and dry the kale; shred it if necessary. Store in the fridge.

- Up to 1 hour ahead: Cook the bacon and make the dressing; make the toast batons; cook the eggs.

- About 15 minutes ahead: Dress the kale.

- At the last minute: Assemble the salads.

4   Add ½ inch of water to a medium saucepan and fit the pan with a steamer basket. Bring to a boil over medium heat. Place the eggs in the basket, cover tightly, and steam for 6½ minutes. Transfer to a bowl of ice water and let cool for 1 to 2 minutes, then peel and rinse.

5   Toss the kale with enough dressing to coat the leaves, season with salt and pepper, add the croutons, and mix thoroughly. Divide among 4 plates and top with the bacon. Tear or cut an egg in half and place on top of each salad. Serve immediately and pass extra dressing on the side.

WINTER CITRUS SALAD WITH RED ENDIVE, AVOCADO, DATES, AND OLIVES

SERVES 4 TO 6

This salad is a symphony of flavors and textures, as any good salad should be. The dressing, which is almost a relish, has bits of salty olives and jammy sweet dates vying for your attention. Played against the slightly bitter and crunchy endive, juicy sweet-tart citrus, and creamy avocado, it truly sings, and is an absolutely perfect thing to brighten up the winter doldrums. I love the way red endive looks in this salad, but if you can't find it, white Belgian endive will be fine. Place the endive (whether it is red or white) in a bowl of ice water for at least ten minutes before assembling the salad to crisp it up.

2 blood oranges

1 Cara Cara orange

1 Minneola tangelo

2 Medjool dates, pitted and finely chopped

½ cup pitted black oil-cured olives, finely chopped

1 small shallot, minced

¼ cup finely chopped fresh Italian parsley

3 tablespoons red wine vinegar

3 tablespoons extra-virgin olive oil

Zest of 1 orange

1 tablespoon citrus juice (from the fruit)

Freshly ground black pepper

2 heads Belgian endive, preferably red, petals separated

1 ripe avocado, pitted and sliced

¼ cup toasted walnuts

Flaky sea salt

1 Zest one of the blood oranges into a small bowl. Peel all of the citrus, removing all of the white pith. Cut some of the fruit into wheels and supreme the others (cut the sections of fruit out, leaving the membrane and pith behind). Remove any seeds. Set aside.

2 To the bowl with the zest, add the dates, olives, shallot, parsley, vinegar, oil, orange zest, and citrus juice and season with pepper.

3 Spread out the endive petals in a large, shallow serving bowl. Arrange the avocado over the endive and spread the citrus over the top. Spoon half of the date mixture over the top and sprinkle with the walnuts and some flaky salt and pepper. Serve the remaining date mixture on the side.

TIMING TIPS:

• Up to 1 day ahead: Make the dressing; store in the fridge.

• Up to a few hours before: Prep the citrus and endive; toast the walnuts.

• At the last minute: Cut up the avocado and assemble the salad.

SUGAR SNAP PEA AND RADISH SALAD

SERVES 4 TO 6

When sugar snaps are in season, I tend to eat them raw, because they're so sweet and tender. I do like to crisp them up a little, though, in a bowl of salted ice water for ten or fifteen minutes before slicing them. Of course, if you prefer, you can cook them first by dropping them into a big pot of boiling water and letting them cook no longer than ten seconds, giving them one good stir, then immediately draining and transfering to a big bowl of ice water. You might balk at the thought of slivering all those peas, but please don't! It really only takes a few minutes and it will give you a chance to practice your knife skills. Personally, I look forward to meditative tasks like this one, and I don't think of them as drudgery. Cutting the snap peas in this way makes them a joy to eat, and to look at, and also lets them absorb the dressing in a way that whole snap peas never could.

1¼ pounds sugar snap peas, strings removed

Salt

1 tablespoon minced shallots

1 tablespoon unseasoned rice wine vinegar

2 teaspoons honey mustard

Freshly ground black pepper

2 tablespoons neutral oil, such as safflower or grapeseed

½ cup slivered fresh mint leaves, plus whole leaves for garnish

6 to 8 radishes, sliced paper thin, preferably on a mandoline

1 Remove the strings from the sugar snap peas and soak the peas in salted ice water for 15 to 20 minutes. Drain well and pat dry with a paper towel. Slice the sugar snaps lengthwise into 2 or 3 slices, depending on their size, keeping track of the little peas that jump out.

2 In a small bowl, combine the shallots, vinegar, honey mustard, and ¼ teaspoon salt and season with pepper. Let sit if you're not in a rush to let the shallots soften. Otherwise, slowly whisk in the oil. Toss the dressing with the snap peas and toss in the slivered mint and radishes. Sprinkle on more salt and pepper and some whole mint leaves.

TIMING TIPS:

- Up to 1 day ahead: Make the dressing and string the snap peas.

- Up to a few hours ahead: Crisp and cut the peas; store in the fridge.

- At the last minute: Toss everything together.

MIXED PEAS OVER WHIPPED FETA

SERVES 4

This salad is a pure expression of springtime, so save it for that wonderful moment when you go to your farmer's market and find all the beautiful and tender spring things all at once.

8 ounces sugar snap peas

4 ounces snow peas, left raw if very young

1 cup shelled fresh English peas

8 ounces feta cheese, crumbled

4 to 6 tablespoons milk or heavy cream

1 to 2 tablespoons fresh lemon juice, to taste

2 tablespoons olive oil, plus more for drizzling

Freshly ground black pepper

Lemon zest

Flaky sea salt

1 cup loosely packed mixed soft fresh herbs, such as chives, mint, chervil, dill, or parsley

Pea blossoms or tendrils (optional)

1 In a large pot of boiling water, blanch the snap peas, snow peas, and English peas. Cook just 10 to 15 seconds, until bright green, and refresh in a bowl of ice water. Drain well and pat dry on paper towels.

2 Combine the cheese, milk, lemon juice, and oil in the bowl of a food processor and process until completely smooth. Season with pepper. Add more milk if needed to thin to a creamy consistency.

3 Spread the whipped feta on a platter or individual salad plates and top with the mixed peas. Zest a lemon over the top and drizzle with oil. Sprinkle with salt and grind pepper over the top. Finish with the herbs and pea blossoms or tendrils (if using).

TIMING TIPS:

• Up to 1 day ahead: Make the whipped feta; stir before serving.

• Up to a few hours ahead: Blanch the vegetables and keep chilled.

• Just before serving: Assemble the salad(s).

VIETNAMESE WATERMELON AND TOMATO SALAD

SERVES 4 TO 6

I really love purslane in this salad, for its lemony flavor and juicy texture, but I realize it's not always readily available, so using arugula is perfectly fine. We belong to a pick-your-own CSA in eastern Long Island called Quail Hill Farm, and purslane is basically a weed that pops up in between the rows and anywhere it can. I pick it when I see it, as there is plenty of it. I have even seen it growing in urban pavement cracks and my herb pots on the deck! I also have seen it in recent years being sold as a crop in farmer's markets, but you might want to forage in the garden before paying good money for it.

FOR THE SALAD:

2 small shallots, sliced crosswise and separated into rings (about 1 cup)

1 tablespoon all-purpose flour

½ cup vegetable oil

3 pounds seedless watermelon (weighed with rind), or ½ small seedless watermelon

4 cups trimmed purslane or arugula

1 pound heirloom tomatoes (2 to 3), cut into wedges

1 cup fresh mint leaves

1 small red chile, thinly sliced

Black pepper

FOR THE DRESSING:

2 teaspoons white or yellow miso

1 tablespoon fish sauce

Dash of sriracha

2 tablespoons fresh lime juice (from 1 juicy lime)

2 tablespoons vegetable oil

1   To make the salad: Toss the shallots with the flour on a small plate. Have a paper towel–lined plate nearby. If you have a pair of cooking tweezers, now is the time to use them! Heat about ¼ inch of oil in a small (8-inch) heavy skillet over medium heat until a shallot ring sizzles gently when dropped in. When the oil is hot, add all the shallots and fry until browned and crisp, about 4 to 6 minutes. As they cook, stir occasionally; remove any that start to get too brown. Scoop out with a slotted spoon or frying strainer and drain on the paper towels.

2   Cut the watermelon into flat triangular pieces. Spread the purslane on a platter or shallow serving bowl. Arrange the watermelon on top with the tomatoes, mint leaves, and chile.

3   To make the dressing: Whisk all the ingredients in a small bowl and drizzle over the salad.

4   Top the dressing with the shallots, grind pepper over top, and serve.

TIMING TIPS:

• Up to 2 hours ahead: Make the dressing; fry the shallots.

• Just before serving: Assemble the salad.

SHAVED VEGETABLE SALAD WITH TOASTED BUCKWHEAT AND AGED GOUDA

SERVES 6

You really aren't living (or cooking) unless you have a trusty mandoline, which you really need to make this salad (I'm sorry). Make the very small investment to buy one if you don't already have one, and I promise you, you will be using it all the time, for everything. My favorite mandoline is the simplest one, a plastic model with an adjustable ceramic blade (see page 23) that I keep handy in my gadget drawer. However, I highly recommend using a cut-resistant glove to wear while using it (see page 23). Then you can slice with abandon with no worries about a nasty cut ruining your meal, and your week. Now, about the salad. The toasted buckwheat gives the salad a satisfying crunch without adding nuts (I love nuts, just not in every salad). Aged Gouda (or Mimolette, if you can find it) adds a caramel-y goodness that's perfect for early fall—or anytime, really! This is the kind of salad that you can change up the ingredients depending on what's in season—don't feel beholden to the assortment I'm suggesting (though it is a very good combination!).

FOR THE TOASTED BUCKWHEAT:

½ cup whole buckwheat groats

1 tablespoon olive oil

½ teaspoon salt

FOR THE DRESSING:

2 teaspoons honey Dijon mustard

1½ tablespoons fresh lemon juice

2 tablespoons olive oil

Salt and freshly ground black pepper

NOTE:

Most supermarkets have whole buckwheat groats; look for Wolff's kasha, which comes in three grinds, one of them whole.

1 To toast the buckwheat: Preheat the oven to 325°F.

2 Coat the buckwheat with the oil and spread it out on a small baking sheet. Bake, stirring a few times, until golden, 10 to 12 minutes. Scrape into a small bowl and toss with the salt.

3 To make the dressing: In a small bowl, whisk the mustard, lemon juice, and oil and season with salt and pepper.

4 To make the salad: Thinly shave the fennel, radish, kohlrabi, and Asian pear (saving the Asian pear for last) on a mandoline. Celery can be tricky to slice on a mandoline, as the strings get in the way, so slice it as thinly as possible, on a deep bias, by hand. Mix all the shaved vegetables and fruit in a serving bowl and toss in the celery leaves. Drizzle with the dressing and season with salt and pepper.

recipe and ingredients continue

FOR THE SALAD:

1 medium fennel bulb, trimmed and quartered

1 watermelon radish, peeled

1 kohlrabi, peeled

1 Asian pear or crisp apple, quartered and seeded

2 stalks celery, and the leaves from the bunch

Salt and freshly ground black pepper

2 to 3 ounces aged Gouda cheese

5 Shave the cheese, also using the mandoline, over the top. (You also can use a vegetable peeler to shave the cheese, depending on its shape.) Sprinkle with the toasted buckwheat.

TIMING TIPS:

• Up to 2 hours ahead: Toast the buckwheat.

• Up to 1 hour ahead: Prepare the vegetables and fruit for shaving; mix up the dressing.

• At the last minute: Shave the vegetables and assemble the salad.

FAMOUS KALE SALAD

SERVES 8

I originally wrote a version of this recipe in 2011 for *Bon Appétit* magazine as part of a story about Thanksgiving sides. I have always been a believer in having a salad of some sort on the Thanksgiving table to cut through all the heaviness. To make it more "holiday," I included raw shaved Brussels sprouts too, but when I make this in my everyday life, which I do, often, I usually leave them out. It went on to be one of the most popular recipes on Epicurious, and still gets fresh reviews to this day. On more than one occasion, I have met people socially, who, when they hear my name, say, "Oh, I know your salad!" or "I brought it to a party but I didn't get any because it went so fast," or "Wow, I didn't think my husband/kids/in-laws liked kale, but they love this salad." Many people, including me, think this tastes better the next day but certainly after a few hours (but make sure to wait to add the nuts just before serving), making it a great get-ahead. The dressing may taste sharp at first, which is by design, but as the cheese melts into the dressing, it kind of mellows out. That said, use this recipe as a starting point, and change things up to suit your taste. If you like a sweeter dressing, add a little honey or maple syrup, or use honey mustard instead of straight Dijon. Because kale bunches can vary so much in size, only use as much dressing as you need to avoid overdressing it. For more ideas on how to change this salad up, see the variations on page 231. If you are a patient prepper, feel free to stack, roll, and slice the kale leaves by hand, but most of the time I use my food processor with the slicing blade, and the whole thing takes just seconds. In this version, I added some simple roasted carrots to the top (see Note).

¼ cup fresh lemon juice

2 tablespoons Dijon mustard

¼ cup minced shallot

1 small garlic clove, finely grated

¼ teaspoon salt, plus more for seasoning

Freshly ground black pepper

½ cup extra-virgin olive oil

⅓ cup whole almonds with skins, very coarsely chopped

2 large bunches Tuscan kale (about 2 pounds total), center stem removed, leaves thinly sliced

1 cup finely grated Pecorino Romano cheese, plus more for the top

1 Combine the lemon juice, mustard, shallot, garlic, salt, and a few grinds of pepper in a small bowl. Stir to blend; set aside to let the flavors meld.

2 Pour the oil into a cup. Spoon 1 tablespoon of the oil from the cup into a small skillet and heat over medium-high heat. Add the almonds to the skillet and cook, stirring frequently, until golden brown in spots, about 2 minutes. Transfer the nuts to a paper towel–lined plate. Sprinkle the almonds lightly with salt.

3 Slowly whisk the remaining oil in the cup into the lemon juice mixture. Season the dressing with salt and pepper. Cover the dressing and shredded kale separately and chill. Cover the almonds and let stand at room temperature.

recipe continues

NOTE:

To roast carrots, peel them, trim them (leaving the top ½ inch of stem if there is one) and lightly coat with olive oil, salt, and pepper. Spread out on a rimmed baking sheet and roast at 425°F, rolling them around occasionally, until golden brown all over, about 35 minutes.

4 Add the dressing and cheese to the kale; toss to coat, massaging lightly with your hands. Season lightly with salt and pepper. Garnish with the almonds and more cheese.

TIMING TIPS:

- Up to 1 day ahead: Make the dressing; slice the kale. Refrigerate until ready to use.

- Up to 2 hours ahead: Toast the almonds.

- Up to 4 hours ahead: Dress the kale; refrigerate.

- At the last minute: Assemble the salad.

KALE SALAD VARIATIONS

Feel free to mix and match any of these ingredients to create your own salad. If making ahead, leave crispy items like prosciutto or nuts until serving time.

Roasted butternut squash, toasted pepitas (cooked the same way as the almonds) and Parmigiano-Reggiano

Mint leaves (chiffonade or torn), pomegranate seeds and toasted sunflower seeds, with tahini and maple syrup added to the dressing

Grated raw beets, shaved fennel, shaved radishes, and almonds, with anchovy paste added to the dressing

Watermelon radish, crumbled goat cheese, and toasted pecans, with pomegranate molasses added to the dressing

Cooked wheat berries or farro, avocado, thinly sliced pears, and manchego cheese

Julienned or sliced Honeycrisp apples, Mimolette (or aged Gouda) cheese, toasted hazelnuts, thinly sliced celery

Fuyu persimmons, crisp prosciutto crumbles, pistachios, and feta cheese, with Meyer lemon added to the dressing

RADICCHIO, BEETS, AND CRANBERRY BEANS

SERVES 6 TO 8

Some people might like to say that balsamic vinegar is "so '80s ('90s?)," and indeed our tastes have come a long way since it first came into the American culinary lexicon. It really got a bad name from watered-down, caramel-colored supermarket imitations that have nothing in common with the real thing. You don't need to pay $50 (or much more) for a good bottle, but it's worth investing in a decent one, and use it when appropriate, like in this salad, where the sweetness of the vinegar is necessary to balance the bitterness of the radicchio in a harmonious way. This salad is a wonderful way to use fresh cranberry beans when they are in season, a season I look forward to every year, but the dry ones will do fine too. In a pinch, you could make this with canned beans, but as they are a main attraction, I urge you to cook your own (see page 37), and if you happen to have an Instant Pot, there is absolutely no reason why you shouldn't use it to cook the beans.

1 bunch medium beets, trimmed
(about 3; 12 to 14 ounces)

Salt

1 tablespoon good balsamic vinegar

2 teaspoons Dijon mustard

1 tablespoon extra-virgin olive oil

Freshly ground black pepper

1 small shallot, minced

1 large head radicchio

1 cup cooked cranberry beans
(see page 37)

8 ounces bocconcini (optional)

1 Trim the beets and scrub them well. Put them in a small saucepan and cover with water by 2 to 3 inches. Add a big pinch of salt and bring to a boil. Reduce the heat to maintain a brisk simmer and cook until tender when pierced with the tip of a paring knife, about 25 minutes. The timing will greatly depend on both the size and freshness of the beets. Let the beets sit in the cooking water for 10 minutes. Drain off the hot liquid and fill the pot with several changes of cold water. Let sit until cool enough to handle. Put your hands under the water and slip the skins off

recipe continues

NOTE

To cook fresh cranberry beans, combine 1¾ cups shelled beans (1 pound unshelled) with 3 cups water; 2 garlic cloves; ½ small onion (skin on, root on); a few sprigs of rosemary, thyme, or sage; 1 bay leaf; 1 teaspoon salt; and 1 tablespoon olive oil in a medium saucepan. Bring to a boil and then simmer, with a lid askew for 30 to 35 minutes, until the beans are tender all the way to the center but not falling apart, stirring occasionally. Let the beans cool in their liquid. Makes 2 cups beans and 2 cups liquid.

TIMING TIPS:

- Up to 3 days ahead: Cook the beans; store in their own liquid in the fridge.

- Up to 1 day ahead, but preferably only a few hours ahead: Cook and dress the beets.

- Up to 1 hour before serving but preferably at the last minute: Plate the salad; chill until ready to serve if doing it ahead.

the beets. Cut into ¼-inch dice and immediately dress with the vinegar, mustard, and oil and season with salt and pepper. Toss in the shallots. Set aside.

2 Spread the whole radicchio leaves out on a platter, like little cups, and top with the beets, beans, and cheese, if using, and drizzle any extra dressing in the bowl over the top.

SHAVED RHUBARB AND BEET SALAD WITH RHUBARB VINAIGRETTE

SERVES 4 TO 6

I like to serve this in the spring, but as long as the rhubarb looks fresh, it's fine to use the hothouse variety that can be found at almost any time of year. Fresh and pretty, it makes a delicate side salad with other dishes and goes especially well with pork or chicken. If you haven't tried raw rhubarb before, prepare to be pleasantly surprised. It's refreshingly tart and crunchy when balanced with the right flavors. If you have a sharp mandoline and the rhubarb is very fresh and not stringy, you can slice it that way. Otherwise, just try to shave it as thinly as you can using a sharp chef's knife. I like the airy delicacy and subtle flavor of mâche here, but you can substitute baby arugula.

FOR THE VINAIGRETTE:

1 cup sliced rhubarb

¼ cup water

1 tablespoon red wine vinegar

½ teaspoon sugar

2 tablespoons minced shallot

Coarse salt and freshly ground black pepper

½ cup extra-virgin olive oil

FOR THE SALAD:

1 bunch beets, trimmed and scrubbed

Salt and freshly ground black pepper

1 ounce mâche

½ cup fresh mint leaves, shredded

1 stalk rhubarb, very thinly sliced

2 ounces soft goat cheese, crumbled

2 tablespoons roughly chopped pistachios

1 To make the vinaigrette: Combine the rhubarb and water in a small saucepan. Cover and cook over medium-high heat until the rhubarb is completely broken down, about 8 minutes. Push through a fine-mesh sieve into a small bowl. (You should have about 3 tablespoons puree.) Add the vinegar, sugar, and shallot, season with salt and pepper, and whisk until well combined. Slowly whisk in the oil and set aside.

2 To make the salad: Place the beets in a small saucepan. Cover with water by 2 inches and add a generous pinch of salt. Bring to a boil, then reduce the heat to maintain a simmer and cook for about 30 minutes, until the tip of a paring knife slides in easily. (The cooking time will depend on how large and how fresh the beets are.) When the beets are tender, drain and run cold water over them. When cool enough to handle, slip the skins off while under water (this will minimize staining your hands). Dice the beets and dress with some of the rhubarb vinaigrette (save the rest for the salad) to coat well while still warm. Season with salt and pepper.

recipe continues

Dressing the beets while they are still warm allows the dressing to be more readily absorbed, but the side benefit is the juices that exude from the beets mingle with the dressing, enhancing it.

3 Arrange the mâche on a platter or shallow serving bowl. Sprinkle with the mint and scatter the beets over the top. Coat the sliced rhubarb with a bit of the dressing and scatter it over the top. Garnish with the cheese and pistachios. Drizzle with some of the remaining dressing and pass extra dressing on the side, or save for your next salad.

TIMING TIPS:

- Up to 1 day ahead: Make the vinaigrette; store in the fridge.

- Up to 2 hours ahead: Cook the beets and dress them; leave at room temperature. Wash and dry the mâche or arugula; keep chilled.

- At the last minute: Assemble the salad.

SIMPLE BUT EXCEPTIONAL GREEN SALAD

SERVES 4 TO 6

The importance of being able to make a good green salad is underestimated. Often it is the best complement to other dishes you are serving—it literally goes with everything. Sourcing fresh greens is the single most important part, of course! In spring, summer, and fall, local greens are available in my farmer's market and at the farm stands I frequent, and that is what I seek out. I usually go for a mix of textures, flavors, and colors, and I am very partial to dark red lettuces, but sometimes I will feature just one type of lettuce if it is particularly nice looking. I like to keep the leaves whole, or torn into very large pieces, depending on how large they are, and mix in some smaller spicy leaves, like arugula or mizuna. In the winter, I still seek out greenhouse-grown local lettuce if possible, but otherwise I look for the best lettuce I can find in the grocery store, which often is Boston, Bibb or Little Gem (when available), and sometimes romaine. I usually forgo supermarket red leaf lettuce, as it usually seems a little sad and limp to me. I also might supplement with radicchio or other seasonal chicories like Castelfranco, and also red or white Belgian endive during the colder months.

I know people have become accustomed to buying packaged lettuce mixes, but they really are a crime against salad. My biggest peeve about them is that because they (are supposed to) have a long shelf life, there usually is at least one variety of lettuce in there that has turned to slime, even if some of the others are still somewhat fresh. It just can't compare to even a supermarket head of lettuce, which is at least still alive until you cut the bottom off and start washing it. But once you have had freshly harvested lettuce, it's hard to go back. You really can taste the difference.

A simple but classic vinaigrette is all you need to dress a good green salad. The recipe below is infinitely adaptable, but it's a start. Use whatever kind of vinegar you want—add a squeeze of lemon if you want it tart. Let a bruised clove of garlic laze around in the vinaigrette to add some, but not too much, garlic flavor. Use half vegetable oil if you prefer a softer flavor. Add a lot more herbs or none at all. If it's too sharp, add some honey, sugar, or maple syrup. I like to make vinaigrette in a small jar, because then I can easily judge the ratio of acid to oil without measuring—and if it's an almost empty mustard jar, all the better, as the little bit of mustard clinging to the jar is the perfect amount! Generally speaking, vinaigrette is three parts oil and one part acid, but sometimes I like mine a little more acidic and will veer toward a ratio of two to one. Mix the acid with the mustard and shallots first—I like to let it sit for a bit if I can to mellow out the shallots, and then add the oil and shake it up until emulsified.

To make a green salad an hour or two ahead of time for a party, choose a large bowl, preferably wooden, that you can fit in your refrigerator. Pour the vinaigrette into the bottom of the bowl and add the greens on top. Cover with a clean dish towel and chill until ready to serve. At the last minute, use salad tongs to toss the salad, making sure to scoop up the vinaigrette from the bottom of the bowl. Season with flaky salt and pepper as you go and serve immediately. (See photo, page 186.)

BASIC VINAIGRETTE

MAKES ABOUT ½ CUP

1 medium shallot, finely minced (about 2 tablespoons)

1 tablespoon Dijon or grainy mustard

2 tablespoons vinegar (red wine, sherry, white wine, or balsamic)

½ teaspoon salt

Freshly ground black pepper

1 tablespoon chopped fresh soft herbs, such as tarragon, chives, chervil, or parsley (optional)

¼ cup plus 2 tablespoons extra-virgin olive oil

Combine the shallot, mustard, vinegar, salt, pepper to taste, and herbs (if using) in a small jar or bowl. Shake or whisk until well combined. Let sit for a few minutes. Add the oil and shake if using a jar, or slowly whisk it in if using a bowl.

RAW CAULIFLOWER SALAD WITH WARM VINAIGRETTE

SERVES 6 TO 8

I love the way the different colors of cauliflower look in this salad, but honestly, they all taste the same, so if you only have white, or one of the three colors, go with it! You easily could leave one or two ingredients out (because it is kind of a lot), but try not to skip the pepitas and pomegranate seeds, as they add so much texture and color.

FOR THE SALAD:

1 small purple cauliflower (about 8 ounces)

1 small orange cauliflower (about 8 ounces)

1 small green cauliflower or Romanesco (about 8 ounces)

¼ cup extra-virgin olive oil

¼ cup pepitas

¾ teaspoon salt, plus more for the pepitas

4 scallions, white and green parts, trimmed and thinly sliced

5 to 6 radishes, thinly sliced

4 ounces feta cheese, crumbled

One 15.5-ounce can chickpeas, rinsed and drained

Half 10-ounce container white button mushrooms, trimmed and very thinly sliced

1 pomegranate, seeded (about 1 cup seeds)

1 cup packed fresh Italian parsley leaves, very coarsely chopped

Freshly ground black pepper

FOR THE DRESSING:

4 garlic cloves, grated on a Microplane

1 teaspoon Dijon mustard

1 teaspoon anchovy paste (optional)

2 tablespoons red wine vinegar

Juice of ½ lemon (1 tablespoon)

1 To make the salad: Separate the cauliflower into 1-inch florets, then thinly slice each floret either by hand or with the slicing blade of a food processor. You should have about 6 cups.

2 Heat the oil in a small skillet over medium-high heat until a test pepita sizzles. Add the pepitas and cook for 2 to 3 minutes, or until puffed and golden. Scoop out onto a paper towel–lined plate to drain and toss with some salt. Set aside. Set pan of oil aside.

3 In a large bowl, combine the cauliflower, scallions, radishes, cheese, chickpeas, mushrooms, pomegranate seeds, parsley, and salt and season with pepper.

4 To make the dressing: Heat the reserved oil over medium-low heat. Add the garlic and cook, stirring, until it starts to turn golden, about 10 minutes. Stir in the mustard, anchovy paste (if using), vinegar, and lemon juice and let it warm through. Pour over the salad and toss to mix well. Let sit for 1 hour at room temperature before serving, or store in the refrigerator for longer. Sprinkle with the pepitas just before serving.

TIMING TIPS:

- Up to 1 day ahead: Slice the cauliflower; make the dressing; pick the parsley leaves. Refrigerate until ready to use.

- 2 hours before serving: Prep the rest of the ingredients and assemble the salad.

COLD SOBA NOODLE SALAD WITH STRAWBERRIES

SERVES 8

To me, there is nothing more refreshing for a warm-weather lunch or dinner than a cold noodle salad. While adding strawberries to a salad like this may seem unusual, and it is, it really works. The juiciness of the berries adds a cool and sweet-tart contrast to the slight spiciness of the peppers and the salty miso dressing. While the salad can marinate and improve even for several hours, the strawberries won't hold up well, so toss them in just before serving. This is nice plated as a first course or served as a side with anything off the grill, but especially chicken, flank steak, or pork tenderloin.

FOR THE DRESSING:

¼ cup rice wine vinegar

1 tablespoon sugar

1 teaspoon salt

2 tablespoons white miso

1 hot red chile, finely minced, or more to taste

2 tablespoons toasted sesame oil

FOR THE SALAD:

One 8- or 8.8-ounce package soba noodles, cooked and rinsed

4 ounces shishito peppers (if not in season, substitute cubanelle or poblano peppers)

2 Kirby or Persian (mini) cucumbers, peeled, seeded, and thinly sliced on the bias into ¼-inch-thick half-moons

8 ounces strawberries, hulled and cut in half (about 2 cups)

1 small red chile, thinly sliced

2 scallions, white and green parts, trimmed and thinly sliced

¼ cup fresh mint leaves, roughly chopped

¼ cup fresh cilantro leaves, roughly chopped if large

1 To make the dressing: Stir the vinegar, sugar, and salt together in a small bowl until dissolved. Add the miso, chile, and oil and whisk to combine. Set aside.

2 Place noodles in a serving bowl and toss with the dressing.

3 Grill the shishito peppers on a hot grill, grill pan, or cast-iron skillet for 2 to 3 minutes per side, until blistered and softened. Cool, then slice on a bias, avoiding the seeds.

4 Top the dressed noodles with the grilled peppers, the cucumbers, strawberries, chile, scallions, mint, and cilantro and mix gently to combine.

TIMING TIPS:

- Up to 1 day ahead: Cook the soba noodles; rinse them with cool water, lightly oil them, and store in a resealable bag or container in the fridge. When ready to serve, put in the colander and run cold water over them to loosen, if needed. Make the dressing; refrigerate.

- A few hours ahead: Blister the shishitos.

- 1 hour ahead: Prep the herbs and strawberries.

- At the last minute: Toss all the salad ingredients together. Don't add the strawberries until just before serving.

SHAVED ASPARAGUS SALAD

SERVES 4

When asparagus is abundant and snappy fresh, here's a fantastic way to use it. You will need a sharp, preferably U- or V-shaped vegetable peeler, which is the best tool to peel the asparagus into thin shavings. It's impossible to peel the whole thing into thin slices, so you can either toss the thicker pieces into the salad or save them for a soup or omelette. Choose thicker asparagus for this, as it will be easier to shave. Don't trim the bottoms as you usually would, so you'll have something to grab onto, and pull the peeler from a few inches from the bottom of the stalk toward the tip. Turn the stalk over when you reach the middle, and then shave the sides.

1 lemon, preferably organic, scrubbed

1 small shallot, thinly sliced on a mandoline

¼ cup extra-virgin olive oil

½ teaspoon salt

Freshly ground black pepper

1 pound asparagus (about 1 bunch)

2 ounces Parmigiano-Reggiano cheese

2 tablespoons roasted salted pistachios (I love the Wonderful Pistachios brand), slightly crushed

½ cup fresh mint leaves, torn

1 Zest the lemon into a small bowl. Set aside. Juice the lemon (you should have about 2 tablespoons juice). In a large bowl, combine the shallot, lemon juice, oil, and salt and season with pepper. Thinly shave the asparagus, as described above. Toss with the dressing and season with more salt and pepper.

2 Transfer to a serving bowl and shave the cheese over the top using the vegetable peeler. Sprinkle with the pistachios and mint leaves and serve.

TIMING TIPS:

• Up to 3 hours ahead: Shave the asparagus and chill.

• Up to 1 hour ahead: Make the dressing.

• At the last minute: Assemble the salad.

GRILLED CHICORIES AND LETTUCES WITH MELTED PARM AND ANCHOVY VINAIGRETTE

SERVES 6 TO 8

A big platter of various halved and grilled heads of slightly bitter greens is a sight to behold and a cinch to prepare. I like to add the cheese while the chicories are cooking on the second side, so the heat of the grill melts it slightly. Juicy tomatoes—any kind you want—add a nice contrasting and sweet note to balance the bitterness, but leave them off if they're not in season. If it's not grilling season, or you don't have an easy-to-fire-up gas grill, you can do this under the broiler instead.

FOR THE DRESSING:

1 garlic clove, grated on a Microplane

½ shallot, finely minced
(about 1 tablespoon)

1 tablespoon anchovy paste
or 4 anchovies, mashed

1 tablespoon capers, chopped

1 tablespoon Dijon mustard

1½ tablespoons fresh lemon juice

Pinch of salt

Freshly ground black pepper

4 tablespoons olive oil

FOR THE SALAD:

2 heads radicchio or Treviso

1 to 2 heads romaine or Little Gem
lettuce

1 bunch dandelion greens

2 tablespoons olive oil

Salt and freshly ground black pepper

2 ounces Parmigiano-Reggiano cheese,
thinly shaved

8 ounces juicy tomatoes, chopped

1 To make the dressing: Combine the garlic, shallot, anchovy paste, capers, mustard, lemon juice, salt, and pepper to taste in a small bowl; whisk to combine. Slowly whisk in the oil until emulsified. Set aside.

2 To make the salad: Heat a grill to high.

3 Halve the radicchio heads, leaving the cores intact so the heads hold together. Repeat with the lettuce. Lightly oil the radicchio, dandelion greens, and lettuce and season with salt and pepper. Grill the heads cut side down for 2 minutes, or until lightly charred. Carefully turn, add the cheese to the tops, and grill for 2 minutes more. Arrange on a platter cut side-up, drizzle with the dressing (you may not need all of it), and top with the tomatoes. Crack some pepper over the top and serve, with extra dressing on the side.

TIMING TIPS:

- Up to 1 day ahead: Make the dressing and store in the fridge.
- Up to 1 hour before serving, but preferably just before serving: Grill the chicories and lettuces.
- At the last minute: Assemble and dress the salad.

VEGETABLES

KABOCHA CANDY WITH YOGURT AND TOASTED PEPITAS

SERVES 6 TO 8

No, it's not really candy, but Steve and I started calling it that after enjoying it out of hand as a snack after bringing home a surplus from our CSA farm near our home in Amagansett. It has a uniquely dry texture, similar to chestnuts, and a sweet and nutty flavor that sets it apart from other squash varieties, with a thin and tender skin that doesn't need to be peeled (woo hoo!). Here it's gussied up as a side dish, but feel free to skip the embellishments and just eat the squash straight!

1 medium kabocha squash, about 2½ pounds, well scrubbed

2 tablespoons olive oil, plus ¼ cup for frying the seeds

½ teaspoon kosher salt

Freshly ground black pepper

1 tablespoon maple syrup

¼ cup pepitas

½ cup plain Greek yogurt or labneh

Flaky sea salt

Lime wedges

1 Preheat the oven to 425°F.

2 Carefully cut the squash in half through the stem and scoop out and discard the seeds (see Tips). Cut into wedges, about 1½ inches at the widest point. In a large bowl, toss the squash with 2 tablespoons of the oil, the kosher salt, and pepper. Arrange wedges in a single layer on a rimmed baking sheet. Roast for 15 minutes, until they start to turn deep golden brown on the underside. Remove from the oven and carefully turn all the pieces. Drizzle the maple syrup over the squash and return to the oven for 10 minutes, or until deep golden brown on both sides.

recipe continues

SQUASH TIPS

It can be intimidating to cut a hard winter squash, but here's the thing—you don't have to worry about cutting it in half perfectly, as a few rough pieces are fine in the mix. You do need a large, sharp knife, but to cut it in half safely, gently rock the blade of your knife into the squash before applying any pressure to make sure your knife doesn't slip. Once it is securely into the flesh, then you can start applying pressure. If it's very hard and the knife seems stuck, just pick up the whole unit (knife in squash) and bang it down on your work surface. Eventually the squash will cleave in half. I like to scoop out the seeds with an ice cream scoop. Then use the flat surfaces created to make a stable base to continue cutting.

3 Pour the remaining ¼ cup oil into a small skillet and heat over medium heat. Add the pepitas and cook until they sizzle and pop and turn slightly brown (but don't overcook!), about 3 minutes. Using a slotted spoon, scoop out onto a folded paper towel and sprinkle with kosher salt. Let the oil cool in a small bowl.

4 Spread the yogurt on the bottom of a serving platter, and arrange the squash slices on top. Drizzle with about 2 tablespoons of the reserved oil, and sprinkle with the pepitas, and some flaky salt. Serve with lime wedges.

TIMING TIPS:

- Up to 1 day ahead: Cut up the squash and store it in the fridge.

- Up to 2 hours before serving: Roast the squash; fry the pepitas.

- At the last minute: Assemble the platter.

BRUSSELS SPROUT GRATIN WITH SPECK AND RYE CRUMBS

SERVES 6 TO 8

This dish packs a lot of flavor into one baking dish with a pretty short ingredient list. It is pleasantly reminiscent of a pastrami on rye sandwich (or maybe it's a Reuben?), thanks to the speck, which is smoked, the mustard, rye croutons, and caraway seeds. This would be great anytime Brussels sprouts are around, but it would be right at home on the Thanksgiving table. Look for a moist, handmade loaf of rye bread for the croutons—it will make all the difference. Carissa's Salty Soured Pickled Rye (page 356) is a favorite.

1½ pounds Brussels sprouts, trimmed

3 tablespoons olive oil

2 shallots, sliced lengthwise

2 ounces thinly sliced speck, cut into 1-inch-thick ribbons

Salt and freshly ground black pepper

1 cup heavy cream

3 tablespoons grainy mustard

2 slices good rye bread, cut or torn into small pieces

2 teaspoons caraway seeds

1 Preheat the oven to 375°F.

2 If using a food processor, shred the Brussels sprouts using the slicing blade. If not, shred them by hand by slicing them as thin as possible. Set aside.

3 Add 1 tablespoon of the oil and the shallots to a large (3-quart) baking dish, place in the oven, and roast, stirring once or twice, for 15 minutes, or until golden brown. Remove the dish from the oven, stir in the Brussels sprouts and speck, and season with ½ teaspoon salt and pepper to taste. Whisk the cream and mustard in a small bowl and evenly drizzle it over the Brussels sprouts. Gently toss together to combine thoroughly.

4 In a small bowl, combine the remaining 2 tablespoons oil with the rye crumbs. Sprinkle over the top of the baking dish, then sprinkle on the caraway. Return to the oven and bake for 35 to 40 minutes, until golden brown and bubbling. Serve immediately.

TIMING TIPS:

• Up to 1 day ahead: Shred the Brussels sprouts; store in the fridge.

• Up to 1 hour before serving: Assemble the gratin and bake.

ROOT VEGETABLE TIAN

SERVES 6 TO 8

This is the winter version of the well-known late summer classic made with tomatoes, eggplant, onion, and zucchini. It takes a bit of care to assemble, but the results—concentric circles of jewel-toned vegetables—are showstopping. The addition of a creamy layer of chickpeas gives it enough heft to serve as a meatless main, but it's also a delightful side dish or lunch. It travels really well and is good at room temperature, making it an excellent potluck choice.

One 15.5-ounce can chickpeas, drained, liquid reserved

2 small sweet potatoes, peeled and sliced ⅛ inch thick

3 medium beets, peeled and sliced ⅛ inch thick

3 large parsnips, peeled and sliced ⅛ inch thick

2 small red onions, sliced ⅛ inch thick

1 tablespoon fresh thyme leaves, roughly chopped (or substitute 1 teaspoon dried thyme)

½ cup grated Parmigiano-Reggiano cheese

2 tablespoons extra-virgin olive oil

1 teaspoon salt

Freshly ground black pepper

3 garlic cloves, minced

1 Preheat the oven to 375°F.

2 Puree the chickpeas in a food processor with ¼ cup of the reserved liquid. Spread the puree evenly on the bottom of a 9-inch round (2-quart) baking dish. Grab 2 or 3 slices each of sweet potato, beet, parsnip, and onion ring. Starting at the outer edge of the dish, arrange the slices standing up. Repeat, moving in a concentric circle until the ring is complete. Arrange the vegetables in a similar manner to fill up the center of the dish. Combine the thyme and cheese in a small bowl.

3 Brush the vegetables with the oil and season with the salt and some pepper. Scatter the garlic and the cheese mixture over the top. Cover tightly with foil, set on a baking sheet, and bake for 35 minutes. Uncover and bake for 25 to 30 minutes more, until the top is lightly browned and the vegetables are tender when pierced with the tip of a paring knife. Use a spoon to serve warm or at room temperature

TIMING TIP:

Up to one day ahead: The tian can be assembled or completed completely ahead of time. Reheat if desired.

CARAMELIZED FENNEL WITH CITRUS AND OLIVES

SERVES 6

Fennel is one of my favorite vegetables—part of what I love is how its character is so completely different depending on whether it is raw or cooked. Here it is cooked until soft and almost creamy, as it absorbs the liquid in the pan. If you have homemade chicken stock, this is a good time to use it, as the flavors are simple and few and the fennel drinks up the chicken stock.

1 Cara Cara orange or pink grapefruit

1 blood orange

1 large or 1½ small fennel bulbs (about 2 pounds), fronds reserved

2 tablespoons unsalted butter

1 tablespoon honey

½ teaspoon salt

1 cup chicken stock (see page 31) or vegetable stock

12 Kalamata olives, torn in half and pitted

Freshly ground black pepper

Fennel pollen (optional)

1 Use a knife to cut away the peel and pith from the oranges. Cut in between the membranes using a small sharp knife, holding your hand over a bowl to catch all the juices.

2 Cut the fennel into 1-inch-thick wedges. Heat a large skillet over medium-high heat. Add the butter and honey and cook until melted. Add the fennel and salt and cook for 6 to 8 minutes, turn, and cook for 1 minute more, or until browned. Add the stock and reserved citrus juice.

3 Reduce the heat to low and simmer for 15 minutes, or until the liquid is almost evaporated. Add ¼ cup water and simmer, turning occasionally, for another 5 to 7 minutes, until very tender. Transfer to a platter and top with the citrus, olives, reserved fennel fronds, and some pepper and fennel pollen (if using).

TIMING TIP:
This dish comes together quickly, but even trimming and cutting the fennel an hour to a day before and having it ready to cook is helpful.

TWICE-BAKED CELERIAC

SERVES 4

These gnarly roots, which are baked, scooped out, and baked again, are sure to be a conversation piece at your next gathering! Baseball-size celeriac, which are easier to find in the fall, will be just the right size to serve one per person. If you only can find larger, softball-size ones, cut them in half after cooking for sharing. Look for nice round, not overtrimmed celeriac for this recipe, and scrub thoroughly with a vegetable brush, lightly peeling if there are a lot of fine roots on the surface.

4 large celery roots, trimmed of roots and stems (about 14 ounces each)

2 heads garlic

2 tablespoons olive oil

1 cup grated Parmigiano-Reggiano cheese

2 tablespoons unsalted butter

1 tablespoon fresh thyme leaves

1 teaspoon coarse salt

Freshly ground black pepper

About ¼ cup warm milk or half-and-half

¼ cup grated Gruyère cheese

TIMING TIP:

The stuffed celeriac can be prepared and assembled completely ahead of time. Refrigerate until 1 hour before baking.

1 Preheat the oven to 350°F.

2 Trim the celeriac of any hairy roots and the greens if they are still attached (leave about an inch of green if they are) and scrub thoroughly using a vegetable brush. Trim a thin slice off the bottom of the celeriac so they will stand upright. Pat dry and rub the roots and the garlic with the oil. Wrap 2 celeriac and 1 head of garlic in each of two loosely wrapped foil packets. Place on a baking sheet and bake for 1 hour. Remove the garlic and let cool. Cut the tops off the garlic heads and squeeze out all the roasted garlic. Set aside. Re-wrap the celeriac tightly and bake for another 30 to 60 minutes, until very tender when pierced with the tip of a paring knife.

3 Remove from the oven and cool slightly. Increase the oven temperature to 375°F.

4 Slice off the tops of the celeriac and carefully scoop out the flesh, leaving a ¼-inch-thick wall all around. A melon baller works well for this. Transfer the flesh to a food processor and process until very smooth (and while still warm) along with all of the roasted garlic, the Parmigiano-Reggiano cheese, butter, thyme, salt, and pepper to taste. Slowly add the milk until the puree looks like creamy mashed potatoes (you may not need all of the milk). Divide among the celeriac shells and top with the Gruyère cheese. Bake until the stuffed celeriac is very hot and the cheese has started to brown, 40 to 45 minutes (or about 1 hour if they've been refrigerated). Serve immediately.

ROASTED FAIRY TALE EGGPLANT WITH TOMATOES

SERVES 6

When I first saw the amazing array of unusual varieties of tiny eggplants that farmers were starting to grow, I just had to find a way to use them. It's what my husband would call a "hot-cold salad." The roasted eggplants are topped with a juicy tomato salad—everything melds together in a creamy, juicy, meaty, spicy, herby mess. If you can't find little heirloom eggplants, buy the smallest ones you can find, prick with a fork, and cook them whole until they are soft. Scoop out the flesh and top the yogurt with it.

1 cup plain Greek yogurt
(any fat content)

2 tablespoons tahini

1 tablespoon fresh lime juice
(from 1 lime)

¼ cup pitted Kalamata olives, chopped

¼ cup fresh mint leaves, chopped,
plus more for garnish

½ teaspoon ground toasted cumin

1 small garlic clove, grated on a
Microplane

Kosher salt and freshly ground black
pepper

1½ pounds small eggplant, such as
Fairy Tale or Thai

2 tablespoons olive oil

2 pounds assorted tomatoes, cut into
wedges

Flaky sea salt

1 Combine the yogurt, tahini, lime juice, olives, mint, cumin, and garlic in a small bowl. Season lightly with kosher salt and some pepper.

2 Leave the eggplant whole (with the tops, unless they bother you), toss them with 1 tablespoon of the oil, and season with kosher salt and pepper.

3 Heat a grill to medium-high.

4 Put the eggplant on the grill and cook, turning frequently, until lightly charred and soft. It will take only 2 to 3 minutes per side for small ones and up to 15 minutes for larger ones.

5 Toss the tomatoes with the remaining 1 tablespoon oil, ½ teaspoon kosher salt, and pepper to taste. Spread the yogurt mixture on a platter and top with the warm eggplant. Spoon the tomatoes, along with their juices, over the eggplant and top with mint. Sprinkle with flaky salt and pepper.

TIMING TIPS:

• Up to 1 hour ahead: Make the yogurt mixture; grill the eggplant.

• 30 minutes before serving: Dress the tomatoes.

• At the last minute: Assemble the platter.

ROASTED RADISHES WITH RADISH GREEN PESTO AND CRÈME FRAÎCHE

SERVES 6 TO 8

I know I am not alone in my love for cooked radishes, or radishes in general, but I must say they have taken on a whole new dimension since I have started cooking them. Not only are they beautiful to look at, but they are delicate and juicy and complement simple meat and fish dishes so well, especially in spring. When good local radishes pop up in farmer's markets (and supermarket ones are usually pretty good too), their greens are too good to throw away—this pesto makes good use of them, and the leftovers (you won't need all of it here) can be used to dress a pasta dish, spread on toast, or whisk into salad dressings.

FOR THE RADISHES:

2 bunches radishes, ½ inch of stem left on, cut in half lengthwise if large, and greens reserved

1½ tablespoons extra-virgin olive oil

¼ teaspoon salt

Freshly ground black pepper

⅓ cup crème fraîche

FOR THE PESTO:

2 bunches reserved radish greens

½ cup pistachios, plus more for garnish

½ cup extra-virgin olive oil

Zest of 1 lemon, preferably organic

½ cup grated Parmigiano-Reggiano cheese

½ teaspoon salt

Freshly ground black pepper

1 Position a rack in the center of the oven and preheat the oven to 425°F.

2 To roast the radishes: Toss the radishes with the oil, salt, and some pepper on a baking sheet, coating the radishes well. Spread out evenly on the baking sheet. Roast for 25 to 30 minutes, tossing once or twice, until golden brown.

3 Meanwhile, make the pesto: Pick over the radish greens, discarding any yellow or brown ones. Immerse them in cold water, swishing them around to remove the sand and grit. Repeat if needed, and if they were at all wilted, let them sit in the water until they are lively again. Spin dry, then place in the bowl of a food processor along with the pistachios, oil, lemon zest, cheese, salt, and pepper to taste. Process until nearly smooth.

recipe continues

When arranging vegetables for roasting, leave a little more negative space toward the center of the baking sheet and crowd the edges a bit more. The center tends to steam, while the edges brown better.

4 To assemble: Spread the crème fraîche on the bottom of a flat platter. Put the radishes on top and drizzle with 2 to 3 tablespoons pesto, or as desired. Sprinkle with chopped pistachios and serve.

TIMING TIPS:

- Up to 1 day ahead: Make the pesto; trim the radishes and store them in water in the fridge.

- Up to 1 hour ahead: Roast the radishes.

- At the last minute: Assemble the platter.

MARTHA'S ROASTED VEGETABLES

SERVES 4 TO 6

No, not *that* Martha. My good friend Martha McCully brought a version of this to a fall potluck, and I thought, *Why didn't I think of that?* Actually, she got the idea from a friend of hers—sorry, Martha's friend, but I don't know who you are—the simple twist of adding almonds (yum), pancetta (ditto), and dried figs (my favorite) to the usual array of oven-friendly vegetables turns this into an excellent side to go with any protein, and one that especially complements pork. Of course you can omit the pancetta if serving vegetarians.

2 delicata squash, cut in half crosswise, seeds scooped and cut into rings

1 fennel bulb, cut into thin wedges

2 to 3 shallots, cut into thick lengthwise slivers

2 tablespoons fresh rosemary leaves

1 cup raw almonds

8 to 10 dried figs

Handful of fresh sage leaves

Whole rosemary sprigs

½ teaspoon salt

Freshly ground black pepper

One ¼-inch-thick slice pancetta, cubed (about 4 ounces)

2 tablespoons olive oil

1 Preheat the oven to 425°F.

2 Combine the squash, fennel, shallots, rosemary leaves, almonds, figs, sage leaves, rosemary sprigs, salt, pepper, pancetta, and olive oil in a large bowl. Spread out on a baking sheet and roast for 30 minutes. Stir and toss, then continue to roast until everything is nicely caramelized, another 25 to 30 minutes. Serve immediately.

> **TIMING TIP:**
> This all comes together quickly at the last minute, but you can prep all the veggies a few hours ahead of time.

STARCHY SIDES

QUAC 'N CHEESE

SERVES 8 TO 10

Let's not call this mac 'n cheese, because it has no mac. Quinoa stands in here, but really it is a dish all unto itself. It's full of flavor, great as a side, and any veg head would be very happy making this their main course, along with a salad or two. It is trying to be healthy, with olive oil replacing the butter in the béchamel, and can be made gluten free by subbing gluten-free flour in the béchamel and gluten-free breadcrumbs for the topping.

4 tablespoons extra-virgin olive oil, plus more for the pan

1 small onion, minced

3 tablespoons all-purpose flour

3 cups whole milk

10 ounces sharp white cheddar cheese, shredded

1¼ teaspoons salt

Freshly ground black pepper

Freshly grated nutmeg

Pinch of cayenne pepper

1½ teaspoons dry mustard

4 cups cooked tri-color quinoa

2 cups shredded kale

⅓ cup panko breadcrumbs

⅓ cup grated Parmigiano-Reggiano cheese

1 Preheat the oven to 375°F.

2 Heat 3 tablespoons of the oil in a large saucepan over medium heat. Add the onion and cook for 5 to 6 minutes, until translucent. Add the flour and cook, stirring, for 2 to 3 minutes. Pour in the milk in a slow stream, whisking continuously. Cook, stirring frequently, until the mixture comes to a boil. Lower the heat and simmer for 6 to 8 minutes, until thickened. Add 8 ounces of the cheddar cheese, whisking until fully melted. Turn off the heat, stir in the salt, pepper and nutmeg to taste, the cayenne, and mustard powder. Transfer to a large bowl, add the quinoa and kale, and mix well.

3 In a small bowl, stir the remaining 1 tablespoon oil with the panko. Mix in the Parmigiano-Reggiano and set aside. Butter a 10-inch cast-iron skillet or similar-size baking dish. Transfer the quinoa mixture to the skillet and scatter the panko topping over it. Top with the remaining cheddar cheese. Bake uncovered for 40 to 45 minutes (or up to 55 minutes if taken from the fridge), until golden brown and bubbling at the edges. Serve immediately.

NOTE:

I call for cooked quinoa in this recipe, because the volume can vary depending on what color you use and how it is cooked. I usually cook 1½ cups dry with 2¾ cups water, rice style, for 15 minutes, covered, which will yield a bit (about 1½ cups) more than what's needed for this recipe. Use the extra in a salad or a grain bowl.

TIMING TIP:

- Up to 2 days ahead: Make the béchamel, shred the kale, and cook the quinoa.
- Up to 1 day ahead: Assemble the dish; keep refrigerated.
- Just before serving: Bake the dish.

FREGOLA SALAD WITH OIL-CURED OLIVES, BROCCOLINI, AND SALSA VERDE

SERVES 6 TO 8

I just love fregola Sarda, which is really just a variant on Israeli (large-grain) couscous. It comes from Sardinia, and is a staple in seafood dishes there. It's deeply toasted, giving it an almost smoky flavor, and has a rough and pebbly surface that makes it a bit less slippery than couscous. You may not find it in your supermarket, but it is worth seeking out from an Italian grocer or online. It's great with clams and seafood, but here I use it in a salad that makes an excellent side to just about anything. It comes in different size grains, but medium is the most common. I love the sweet crunch of raw broccolini here, but you could blanch it briefly if you don't agree.

2 cups (one 10.5-ounce container) cherry or grape tomatoes, cut in half (see page 26)

1 tablespoon extra-virgin olive oil

Salt and freshly ground black pepper

Pinch of sugar

1½ cups medium-grained fregola sarda or Israeli couscous

6 tablespoons Salsa Verde (page 34)

2 cups chopped raw broccolini

½ cup oil-cured black olives, pitted and torn in half

2 tablespoons fresh lemon juice

1 Preheat the oven to 300°F. Line a baking sheet with parchment paper.

2 Toss the tomatoes with the oil, ½ teaspoon salt, pepper to taste, and the sugar, coating well. Spread out on the prepared sheet with the cut sides up. Roast for 45 to 60 minutes, until the edges shrivel but they retain their juiciness. Set aside to cool slightly.

3 While the tomatoes are roasting, cook the fregola in abundant salted water until al dente, 8 to 10 minutes. Drain and rinse in cool water. Transfer to a serving bowl and toss with the salsa verde, Broccolini, olives, and tomatoes, saving a few to garnish the top. Add the lemon juice and season with salt and pepper. Toss the remaining tomatoes on top and serve.

TIMING TIPS:

• Up to 1 day ahead: Make the salsa verde, cook the fregola, pit the olives, and roast the tomatoes. Store in the fridge.

• At the last minute: Toss all the salad ingredients together.

FREEKEH SALAD WITH PICKLED ONIONS, FETA, AND HERBS

SERVES 6 TO 8

This fluffy grain salad is an explosion of flavors, textures, and colors, and is a great acidic foil for the rich Slow-Roasted Lamb Shoulder with Pomeganate Molasses (page 107). Everyone should have a jar of preserved lemons (see page 15) in their fridge, but if you don't, use the zest of one lemon and some finely chopped green olives in the vinaigrette to approximate the flavor. (See photo, page 107.)

FOR THE QUICK-PICKLED ONIONS:

⅔ cup red wine vinegar

1 tablespoon sugar

1½ teaspoons salt

1 small red onion, cut lengthwise into ¼-inch-thick wedges

FOR THE SALAD:

¼ teaspoon salt, plus more to taste

1½ cups cracked freekeh or bulghur

3 tablespoons finely chopped preserved lemon

2 tablespoons fresh lemon juice

4 tablespoons extra-virgin olive oil

Freshly ground black pepper

4 ounces feta cheese, crumbled

½ cup packed fresh dill sprigs

½ cup packed fresh mint leaves (torn if large)

½ cup packed fresh Italian parsley leaves, roughly chopped

1 cup pomegranate seeds

1 Make the pickled onions: Combine the vinegar, sugar, and salt in a small skillet and bring to a boil over medium heat. Add the onions, turn off the heat, and cover until wilted, about 5 minutes. Let cool in the liquid until ready to use.

2 To make the salad: Bring 2½ cups water to a boil in a medium saucepan. Stir in the salt and freekeh, cover, and reduce the heat to maintain a simmer. Cook for 18 to 20 minutes, or until the grains are tender and all the water has been absorbed. Transfer to a large bowl and toss occasionally with a fork until mostly cooled.

3 Whisk together the preserved lemon, lemon juice, and oil and season with pepper. Toss the dressing with the freekeh and add the drained pickled onions, cheese, herbs (saving some for the top), and pomegranate seeds (saving some for the top). Season with salt and pepper. Transfer to a serving bowl and top with the reserved herbs and pomegranate seeds.

TIMING TIPS:

- Up to 1 day ahead: Cook the freekeh, make the pickled onions and the dressing, and prep the pomegranate seeds. Refrigerate all.

- Up to 1 hour ahead: Pick the herbs; refrigerate.

- At the last minute: Toss all the salad ingredients together.

OVEN-BAKED POLENTA

SERVES 6 TO 8

Even though making stovetop polenta is "easy," many people, including myself, shy away from it because of the constant stirring and the inevitable spitting and spattering, which can result in a nasty burn. I prefer this all-in-the-oven method, as it works perfectly, producing a creamy porridge that goes really well with any braise, but especially the Osso Buco Sugo with Orange Gremolata (page 103), French Beef Stew (page 101), and Baked Turkey-Spinach Meatballs (page 113). You also could just throw some roasted vegetables on top and call it a meal. Don't be skeptical when you see all that water sloshing around—the polenta will absorb every bit of it. Have faith!

1½ cups coarse-grind polenta (I like Bob's Red Mill corn grits/polenta)

6 cups cool water or chicken stock

1½ teaspoons salt

½ cup whole milk or heavy cream

3 tablespoons unsalted butter

½ ounce Parmigiano-Reggiano cheese, grated (¾ fluffy cup)

1 Preheat the oven to 350°F.

2 Combine the polenta, water, and salt in an 8 by 11-inch (2-quart) baking dish. Place the baking dish on a baking sheet (just in case!) and bake uncovered for 45 minutes. Remove from the oven, stir well, and stir in the milk, butter, and cheese until the butter is melted. Continue baking for 45 minutes longer. If you want the top to be browned, run under the broiler for a couple minutes.

TIMING TIPS:

The beauty of this polenta is that it is almost completely hands off, so you can simply put it in the oven to bake as you finish the rest of your menu. It will stay quite hot for about 15 minutes, or it can be left in a warm oven until ready to serve. You can measure everything into the baking dish an hour before, so all you have to do is pop it in the oven.

CRISPY SEMOLINA POTATOES

SERVES 6

People love potatoes, especially really hot and crispy ones, so I suggest you have some very good and easy potato recipes in your arsenal. By now, just about everyone knows how to make a smashed potato (which I adore, and included in my first book, *Recipes*), but lately I've been enjoying another two-step potato recipe, and here it is.

2 pounds thin-skinned baby potatoes

Salt

3 tablespoons melted duck fat, or peanut or grapeseed oil

2 tablespoons fine semolina

3 to 4 garlic cloves, smashed into large pieces

Flaky salt

Handful fresh sage leaves

1 Preheat the oven to 425°F.

2 Bring a large saucepan of water to a boil. Add the potatoes and a good handful of salt and cook for about 10 minutes (depending on size), until they are softening on the outside but still hard in the center. Drain in a colander, banging them around to break the skins. Pull any big pieces of skin off, leaving at least 50 percent of the potato flesh exposed.

3 Heat the fat in a large cast-iron skillet in the oven for 5 minutes. Transfer the potatoes to a large bowl and toss with ½ teaspoon salt and the semolina. Carefully transfer to the hot pan, add the garlic and sage, give it a stir, leaving any loose semolina in the bowl (this will burn), and return to the oven to roast for about 40 minutes, shaking the pan every 10 minutes, until golden brown all over. Season with flaky salt, garnish with the sage, and serve.

TIMING TIP:

- Up to 1 day ahead: Par-cook and peel the potatoes; store in the fridge.

- About 1 hour before serving: Preheat the pan and cook the potatoes so they're done as close to serving time as possible.

- Reheat at the last minute.

TOASTED FARRO PILAF WITH MUSHROOMS

SERVES 6

I'm sad to say I don't come from a long line of great cooks, but I did look forward to my grandmother Essie's Sunday dinners. She lived in a high-rise apartment building in Philadelphia, where I grew up, so when we got out of the elevator on her floor, I could smell the dinner she was cooking, which usually was rump roast and barley pilaf, which I loved. This dish is an homage to her and that barley pilaf. I'm using farro, adding a lot more mushrooms, and fresh dill, which Essie didn't use, but it makes sense with the Eastern European accent of this dish. This is comfort food for me.

3 tablespoons olive oil

1 tablespoon unsalted butter

1 cup farro

4 small shallots, trimmed and sliced lengthwise

8 ounces mushrooms (any kind!), sliced

Salt and freshly ground black pepper

1¾ cups homemade or low-sodium boxed chicken stock

1 tablespoon balsamic vinegar

½ cup chopped walnuts

½ cup fresh dill leaves

1 Heat 1 tablespoon of the oil in a large, wide saucepan over medium heat. Add the butter and farro and toss to coat. Toast, stirring occasionally, until deep golden brown, 8 to 10 minutes. If the farro starts getting too dark, reduce the heat to medium-low. Transfer to a bowl.

2 Add another 1 tablespoon of the oil to the pan, increase the heat to medium, and add the shallots. Cook for 5 minutes, or until golden. Add half of the mushrooms, increase the heat to medium-high, and cook until browned, 4 to 6 minutes. Add 1 teaspoon salt and pepper to taste. Return the farro to the pan and add the stock and vinegar. Scrape up any browned bits from the bottom of the pan and bring to a boil. Reduce the heat to maintain a simmer, cover, and cook for 35 minutes, or until all the liquid is absorbed. Set aside.

3 In a small nonstick skillet, heat the remaining 1 tablespoon oil over high heat. Add the remaining mushrooms and cook, tossing frequently, for about 5 minutes, until browned and crispy. Add the walnuts, ⅛ teaspoon salt, and pepper to taste and cook, tossing, for 3 minutes more.

4 Stir half of the dill into the pilaf and transfer to a serving bowl. Top with the mushroom mixture and the remaining dill and serve.

TIMING TIPS:

- Up to 2 hours ahead: Cook the farro with the liquid and set aside. Reheat before serving, adding a bit of liquid if needed to loosen.

- At the last minute: Cook the mushrooms for the topping. Reheat the pilaf if it has been sitting. Don't put the dill on until just before serving.

DUCK FAT OVEN FRIES

SERVES 6 TO 8

While you can use olive oil to make these oven fries, duck fat takes them to the next level. You can buy duck fat frozen or fresh (see page 16), or save the fat if you ever cook duck. It makes potatoes very, very crispy and tasty.

4 large russet potatoes (about 12 ounces each), scrubbed

4 tablespoons melted duck fat or olive oil

½ teaspoon salt, plus more to taste

About 2½ cups loosely packed fresh herbs: parsley, sage, and/or rosemary

½ ounce Parmigiano-Reggiano cheese

4 thin slices prosciutto, cut into ½-inch strips

¼ cup sliced pepperoncini

1 Preheat the oven to 425°F.

2 Cut the potatoes into ½-inch-thick French-fry shapes, leaving the skin on. Divide between 2 rimmed baking sheets and toss the potatoes on each sheet with half the duck fat and the salt. Arrange in a single layer. Bake for 35 to 40 minutes, until the potatoes are nice and browned on the bottom. Stir with a spatula and add the herbs, cheese, prosciutto, and pepperoncini on top and bake for 10 to 15 minutes longer, until the potatoes are browned and crisp and the herbs are crunchy. Add more salt to taste. Serve immediately.

TIMING TIP:

These should be made at the last minute. Don't cut up the potatoes ahead of time and leave them in water, as it will hinder the crispiness.

TIP:

For this recipe, avoid the type of rosemary that looks like thin pine needles, and opt for the kind that has broader, softer leaves. The former can become unpleasantly sharp (pointy) when roasted.

SPRING POTATO SALAD WITH GREEN GARLIC DRESSING

SERVES 6 TO 8

Green garlic is young garlic that looks like big, woody scallions. It has a mild garlic flavor, which makes it perfect for using raw, like in this beautiful green dressing. The season is short, though, so if you don't catch it, you can use garlic scapes for the same effect. If you don't have either, use a few scallions and a small garlic clove instead.

FOR THE VINAIGRETTE:

2 stems green garlic or 4 stems garlic scapes, roughly chopped

1 cup loosely packed fresh Italian parsley leaves

2 tablespoons white wine vinegar

2 tablespoons fresh lemon juice, preferably Meyer

¼ teaspoon salt and freshly ground black pepper

Pinch of sugar

½ cup extra-virgin olive oil

2 tablespoons vegetable or other neutral oil

FOR THE SALAD:

2 pounds baby potatoes (smaller than golf balls)

1½ teaspoons salt

1 bunch scallions, white and green parts, trimmed and thinly sliced

1 small bunch fresh chives (with blossoms if available), snipped (about ½ cup)

1 bunch arugula or 2 cups baby arugula

1 To make the vinaigrette: Combine the green garlic, parsley, vinegar, lemon juice, salt, pepper, and sugar in a mini food processor and pulse until everything is well chopped. Slowly add the oil through the hole in the lid until emulsified. Adjust the seasonings.

2 Place the potatoes in a large saucepan and cover with cold water by 2 inches. Add 1½ teaspoons salt and bring to a boil. Simmer for 12 to 15 minutes, stirring occasionally, or until tender when pierced with the tip of a sharp paring knife (if potatoes are larger, you may need a little more time). Let cool in the water for 15 minutes. Drain, cut the potatoes in half, and toss with enough dressing to coat generously while still warm. Season with salt and pepper and toss with the scallions and chives.

3 Place the arugula in a serving bowl and top with the potato mixture. Drizzle more dressing over the top. Sprinkle with the chive blossoms, if you have them, and pass extra dressing on the side.

TIMING TIPS:

- Up to 1 day ahead: Make the dressing; store in the fridge.
- Up to 2 hours ahead: Cook the potatoes and dress them.
- At the last minute: Assemble the salad.

NOT ACTUALLY BAKED CRANBERRY BEANS

SERVES 8

I love cranberry beans, whether they are fresh or dried. I use the dried ones in this recipe for a more modern take on baked beans to serve with the ribs on page 95 (trim a small rib from the rack to use to flavor the beans; see below). They are creamy beans with a thin skin, and they create a rich and flavorful broth. They can be a little hard to find at retail stores (see page 356), unless you know where to look. My supermarket has them in the Goya section, labeled "Roman Beans." I like these straight from the pot. (See photo, page 95.)

1 pound (2½ cups) dried cranberry beans

1 bay leaf

6 whole garlic cloves, peeled

3 tablespoons olive oil

A few sprigs of thyme and/or sage

Salt

1 raw or cooked pork rib (optional)

1 medium onion, thinly sliced

2 teaspoons smoked paprika

1 teaspoon dry mustard

Pinch of Aleppo pepper, or red pepper flakes

1 tablespoon tomato paste

Splash of balsamic vinegar

Freshly ground black pepper

1   To cook the beans: Soak the beans in water to cover overnight, or do a quick soak by bringing them to a strong boil and letting them sit for 1 hour. Drain and put them in a large saucepan with 7 cups water, the bay leaf, garlic, 2 tablespoons of the oil, the herbs, and 1 teaspoon salt. Add the pork rib (if using), bring to a boil over high heat, then reduce the heat to a steady, visible simmer. Cover partially and cook for 40 to 45 minutes, until the beans are soft. Cut through a bean—the center shouldn't look white and should feel completely soft when you bite into it. Let the beans cool in their liquid—do not drain. Discard the bay leaf, thyme stems, and whole sage leaves. Smash the garlic and some of the beans against the side of the pan with a wooden spoon to help thicken the liquid.

2   Meanwhile, heat the remaining 1 tablespoon oil in a medium (10-inch) skillet over medium-high heat. Add the onions and ½ teaspoon salt and cook, stirring occasionally, until they have started taking on a lot of color, 10 to 12 minutes. Turn the heat down to medium-low and continue cooking until completely soft, another 3 to 5 minutes. Add the paprika, mustard, and Aleppo pepper. Deglaze with ½ cup water and add the tomato paste. Cook until thickened, 1 to 2 minutes.

TIP:

To make garlic chips, slice 4 garlic cloves thinly, lengthwise. Place a paper-towel-lined plate near the stove. Heat ¼ cup of any kind of oil in a small skillet over medium heat until hot enough for a garlic slice to sizzle in the oil, about 5 minutes. Carefully add all the garlic slices at once, and cook, stirring gently, until they are golden brown all over, about 5 minutes. Remove with cooking tweezers, mesh spatula, or slotted spoon and drain on paper towels. Besides using to top the beans, add them to salads, on top of pizza, to garnish a soup, or mixed into fried rice.

3 Add the onions to the bean mixture along with the vinegar and cook for 15 to 20 minutes, until fairly thick but still soupy. If the beans get too thick, you may need to add water. If they are too thin, continue cooking until they're as thick as you want them. Season with salt and pepper. Cover until ready to serve. Sprinkle with garlic chips if desired.

TIMING TIPS:

- Up to 2 days ahead: Cook the beans through the first step; store in the fridge.

- 1 to 2 days ahead: Cook the entire bean mixture; store in the fridge.

SUMMER CORN PUDDING

SERVES 8 TO 10

This pudding is just the essence of August, and it could serve as a main course with salad for lunch or alongside any kind of grilled meat or fish for dinner. If you don't have any squash blossoms, and even if you do, basil sprinkled over just before serving would be fine. It will be quite loose when it goes into the oven, but it will firm up as it bakes. You want it to be just setting when you pull it out to add the cherry tomatoes and roasted corn to the top. The idea is for them to stay on top rather than sink in.

Unsalted butter, for the baking dish

4 ears corn, kernels cut from cobs (about 5 cups), plus 1 more ear for the top

2 cups milk

4 large eggs

1 cup sliced trimmed scallions, white and green parts (1 bunch)

1 tablespoon fresh thyme leaves, chopped

½ cup stone-ground cornmeal

1 teaspoon plus a pinch of salt

Pinch of cayenne pepper

1 cup grated Parmigiano-Reggiano cheese, plus more for the top

¾ cup halved cherry tomatoes

1 teaspoon olive oil

6 squash blossoms (optional)

1 Preheat the oven to 350°F. Butter a 3-quart baking dish and line a baking sheet with parchment paper.

2 Combine 2 cups of the corn kernels, the milk, and eggs in a blender and blend until smooth. Transfer to a large bowl and stir in the remaining corn kernels, the scallions, thyme, cornmeal, 1 teaspoon of the salt, the cayenne, and cheese. Stir with a rubber spatula until well combined. Pour into the prepared baking dish.

3 In a medium bowl, combine the tomatoes and extra ear of corn with the oil and the pinch of salt. Spread out, tomatoes cut-side up, on the prepared baking sheet. Place in the oven along with the corn pudding.

4 Remove the squash blossoms from the stems and discard the pistils. Tear vertically into 2 or 3 pieces each.

5 After 20 minutes, remove both the pudding and the tomatoes from the oven. Sprinkle more cheese over the top and scatter the squash blossoms and tomato-corn mixture on the surface. Return to the oven and bake until just set, about another 20 minutes. Serve warm or at room temperature.

TIMING TIP:
The entire pudding can be made 1 day ahead; reheat or serve at room temperature.

GRAIN SALAD WITH MANY FLAVORS (THAT HOLDS UP FOR HOURS)

SERVES 6 TO 8

I love a chewy grain salad (this one has lentils too) with a lot of contrasting flavors and textures. Sweet, sour, chewy, crunchy, salty. You can go crazy and add more ingredients here; just don't add toasted nuts or seeds ahead of time, as they will get soggy—throw them on top just before serving.

FOR THE SALAD:

1 cup uncooked farro

½ teaspoon salt

1 cup French green lentils or beluga lentils, cooked

1 seedless cucumber, peeled and diced

2 tablespoons capers, drained and rinsed

1 cup pomegranate seeds (optional)

1 cup golden raisins and/or currants

3 large carrots, grated (about 1 cup)

⅓ cup pitted Kalamata olives, slivered lengthwise

⅓ cup chopped fresh Italian parsley

FOR THE DRESSING:

2 tablespoons fresh lemon juice

1 tablespoon minced shallot

1 tablespoon red wine or sherry vinegar

¼ cup plus 1 tablespoon olive oil

½ teaspoon salt

Freshly ground black pepper

1 To make the farro: In a large saucepan, combine the farro, salt, and an abundant amount of water. Bring to a boil, then reduce the heat to maintain a simmer and cook for about 20 minutes, until the grain is tender but still firm. Drain well and let cool to room temperature. Transfer to a bowl.

2 Make the dressing: Combine the lemon juice, shallot, and vinegar in a small bowl. Slowly add the oil while whisking, then add the salt and pepper. Set aside.

3 To assemble the salad: Add the lentils, cucumber, capers, pomegranate seeds (if using), raisins, carrots, olives, and parsley to the farro and toss with the dressing. Adjust the seasonings. The salad will keep well for up to 3 days.

TIMING TIPS:

• Up to 1 day ahead: Cook the farro and lentils.

• Up to 6 hours ahead: Prep the rest of the ingredients and assemble the salad. Refrigerate until 1 hour before serving.

DESSERTS

FOUR
GOOD
COOKIES

MULTI-NUT SHORTBREAD
MAKES ABOUT 3 DOZEN

I have always been a sucker for salty-sweet shortbread; in fact, this recipe is a variation on one from my first book. It may seem excessive (that's me!) to make *six* different flavors of shortbread, but you don't have to—pick any nut and go with it. Each nut has a flavor all its own and also, when whole, will vary in volume, so I highly recommend that you weigh rather than measure the nuts, so you know how much you need to start with. Once ground, you will need ½ cup of any of them. See the guide below for approximate volumes for each nut. Since each batch is fairly small, this is a dough I prefer to mix by hand with a wooden spoon in a small bowl. If the butter is softened to room temperature, it is easy to do (just make sure it isn't softened to the point of almost melting).

1¾ ounces nuts, plus more for garnish (½ cup ground)

½ cup (1 stick) unsalted butter, softened

¼ cup light brown sugar

¼ cup granulated sugar, plus more for sprinkling

½ teaspoon vanilla extract

½ teaspoon salt

1¼ cups all-purpose flour

1 large egg white, lightly beaten with a fork

NOTE:

Try these with walnuts, hazelnuts, almonds, cashews, pistachios, sunflower seeds, or pecans, as shown. Peanuts work too!

Volume measurements for whole nuts:

- Walnuts=slightly heaping ½ cup
- Hazelnuts=⅓ cup
- Almonds=slightly heaping ⅓ cup
- Pistachios=heaping ⅓ cup
- Sunflower seeds=heaping ⅓ cup
- Pecans=level ½ cup
- Peanuts=heaping ⅓ cup
- Cashews=heaping ⅓ cup

1 Preheat the oven to 300°F.

2 Finely grind the nuts in a mini food processor or coffee/spice grinder. Be careful not to overdo it and turn it into nut butter.

3 In a small, heavy bowl, using a wood spoon, cream the butter, brown sugar, and granulated sugar until smooth and creamy. Add the vanilla and salt and stir to combine. Mix in the nuts and the flour. Knead a few times to mix thoroughly.

4 Immediately roll the dough out on a silicone baking mat or a piece of parchment paper to an even ¼-inch thickness. Slide onto a cookie sheet, cover with plastic wrap, and chill until firm, at least 30 minutes.

5 Cut circles using a 2-inch cookie cutter with a fluted edge. Because the dough will be cold, they should be easy to handle. Transfer to another lined cookie sheet, brush sparingly with egg white a few at a time, and press a few pieces of nut into the center of each cookie. Sprinkle with granulated sugar and repeat until all the cookies are done. Chill or freeze again until firm. Re-roll the scraps and repeat until all the dough is used. Bake for 20 to 25 minutes, or until the tops are crackled and the cookies are just turning slightly golden at the edges. Let cool slightly on the baking sheets, then transfer to a cooling rack to cool completely.

TRIPLE-GINGER CHOCOLATE CHUNK COOKIES

MAKES 24 LARGE COOKIES

I'm kind of famous for these cookies. The first version was created many years ago, when I was food editor at *Martha Stewart Living*. They were a favorite of the staff, and even ended up gracing the cover of an *MSL* cookie book. I grew up loving a chewy crinkly molasses cookie, and it was one of my favorite childhood baking projects (when I learned that vegetable oil was not a good substitute for vegetable shortening). This version uses butter, of course, and is studded with chunks of chocolate and nubbins of chewy candied ginger that get stuck in your teeth (in a good way). The recipe has evolved a bit from the original, and is moister and gooier. I store a big batch of this dough in my fridge around the holidays and bake off a plate at a time to bring to parties and gatherings (warm). I like to serve them as close to baking time as possible, but of course they are still good for a few days stored in an airtight container.

2 cups plus 2 tablespoons all-purpose flour (see Tip)

2 teaspoons baking soda

½ teaspoon salt

1½ teaspoons ground ginger

1 teaspoon ground cinnamon

¼ teaspoon ground cloves

1 tablespoon unsweetened cocoa powder

¾ cup (1½ sticks) unsalted butter, softened

²⁄₃ cup packed light or dark brown sugar

1 tablespoon grated fresh ginger

2 large egg yolks

½ cup unsulphured molasses

1 teaspoon vanilla extract

8 ounces dark chocolate chunks (chop a quality chocolate bar for the best results)

⅓ cup coarsely chopped candied ginger

Granulated sugar

1 Whisk together the flour, baking soda, salt, ground ginger, cinnamon, cloves, and cocoa powder in a large bowl. Set aside.

2 With a stand or hand mixer, cream together the butter and brown sugar until light and fluffy, 2 to 3 minutes. Beat in the fresh ginger and egg yolks until combined. Add the molasses and vanilla, then add the flour mixture and mix on low speed just until no flour pockets remain. Stir in the chocolate and candied ginger. Chill the dough until firm, at least 3 hours, but preferably overnight.

3 Preheat the oven to 350°F. Line a cookie sheet with parchment paper.

4 Place some granulated sugar in a bowl. Pinch off 6 pieces of dough about the size of a golf ball (about 1½ ounces) and roll in the sugar. Place on a plate and freeze while the oven heats up

recipe continues

This recipe is particularly sensitive to the amount of flour you use, so measure carefully, using the spoon and level technique (page 16), or better yet, weigh it out for the best results.
Use 10 ounces or 285 grams of flour.

(about 10 minutes). Roll in the sugar again and place the cookie dough balls 2 inches apart on the prepared cookie sheet. Bake the cookies for 10 to 12 minutes, 1 sheet at a time, rotating the pan after 5 minutes, until the tops begin to crack and the edges are just set. Be careful not to overbake. Let the cookies cool for about 5 minutes on the baking sheet, then transfer to a cooling rack to cool completely. Repeat with the remaining dough, keeping it in the refrigerator between batches.

TIMING TIPS:

- Up to 3 days ahead: Make the dough and store in the fridge.

- Up to 2 days ahead: Scoop the balls and roll in sugar. Place in an airtight container and return to the fridge.

- Just before serving: Bake the cookies.

CORNMEAL THUMBPRINTS WITH PRESERVES

MAKES 3½ DOZEN

I started using membrillo as a filling for these little cookies when I was looking for something a little Spanish to bring to my friend Claudja's annual paella party, and it has become a favorite. It does take a little more melting than other jams and preserves and a little more water to make it spoonable. It also gets really hot, so handle with care. Most other preserves or jams will only take about twenty to thirty seconds and a few teaspoons of water to melt them enough to spoon into the centers of these cookies.

2 cups all-purpose flour

½ cup fine yellow cornmeal

½ teaspoon coarse salt

10 tablespoons unsalted butter,
   at room temperature

⅔ cup sugar

2 teaspoons grated lemon zest

3 large egg yolks

½ teaspoon vanilla extract

⅓ cup membrillo (quince paste) or
   any jam or preserves of your choice

TIMING TIPS:

• Up to 2 weeks ahead: Make the dough and freeze.

• Up to 2 days ahead: Make the dough and refrigerate.

• Up to 1 day ahead: Bake the cookies.

• Up to 6 hours ahead: Fill the cookies.

1 Preheat the oven to 350°F. Line 2 baking sheets with parchment paper.

2 Whisk together the flour, cornmeal, and salt in a large bowl. Set aside.

3 In a stand mixer, on medium-high speed, cream together the butter, sugar, and lemon zest until light and fluffy, 2 to 3 minutes. Beat in the egg yolks and vanilla. Add the flour mixture. Mix until combined and no flour pockets remain.

4 Shape heaping teaspoonfuls of the dough into rough balls (about 1-inch in diameter). Place on the cookie sheets 1 inch apart and bake for 5 minutes. If you can take the heat, use your thumb to make a deep indentation in each cookie (switching thumbs or dipping in ice water in between makes it easier). You can use the end of a wooden spoon handle too. The edges will crack when you do this. Rotate the baking sheet and return to the oven for 5 to 8 minutes more, until barely golden around the edges.

5 Remove the cookies from the oven. Re-indent the thumbprints. Warm the preserves in the microwave for 15 seconds, adding a little water if needed to loosen, stirring, and heating again if needed until smooth and spoonable. If using membrillo, you will need more water (3 to 4 teaspoons)). Using a small spoon, spoon a little filling into the center of each cookie while they're still warm. Transfer to a cooling rack to finish cooling.

BLACK AND WHITE TAHINI SWIRL COOKIES

MAKES ABOUT 60 COOKIES

Black tahini, which usually is available at Whole Foods (and Amazon, of course) is inky black and typically quite a bit looser and oilier than white tahini, hence the extra flour in the black dough. The two doughs need to be more or less the same consistency so they can be kneaded together easily to create a marbled effect. If you can't find black tahini, just double the white dough and forgo the marbling. They still will look cool (and taste great) with black sesame seeds around the outside.

FOR THE WHITE DOUGH:

½ cup (1 stick) unsalted butter, softened

½ cup sugar

½ cup regular sesame tahini

¾ teaspoon salt

½ teaspoon vanilla extract

1¼ cups all-purpose flour

FOR THE BLACK DOUGH:

½ cup (1 stick) unsalted butter, softened

½ cup sugar

¾ teaspoon salt

½ cup black tahini

½ teaspoon vanilla extract

1½ cups all-purpose flour

FOR FINISHING THE COOKIES:

1 large egg white

6 tablespoons black sesame seeds

Flaky sea salt

1 To make the white dough: In the bowl of a stand mixer using the paddle attachment, cream the butter and sugar until light and fluffy. Add the tahini, salt, and vanilla, and beat to blend, scraping the bowl once or twice. Add the flour all at once (with the machine turned off) and beat on low speed just until incorporated. Knead lightly in the bowl if needed to bring the dough together into a soft mass. Scrape onto a piece of parchment paper and set aside.

2 To make the black dough: Without cleaning the bowl, repeat the process for making the white dough above.

3 To combine the doughs: Divide each dough in half and pat one portion of the white dough out into an 8 by 4-inch rectangle. Top with a portion of the black dough, patting it out on top to fit. It doesn't need to be perfect! Repeat the process so you have a rectangle with 4 alternating layers. Fold over and lightly knead once or twice, give it a quarter turn, and knead again once or twice. You are trying to create a marbled effect, so be careful not to overdo it, or you will wind up with gray dough.

4 Divide into 4 equal pieces. Now, this may sound confusing or complicated, but just bear with me and follow along and it all will make sense. Take a sheet of parchment paper about 20 inches long and lay it on the counter in front of you with the short end facing you. Place a dough piece on the lower quarter of the paper, then fold the paper over the dough. Get a small baking sheet with a straight edge (no protruding handles). Now place

recipe continues

your hand under the fold, and firmly hold the bottom part of the sheet in place. Using the short end of the baking sheet, tap kind of vigorously against the paper-covered dough, forming it into a tight log. Use the parchment to roll the log back to the starting position and repeat the process 3 or 4 times until you have a perfectly cylindrical log about 7 inches long and 1½ inches in diameter. If it becomes too long, simply push the ends together to shorten it, then tap a few more times. Roll the log up in the sheet of parchment, twist the ends, and refrigerate until firm, at least an hour or two. Repeat with the remaining dough. You will have 4 logs.

5 To form and bake the cookies: Preheat the oven to 325°F and line 3 baking sheets with parchment paper.

6 When ready to bake, beat the egg white using a fork, with a teaspoon of water to thin it out. Spread the sesame seeds out on a small baking sheet. Very lightly brush the outside of a log with the egg white. Roll in the sesame seeds, pressing hard to coat the log completely. Repeat with the remaining logs. Cut the log into generous ¼-inch-thick slices and arrange on the prepared baking sheet about 1 inch apart. Very lightly brush the tops of the cookies with egg white (you should be able to do about 6 cookies with every dip of the brush) and sprinkle judiciously with flaky salt. Repeat until all the dough has been sliced. Bake for 17 minutes if baking one sheet at a time, or 20 minutes if baking 2 at a time, or until the cookies are barely starting to brown around the edges and they are slightly puffed and crackled. Let cool on the sheet for 5 minutes, then transfer to a cooling rack to cool completely.

QUINOA ALMOND TUILES

MAKES 16

These lacy cookies are quite easy and quick to make, despite their impressive appearance. The addition of popped quinoa not only gives this stalwart of the French kitchen a very "now" update, but the crunchy texture is habit forming. If you have a silicone baking mat (or two), now is the time to use it. Make sure you bake the sheets one at a time—they simply don't bake right if you try to bake two at once. Take my word for it! Also, be very precise about measuring the butter—if you have a digital scale, use it—a little too much and they will become too fragile to work with. All that said, if tuiles seem too fussy, you could spread the mixture out on two baking mats in one thin layer and make brittle (see Notes), which you can break into shards that have a charm all their own.

½ cup prewashed white quinoa
    (see Notes)

2 tablespoons sesame seeds

⅓ cup sliced (untoasted) almonds

¼ cup honey

½ teaspoon vanilla extract

Big pinch of salt

1 tablespoon unsalted butter,
    plus melted butter if using foil

1 To pop the quinoa, spread it out on a microwave-safe dinner plate. Place in the microwave and cook on high for 1 minute and 30 seconds. The quinoa will be popped, but it won't look that much different. (Alternatively, heat a dry 12-inch skillet over medium heat for 45 seconds. Add the quinoa in an even layer and shake the pan to roll the grains around until they are a little toasty but not browned, about 1 minute. Immediately pour into a medium bowl). Add the sesame seeds and almonds to the bowl.

2 Put the honey in a microwave-safe bowl or cup and cook for 30 seconds (or heat in a small pan until hot). Add to the bowl, along with the vanilla, salt, and butter. Stir until everything is well coated and the butter is melted.

3 Preheat the oven to 325°F. Line two baking sheets with silicone baking mats. If you don't have baking mats, line the sheets smoothly with foil and brush them with melted butter.

4 Place about a scant tablespoon of the batter into 12 separate piles (6 on each sheet), evenly spaced 2 inches apart. Flatten slightly using your fingers. Bake one sheet at a time on the center rack for 15 to 17 minutes, turning the baking sheet halfway through baking, until the tuiles are deep golden brown all the way to the center but not burnt. Repeat using the remaining batter; you should have enough for 4 more.

recipe continues

Most quinoa is prewashed, removing the saponins, substances that taste bitter and may upset your stomach. Because of quinoa's popularity and ubiquity, it may not even be labeled as such. Stick to packaged quinoa rather than getting it from the bulk bins, as that may not be washed, and it is important to start with dry grains here.

To make brittle, divide the quinoa batter between two baking sheets lined with silicone baking mats. Spread the batter out using a small offset spatula in an even layer. Bake according to the instructions above. Let cool on the mats, then break up into pieces.

5 Remove from the oven and let cool, undisturbed, for 3 to 5 minutes, until the tuiles can be lifted without falling apart. Use a little spatula to test the edge starting at 3 minutes. It will be impossible to lift until all of a sudden it isn't. Carefully run a small offset spatula under each tuile, lift it up, and flip over onto a rolling pin or a wine bottle with the shiny (bottom) side up to continue cooling. After a few minutes they will have set, and you can transfer them to a cooling rack or plate. When completely cooled, transfer to an airtight container to store until ready to serve. If you don't care about them being curved, you can just let them cool until firm.

TIMING TIP:

These can be made up to 2 days ahead and stored in an airtight container.

BANANA BUCKWHEAT LOAF

MAKES 1 STANDARD LOAF

Does the world really need another banana bread recipe? Is there anything more to say on the subject? As I was pondering this, I noticed a bowl of blackening bananas on my counter, and I remembered why we need an endless supply of banana bread recipes. Looking for inspiration, I opened my baking pantry and surveyed the many half-used bags of this and that. A bag of buckwheat flour was staring back at me, and I decided that was just what my banana bread needed. The resulting loaf, laced with cardamom and moistened by roasted walnut oil, was better than any I had eaten, made more tender and crumbly (in a good way) by the gluten-less buckwheat flour. And to top it off (only if you're so inclined) a lip-smacking glaze flavored with tahini and maple with little crunchy nubbins of toasted buckwheat groats sprinkled all over it. This combination of flavors and textures was so good, I found myself spreading extra glaze on each slice and sprinkling with more toasted buckwheat. If you want to do that, you'll have to double the glaze and the toasted buckwheat. Feel free to substitute any other fat for the walnut oil if you don't have it on hand or don't want to buy it. Vegetable oil, mild olive oil, melted butter, or especially browned butter all will work fine. And don't worry about buying that bag of buckwheat flour—you'll be using it often.

FOR THE LOAF:

2 tablespoons whole buckwheat groats

1 cup walnuts

1¼ cups all-purpose flour

½ cup buckwheat flour

2 teaspoons baking powder

½ teaspoon ground cardamom, plus more for the top

¾ teaspoon salt

2 large eggs

½ cup roasted walnut oil, other neutral oil, or melted and cooled butter

1 cup light brown sugar

3 small, ripe bananas, mashed (1¼ cups)

1 teaspoon vanilla extract

1 Preheat the oven to 350°F. Butter a standard (8½ by 4½ by 2½-inch) loaf pan.

2 Spread the buckwheat groats out on one side of a small baking sheet and spread the walnuts out on the other side and toast until lightly browned, shaking the pan once or twice (but being careful to keep the buckwheat and walnuts separate), 8 to 10 minutes. Set aside. When cooled, roughly chop the walnuts.

3 In a medium bowl, whisk together both flours, the baking powder, cardamom, and salt. In another medium bowl, whisk together the eggs, oil, brown sugar, bananas, and vanilla. Fold in the dry ingredients and the walnuts and transfer to the prepared loaf pan. Place on a small baking sheet and bake until a wooden skewer comes out clean, 55 to 60 minutes.

recipe and ingredients continue

FOR THE GLAZE:

½ cup confectioners' sugar, plus more
    if needed

1 tablespoon tahini

1 tablespoon maple syrup

2 tablespoons heavy cream
    or 1 tablespoon milk

NOTE:

If your bananas are large, measure out and use only 1¼ cups of mash, otherwise it may be too much batter for the pan.

4 Transfer the loaf to a cooling rack and run a butter knife around the sides of the cake to loosen. After 5 minutes, turn the loaf out and let it cool completely, right-side up, on the cooling rack.

5 Wait, if you can, until it's nearly cooled to mix up the glaze. Combine the confectioners' sugar, tahini, maple syrup, and cream in a small bowl and stir until smooth. Add drops of water if it still is too stiff or more confectioners' sugar if it is too loose. It should be just pourable.

6 Drizzle the glaze over the loaf and immediately sprinkle with the buckwheat groats. Lightly sift more cardamom over the top.

TIMING TIPS:

This keeps well, so you could make the loaf a day ahead of time, but I think of banana bread as more of a spur-of-the-moment thing, as it is easy to put together. Glaze about 30 minutes before serving, and make sure to sprinkle the toasted buckwheat right after, when the glaze is still wet.

ANY FRUIT CRISP

SERVES 8 TO 10

The beauty of a fruit crisp is that it is infinitely adaptable—a crowd-pleasing dessert that can be whipped up on (a few) moment's notice—especially if you make a batch or two of crisp topping and leave it in the freezer to top last-minute farmer's market or farm stand finds. If you are a lover of cooked fruit, as I am, and as most people are (I have met a few haters, but, hey, more for us!). It is also the perfect thing to transport to a friend's house or a picnic—provided you allow adequate cooling time so it's not sloshing onto your back seat. There are a few things to remember to ensure crisp perfection every time. Use this recipe as a guide, but if the fruit is exceptionally sweet or sour, adjust the sugar used to sweeten the fruit accordingly. Similarly, if the fruit seems especially juicy, which seasonal fruit tends to be, either pour off some of the accumulated juice and/or add an extra tablespoon or two of flour to make sure the fruit juices thicken properly. Why thicken, you ask? Well, if you don't, all that beautiful crisp topping will just sink in the juice and get soggy from all the excess moisture.

In this version, I've used sour cherries, which are delicious to catch during their fleeting season, and beautiful, velvety plumcots, but you can use whatever you like—all one fruit or a combination of two (or three). It's also fairly important to let the crisp (aka crumble, but not aka cobbler, please) cool a while before serving, to let the filling thicken a bit. An hour of cooling is a good rule of thumb, at which point it still will be warm and at a perfect serving temperature. Pour some cold heavy cream over the top or serve with whipped cream, ice cream, Greek yogurt, or crème fraîche.

FOR THE TOPPING:

1 cup plus 2 tablespoons all-purpose flour

⅓ cup light brown sugar

2 tablespoons granulated sugar

¾ teaspoon ground cinnamon

½ teaspoon ground ginger

¼ teaspoon baking powder

¼ teaspoon coarse salt

½ cup (1 stick) cold unsalted butter, cut into pieces

⅓ cup rolled oats (optional)

2 tablespoons chopped or slivered candied ginger (optional)

1 To make the topping: Combine the flour, both sugars, the cinnamon, ginger, baking powder, and salt in the bowl of a food processor and pulse to combine. Add the butter and pulse until the mixture becomes clumpy and looks moist throughout. Add the oats (if using) and pulse a few times to combine. Toss in the candied ginger (if using). Refrigerate or freeze until ready to use.

2 Preheat the oven to 375°F.

recipe and ingredients continue

FOR THE FILLING:

2 pounds (2 quarts) sour cherries, pitted (about 6 cups)

1 pound plumcots or plums, cut into wedges (about 3 cups)

½ to ¾ cup sugar

3 to 4 tablespoons all-purpose flour

Grated zest of 1 lemon, preferably organic (add some of the juice too if the fruit lacks tartness)

NOTE:

To use any fruit: Use approximately 3 pounds, or 9 cups, of fruit. Adjust the sugar and flour as needed. Some other good combinations are blueberries and peaches, strawberry and rhubarb, plum and apple, or pear and raspberry.

3 To make the filling and bake: In a medium bowl, combine the cherries, plumcots, sugar, flour, and lemon zest. Spread the fruit out in a 3-quart baking dish and sprinkle with the topping. Bake for 35 to 40 minutes, until the fruit is bubbling all over and the topping is golden brown. Let cool slightly before serving.

TIMING TIPS:

• Up to 3 days ahead (or longer if freezing): Make the topping.

• Up to 1 day ahead: If using sour cherries, it's OK to pit them the day before. They may discolor a little, but you won't notice in the final crisp.

• About 2 hours ahead: Assemble and bake the crisp.

CHOCOLATE BEET SHEET CAKE WITH GANACHE

SERVES A CROWD

This cake is a real showstopper, with a light dusting of beet powder gracing the top. You can order the beet powder from Kalustyan's (see page 356), but I recently saw it being sold at CVS in the nutritional supplement aisle! It still looks pretty spectacular without it too. The beets in the batter keep the sweetness in check, add a note of earthiness, and keep the cake moist. If you want to make this cake for a smaller crowd, bake the whole cake, cut it in half, and freeze half. Halve the ganache recipe for the top.

FOR THE CAKE:

½ stick (1 cup) unsalted butter, softened, plus more for the pan

3 large (baseball-size) red beets (about 1½ pounds trimmed, to make 2 cups puree)

¼ teaspoon salt, plus more for cooking the beets

2¼ cups sugar

4 large eggs, at room temperature

½ cup sour cream

1 teaspoon vanilla extract

¾ cup unsweetened Dutch-process cocoa powder

2½ cups all-purpose flour

2 teaspoons baking soda

FOR THE GANACHE:

1 cup heavy cream

6 ounces bittersweet chocolate, chopped

1 tablespoon unsalted butter

2 tablespoons light corn syrup

TO DECORATE:

Chocolate Curls (procedure follows)

Beet powder (optional)

1 To make the cake: Set an oven rack to the center rack and preheat the oven to 350°F. Butter a 9 x 13-inch cake pan, line the bottom with parchment paper, then grease the paper with butter.

2 In a large saucepan, cover the beets with water, lightly salt it, and bring to a boil over high heat. Reduce the heat to maintain a brisk simmer and cook until a paring knife easily slips into a beet, 30 to 50 minutes (or longer if necessary), depending on size and freshness of beets. Let rest in the hot water for 10 minutes, drain, and cover with cold water. When cool enough to handle, slip the skins off the beets under the water (which will lessen any hand staining) and cut into chunks. Place in a food processor and process until very smooth. Measure out 2 cups of the puree and set aside until cooled. Reserve any excess—try adding to hummus.

3 In a stand mixer, cream the butter and sugar until fluffy. Beat in the eggs one at a time, then beat in the sour cream. Add the beet puree and vanilla and mix well. It will look curdled and very pink at this point. Don't worry!

4 In a large bowl, sift together the cocoa, flour, baking soda, and salt. Add the dry mixture to the wet ingredients in the mixer in two additions and beat on low speed until combined and smooth. Remove the bowl from the mixer and fold a few times to make sure it is thoroughly mixed.

5 Spread evenly in the prepared pan and bake for 35 to 40 minutes, rotating halfway through the baking time, until a

recipe continues

toothpick inserted in the center comes out clean. Cool in the pan for 10 minutes, then invert onto a cooling rack and cool completely. Peel off the paper and invert onto a serving platter.

6 To make the ganache: Heat the cream in a small saucepan over medium heat until steaming and bubbling around the edges. Place the chocolate in a small bowl and pour the hot cream over it. Add the butter and corn syrup. Wait 5 minutes, then stir until smooth and glossy. Stir occasionally until it has cooled to a good spreading consistency, then spread over the top of the cake, not quite to the edges.

7 Immediately top with chocolate curls and use a small sieve to lightly dust with beet powder (if using).

CHOCOLATE CURLS
MAKES ENOUGH TO DECORATE A FULL CHOCOLATE BEET SHEET CAKE

You might not believe me, but it actually is easier to temper the chocolate than not for these beautiful chocolate curls. Tempered curls will be easier to handle without melting or breaking them, and because they are hard and dry at room temperature, you will avoid the potential for condensation forming on the curls when you remove them from the freezer, which could then melt the beet powder. If it doesn't work out, you can go to plan B and put the baking sheet in the freezer, but the tempering happens naturally as you spread and scrape the melted chocolate back and forth on the baking sheet, incidentally cooling it as you go. If it is tempered, you will notice it drying to a hard sheen at room temperature (which should be cool-ish). The key thing is to start forming the curls when it hasn't quite hardened, so they actually will curl. If you wait a little too long, it will break into little shards, which are beautiful too! I aim for a mix of shapes, giving the cake a very organic look. If all of this sounds like too much for you, you can just shave a block of chocolate using a vegetable peeler for a still-pretty if less dramatic look. (Try warming the chocolate with your hand before shaving for larger curls.)

To make the curls: Chop 3 ounces bittersweet chocolate and transfer all but a few pieces to a bone-dry microwave-able bowl. (You also can melt the chocolate over a double boiler.) Microwave on high for 1 minute, stir, and microwave in additional 10-second bursts, stirring after each, until it is almost melted. Add the reserved pieces of chocolate and stir constantly with a rubber spatula until melted and smooth. Transfer the chocolate to a clean, flat, uncoated baking sheet and use a bench scraper or offset spatula to smooth the chocolate out. Scrape it up again and smooth it out a few times until the chocolate is cool. At this point, it should start to harden and dry before your eyes. When it looks almost dry and firm, push the baking sheet against the wall for leverage and scrape the chocolate away from you in small sections to form curls and shards, holding the bench scraper at a slight angle. Use a small offset spatula to transfer the curls to a plate. If the chocolate doesn't harden and still looks wet, pop it in the freezer until almost hardened. Remove it and proceed as described above. If it is too hard, run your hand on the bottom of the sheet to warm it slightly and try again. The chocolate does have to be at the perfect temperature to work well, so there is a bit of trial and error involved. But funky shapes look great, so don't worry too much about it. You can always melt it and try again.

BUTTERNUT SQUASH TART WITH CRANBERRY-POMEGRANATE GLAZE

SERVES 10 TO 12

The idea for this tart came to me in a dream. I've been making pumpkin pies and tarts for years, but I always found the top a bit dowdy looking, and I thought why not give it a mirror-like glaze of pomegranate and cranberry? This not only looks incredible with its ruby-red shine, but the tart and juicy topping gives it just the touch of fruity acidity it needs. The chocolate-lined graham cracker crust is not only easy to do, but it is the perfect flavor and textural complement to the filling and topping. The holiday dessert table will never be the same!

FOR THE CRUST:

13 whole graham crackers (to yield scant 2 cups crumbs; 6⅜ ounces), broken into pieces

¼ cup sugar

¼ teaspoon salt

6 tablespoons unsalted butter, melted

4 ounces bittersweet or semisweet chocolate, melted

FOR THE FILLING:

1 pound cubed, peeled butternut squash (OK to use pre-peeled squash)

1 tablespoon unsalted butter, melted

6 tablespoons whole milk

2 large eggs

⅔ cup pure maple syrup

½ teaspoon salt

1 teaspoon vanilla extract

1 teaspoon ground cinnamon

½ teaspoon ground ginger

⅛ teaspoon ground cloves

¼ teaspoon freshly grated nutmeg

1 Preheat the oven to 375°F.

2 To make the crust: In the bowl of a food processor, pulse the graham crackers, sugar, and salt until fine crumbs form. Add the melted butter and pulse to combine. The mixture should feel like wet sand. Spread out in a 10-inch tart pan with a removable bottom and press the crust in, taking care to build up the sides so you'll have a nice top edge. Bake for 8 to 10 minutes, until the crust is golden. Set aside to cool for 10 minutes, then spread evenly with the melted chocolate. Set aside to cool completely while you make the filling. Briefly freeze to harden the chocolate if it hasn't firmed up by the time you're ready to fill it.

3 To make the filling: Toss the butternut squash with the melted butter, spread out on a baking sheet, and roast until tender and golden, turning occasionally, 35 to 40 minutes. The tip of a paring knife should slide in easily when the squash is done. Let cool slightly.

4 Reduce the oven temperature to 350°F and line a baking sheet with parchment paper.

recipe and ingredients continue

1 cup pomegranate juice

1 tablespoon cornstarch

1 cup fresh or frozen cranberries

¼ cup sugar

TO FINISH:

⅔ cup pomegranate seeds

5 Transfer the squash to a blender and add the milk, eggs, maple syrup, salt, vanilla, cinnamon, ginger, cloves, and nutmeg. Blend until smooth. Pour into the cooled crust, place on the prepared baking sheet, and bake until slightly puffed at the edges and the surface looks dry and set in the center, 35 to 40 minutes. Transfer to a cooling rack; when it is cool enough to handle, gently loosen the tart from the ring to make sure it doesn't stick. Leave the ring on and cool completely. Once cooled, put a few toothpicks in the tart to keep the plastic wrap off of the surface and wrap securely in plastic wrap. If not serving right away, you can refrigerate for up to 2 days. I prefer to glaze the tart a few hours before serving no matter what. Once you glaze it, it's better if you don't have to wrap it again.

6 To make the glaze: In a small bowl, slowly whisk the pomegranate juice into the cornstarch until smooth. Place in a small saucepan and add the cranberries and sugar. Bring to a boil over medium heat and cook, stirring occasionally, for 5 to 10 minutes, until the cranberries have all burst and are very soft. Let cool slightly, then pass through a sieve set over a bowl, using a rubber spatula to squeeze out all of the liquid. Scrape the back side of the strainer to get any excess and stir the glaze. If it looks too thick to pour smoothly, add a few drops of water. Pour the glaze over the tart (it can be chilled or just cool enough to handle) and tip it around so the glaze is even. Decorate the edge with a wide band of pomegranate seeds. Chill until ready to serve.

TIMING TIPS:

- Up to 2 days ahead: Bake the tart shell, line with chocolate, and wrap tightly when cooled. Make the filling and glaze and refrigerate.

- Up to 1 day ahead: Fill the tart with squash mixture, bake, and cool. Seed the pomegranate.

- Up to 3 hours ahead: Glaze the tart and garnish with the pomegranate seeds.

BERRY BRITA CAKE

SERVES 10 TO 12

This is a Nordic cake that seems to be little known in the United States, but I was intrigued by the meringue-topped butter cake ever since I first laid eyes on it years ago. When I say meringue-topped, I mean the meringue is spread right on top of the raw cake batter, and they are then baked together, creating a two-layer cake. Just think of it as a variation on strawberry shortcake. You could also top this with juicy peaches. Ideally this cake should be assembled right before serving and eaten all at once, so save it for those times when you are having a big party.

FOR THE CAKE:

1¼ cups all-purpose flour

2 teaspoons baking powder

Pinch of salt

6 tablespoons (¾ stick) unsalted butter, softened

1½ cups sugar

4 large eggs, separated

2 teaspoons vanilla extract

1 lemon, preferably organic, scrubbed

½ cup whole milk

¼ teaspoon cream of tartar

FOR THE BERRIES:

2 pounds strawberries (or any mix of seasonal berries)

⅓ cup sugar

1 tablespoon Aperol or St. Germain (optional)

1 cup heavy cream

8 ounces crème fraîche

1 teaspoon vanilla paste or vanilla extract

Confectioners' sugar, for dusting

1 To make the cake: Preheat the oven to 325°F. Butter a 9 x 13-inch pan. Press a piece of parchment paper large enough to go up the sides of the pan on all sides into the pan, running your hand across the bottom to adhere it.

2 Butter the bottom of the parchment.

3 In a medium bowl, whisk together the flour, baking powder, and salt.

4 In a stand mixer on medium-high speed, using the paddle attachment, cream the butter and ½ cup of the sugar until light and fluffy. Add the egg yolks one at a time, blending well after each addition. Add 1 teaspoon of the vanilla and beat to combine well. Zest the lemon directly into the bowl and beat briefly to combine. On low speed, add half of the flour mixture, then the milk, and then the remaining flour mixture. Mix on low speed just until combined, scraping once or twice.

5 Spread in the prepared pan and set aside. Wash and dry the bowl thoroughly, and using the whisk attachment, beat the egg whites with the cream of tartar on medium speed until foamy. Gradually add the remaining 1 cup sugar and beat on high speed until stiff and glossy. Beat in the remaining 1 teaspoon vanilla. Spoon on top of the cake batter, spreading almost to the edges. Bake for 25 to 30 minutes, until the meringue is beginning to turn golden and the cake is done. A toothpick inserted into

recipe continues

TIMING TIPS:

- Up to 4 hours ahead: Bake the cake.

- Up to 45 minutes ahead: Make the cream mixture and chill. Cut up the strawberries and macerate them.

the cake should come out dry. Let cool in pan 10 minutes. Lift the parchment by the corners and transfer to a cooling rack. Cool completely.

6 To make the berries: When getting ready to serve, hull and halve strawberries and toss with the sugar and Aperol, if using. Let sit until juicy, 15 to 20 minutes. Combine the cream, crème fraîche, and vanilla paste in a clean mixer bowl and whip until softly mounding but holding its shape. Spread the cream on top of the cake, and top with the berries. Dust with confectioners' sugar, if desired.

7 Serve immediately!

CHOCOLATE MALT SEMIFREDDO WITH SALTED CANDIED ALMONDS

SERVES 6 TO 8

I'm not gonna lie, you will need to use a few bowls and pans to make this recipe, but I promise you it will be worth it! Luckily nothing gets too dirty, so it's a pretty easy cleanup. Not only that, but you can make this at least three days (if not a week) ahead of when you want to serve it, so those dishes will be a distant memory. Don't be daunted by this recipe, because it's actually pretty easy, and if you're not already a pro at making caramel, crème anglaise, and meringue, you soon will be. Serve this dessert and you will be a true star, and everyone will be begging you for the recipe.

FOR THE CANDIED ALMONDS:

Butter, for greasing the pan

½ cup whole raw almonds, very roughly chopped

¼ cup sugar

2 teaspoons unsalted butter, plus more to grease parchment

¼ teaspoon vanilla extract

¼ teaspoon flaky sea salt

FOR THE SEMIFREDDO:

1½ cups whole milk

½ vanilla bean, split and scraped

6 ounces extra bittersweet chocolate (70%)

½ cup unsweetened malted milk powder, such as Carnation

4 large egg yolks

7 tablespoons sugar

3 large egg whites

Large pinch of salt

1 To make the candied almonds: Grease a piece of parchment paper or a silicone baking mat and lay it on the counter.

2 In a medium (10-inch) skillet, combine the almonds, sugar, butter, and vanilla. Cook over medium-high heat, stirring occasionally, until the nuts are toasted and the sugar is liquefied and caramel-colored, 5 to 7 minutes. Pour out on the parchment and spread using a metal offset spatula if needed to a single layer. Immediately sprinkle with the flaky salt and let cool. When cooled, chop into smaller pieces (leave half of the almonds a little chunkier and store in an airtight container; these will be for the top).

3 To make the semifreddo: Combine the milk and vanilla pod and seeds in a small saucepan and heat slowly over low heat. Chop the chocolate into small pieces and place in a medium bowl. Set a fine-mesh strainer on top of the chocolate. Set aside.

4 Line a standard (8½ x 4½ x 2½-inch) loaf pan with a large piece of plastic wrap. Leave enough excess so it can be completely folded over once it's filled.

recipe continues

5 Have the malted milk powder ready. Combine the egg yolks with 2 tablespoons of the sugar and whisk until liquefied. When the milk is steaming and bubbling around the edges, slowly whisk it into the eggs and return the mixture to the saucepan. If you're brave and impatient like I am, you'll cook it over medium heat, whisking constantly, until thickened, 4 to 8 minutes. (It will take longer if you want to cook it more gently over low heat.) As the foam starts to subside and the mixture begins to thicken, turn the heat down to low to avoid scrambling the eggs, and cook until creamy, thick, and shiny. Whisk in the malt powder and immediately pour it into the strainer in the bowl of chocolate, leaving any curdy bits in the pan. Push it through the strainer using a rubber spatula. Stir the two mixtures together briefly, let sit for 5 minutes, and stir again until smooth and the chocolate is completely melted. Set the bowl in a larger bowl of ice. If you're not in a hurry, you can stir occasionally until cooled.

6 Heat a large saucepan with a few inches of water in it until simmering. In the bowl of a stand mixer (or just a metal bowl if you are using a hand mixer), combine the egg whites with the remaining 5 tablespoons sugar and the salt and set it over the simmering water. Whisk constantly, hand-holding the whisk attachment until hot to the touch and the sugar is completely dissolved, about 2 minutes, then attach the whisk attachment to the stand mixer and beat the egg whites until stiff and glossy. Fold into the chocolate mixture.

7 Use the rubber spatula to nudge about half the chocolate mixture into the pan. Sprinkle with the more finely chopped half of the candied almonds. Top with remaining chocolate mixture. Fold the plastic over to wrap completely, find a flat, level surface in the freezer, and freeze overnight.

8 Tap the semifreddo out of the pan, unwrap, and place upside down on a serving platter. Scrape the sides to smooth the wrinkles, top with the remaining almonds, and serve immediately.

PARSNIP SHEET CAKE WITH CREAM CHEESE FROSTING AND HOME-CANDIED GINGER

SERVES 12 TO 15

Parsnip cake might seem new, but actually it's been around a long time. There's little difference between parsnip cake and carrot cake (in fact, you could swap carrots in if you want) except that parsnips are more reliably sweet than carrots, and they create a different color cake, of course. This nubby, moist cake is the kind that you keep "trimming" to "even it up." The less sweet than usual cream cheese frosting is the perfect topper for this homey cake, and homemade candied ginger adds a crunchy spicy note to every bite. If you're not up for candying the ginger, finely sliver prepared candied ginger instead.

FOR THE CAKE:

Unsalted butter, for the pan

1½ cups all-purpose flour, plus more for the pan

1½ cups walnuts

¾ cup plus 3 tablespoons roasted walnut or vegetable oil

¾ cup granulated sugar

¾ cup light brown sugar

3 large eggs

2 teaspoons vanilla extract

2 teaspoons ground cinnamon

1½ teaspoons ground cardamom

Generous grating of nutmeg

2 teaspoons ground ginger

¼ teaspoon ground cloves

1½ teaspoons baking powder

¾ teaspoon baking soda

¼ teaspoon salt

3 cups grated parsnips (about 4)

¾ cup golden raisins

1 Preheat the oven to 350°F. Butter a 9 x 13-inch metal baking pan. Line with parchment paper, butter the parchment, and flour the pan, tapping out excess.

2 Place the walnuts on a small baking sheet and toast for 6 to 8 minutes, until fragrant and turning golden brown. Let cool, then coarsely chop.

3 In a medium bowl, whisk together the oil, sugars, eggs, and vanilla. In a large bowl, whisk together the flour, cinnamon, cardamom, nutmeg, ginger, cloves, baking powder, baking soda, and salt. Stir the wet ingredients into the dry ingredients until thoroughly combined. Stir in the parsnips, walnuts, and raisins.

4 Spread the batter in the prepared pan and bake for 35 to 40 minutes, until the top springs back when touched, the cake is turning brown around the edges, and a toothpick comes out dry. Cool in the pan for 15 minutes, then invert onto a cooling rack, peel off parchment, and cool completely. When cooled, invert onto a serving platter.

recipe and ingredients continue

FOR THE FROSTING:

8 ounces cream cheese, at room
 temperature

½ cup (1 stick) unsalted butter, softened

1 cup confectioners' sugar, sifted

2 tablespoons maple syrup

1 teaspoon vanilla extract

Candied Ginger (recipe follows)

TIMING TIPS:

- Up to 3 days ahead: Make the candied ginger.

- The cake can be made 1 day before serving; it actually might even improve. Wrap tightly in plastic wrap.

- Up to 2 hours before serving: Frost and garnish the cake. Briefly chill if needed to set up the frosting.

---

5 To make the frosting: Put the cream cheese in the bowl of a stand mixer fitted with the paddle attachment (or a mixing bowl if using a hand mixer). Cream the cream cheese until smooth, then add the butter, confectioners' sugar, maple syrup, and vanilla. Beat until well combined and fluffy. Spread over the top of the cake almost to the edges. Top with the candied ginger. The cake keeps well for several days.

HOME-CANDIED GINGER

MAKES ABOUT ¼ POUND

1 large piece ginger (about
 5 ounces, 7 inches long, and
 1 to 2 inches in diameter)

1 cup sugar

1 cup water

2 tablespoons light corn syrup

1 Bring a small saucepan of water to a boil. Peel the ginger and slice it lengthwise paper thin and as long as possible using a mandoline. Blanch the ginger for about 20 seconds, then drain. In the same saucepan, combine the sugar, the 1 cup water, and corn syrup and bring to a boil. When the sugar is completely dissolved, add the ginger to the pot. Lower the heat and cook at a brisk simmer, stirring occasionally, for 1 hour, or until very translucent.

2 Preheat the oven to 225°F and line a baking sheet with a silicone baking mat or parchment paper.

3 Drain the ginger very well in a mesh strainer and lay out the ginger pieces as flat as possible on the prepared baking sheet. Bake for 45 to 60 minutes, until pale golden brown and no longer sticky. The timing will vary depending on the thickness of the ginger, so watch carefully toward the end of cooking time and remove them before they brown too much. Remove the baking mat or parchment from the baking sheet and let cool. Store in an airtight container until ready to use.

NOTE:

The syrup can be saved to use for sweetening tea and cocktails.

PLUM BUCKWHEAT BARS

MAKES 24 BARS

These fruity, nubby, grainy bars can be made almost any time of year. Although out-of-season Chilean fruit may not be much good for eating out of hand, when cooked, it is surprisingly delicious. The thing is, out-of-season plums will take considerably more time to cook than juicy summer plums, so use your judgment, and cook just until the fruit has mostly broken down with just a little texture remaining. This could take anywhere from fifteen minutes to an hour.

FOR THE CRUST:

2¼ cups all-purpose flour

¾ cup buckwheat flour

½ cup granulated sugar

½ cup light brown sugar

½ teaspoon salt

1 teaspoon baking powder

½ teaspoon ground cardamom

1 cup (2 sticks) cold unsalted butter, cut into pieces

1 large egg, lightly beaten

FOR THE FILLING:

1½ pounds black or red plums, pitted and cut into 1½-inch chunks

1 heaping cup plum preserves (one 12- or 13-ounce jar)

1 tablespoon cornstarch

Juice of ½ lemon

Confectioners' sugar (optional)

TIMING TIPS:

- Up to 3 days ahead: Make the plum filling.

- Up to 1 day ahead: Make the buckwheat dough; chill until ready to use.

1 Preheat the oven to 375°F. Butter a 9 x 13-inch baking pan and line with parchment paper, leaving 1 inch of overhang over the edge of the pan on the two long sides.

2 To make the crust: Combine the all-purpose flour, buckwheat flour, granulated sugar, brown sugar, salt, baking powder, and cardamom in the bowl of a food processor. Pulse to combine thoroughly. Add the butter and pulse until the mixture resembles coarse meal. Add the egg and pulse until well distributed. Transfer the mixture to a large bowl and continue to mix and work with your fingers until clumps form. It should look like crumb topping at this point. Chill the dough mixture while you make the filling.

3 To make the filling: Combine the plums, preserves, cornstarch, and lemon juice in a small skillet. Cook over medium heat, covered, stirring occasionally, until the fruit has broken down, 15 minutes to 1 hour (see headnote). Transfer to a bowl to cool completely.

4 To assemble the bars: Press half of the dough into the prepared pan, patting with your knuckles to an even thickness. Pour the plum mixture over the dough and distribute it evenly. Sprinkle the remaining dough evenly over the top. Bake for 35 to 45 minutes, until the fruit is bubbling and the top is golden brown.

5 Let cool completely on a wire rack, then cut into 24 squares. Dust with confectioners' sugar (if desired).

WHOLE MEYER LEMON MERINGUE BARS

MAKES 12 TO 16

As a kid, and still, my favorite pie always has been and always will be, lemon meringue. This easy little bar uses a whole lemon and all the yolks and whites, which makes it pretty near perfect for me (or anyone else who likes lemons). Because you will be using the yolks first and the whites either hours or a day or two later, make sure you separate them carefully, store the whites in an ultra-clean glass or metal bowl or jar, and refrigerate until needed. I find the flavor is best using a whole Meyer lemon, which has a milder and thinner rind, with a little regular lemon juice to amp up the acidity.

FOR THE CRUST:

9 whole graham crackers (1 package), broken into pieces (or 1½ cups crumbs)

¼ cup sugar

Large pinch of salt

5 tablespoons unsalted butter, melted

FOR THE FILLING:

1 whole (preferably organic) Meyer lemon, scrubbed

Juice of ½ regular lemon (1 tablespoon)

4 egg yolks

½ cup (1 stick) unsalted butter, melted and cooled

1 cup sugar

1 teaspoon vanilla extract

Pinch of salt

FOR THE MERINGUE TOPPING:

4 large egg whites

1 cup sugar

½ teaspoon vanilla extract

Pinch of salt

1 Preheat the oven to 350°F. Line an 8 by 8-inch baking pan with two pieces of parchment trimmed to fit, going in both directions, with some extra hanging over for easy removal of the bars later.

2 To make the crust: Place the graham crackers, sugar, and salt in the bowl of a food processor and process until fine crumbs form. Add the melted butter and pulse until well blended. It should look and feel like wet sand. Transfer to the prepared pan and mix it up with your hands to make sure the butter is well distributed. Press into the pan, going up the sides a bit, and bake for 10 minutes, or until just golden. Let cool while you make the filling.

3 To make the filling: Trim the stem end of the whole lemon and cut it into 8 pieces. Remove the seeds. Add to a blender jar (preferably of a high speed blender) along with the lemon juice, egg yolks, butter, sugar, vanilla, and salt and blend until very smooth. Pour over the crust (it's OK if it's still warm) and bake for 30 minutes, or until it is bubbling and browning around the edges. It won't look at all set, but it will set up as it cools. Place on a cooling rack. After about 10 minutes, run a small, sharp knife around the edges. Cool completely, then chill until cold. When completely chilled, carefully remove the parchment and, using a spatula, transfer to a small baking sheet (you can do this just before adding the topping).

recipe continues

4 Up to a few hours before serving, make the topping: Combine the egg whites, sugar, vanilla, and salt in the metal bowl of a stand mixer (or just use a metal bowl if using a hand mixer) and set over a pan of simmering water. Keep the mixture moving, hand-holding the whisk attachment until the sugar is completely melted and it's hot to the touch, 1 to 2 minutes. Transfer to a stand mixer and beat on high speed until glossy and very stiff, 2 to 3 minutes. Transfer to the top of the lemon bars, smooth out, and use a large serving fork to create a pattern in the meringue.

5 When you're ready to finish, preheat the broiler and position a rack in upper third of oven.

6 Place under the broiler briefly, watching carefully (or, alternatively, use a kitchen torch), to brown the meringue. Refrigerate until ready to serve. Cut into 12 to 16 squares, depending on how large you want them.

CHAMOMILE FLAN

SERVES 8

This is one of those recipes that proves the pure alchemy that cooking can be. Just a few simple ingredients that you most likely always have in your kitchen are transformed into something so ethereal and delicious.

1 cup sugar

2 tablespoons water

2 cups whole milk

1 cup heavy cream

6 chamomile tea bags or 6 tablespoons dried chamomile flowers or loose tea

6 large eggs

2 large egg yolks

Fresh chamomile flowers (optional)

1 Preheat the oven to 300°F. Have an 8 x 11-inch (2-quart) ceramic or glass baking dish ready by the stove.

2 Combine ½ cup of the sugar and the water in a small saucepan and stir to combine. Cook over medium-high heat until sugar is dissolved and mixture is boiling, 2 to 3 minutes, brushing down the sides of the pan with a wet pastry brush to get rid of any sugar crystals clinging to the sides. Swirl the pan gently to keep the sugar moving, but be careful not to splash yourself. When the sugar starts to color, reduce the heat a bit so it doesn't brown too fast. Cook until it's a deep amber color and beginning to smoke a little. As soon as it reaches the right color, carefully pour it all at once into the dish, tipping it to cover the bottom. Set aside.

3 Pour the milk and cream into a small saucepan and heat over medium heat until bubbles form around the edges and you can see steam rising. Turn off the heat, add the tea bags, cover the pot, and let steep for 30 to 60 minutes. Squeeze out the tea bags (if using loose tea or flowers, strain into a bowl, pressing hard on the solids to extract all the liquid).

4 Combine the eggs, egg yolks, and the remaining ½ cup sugar in a medium bowl and beat vigorously with a whisk until well blended and the sugar has liquefied. Slowly beat the milk mixture into the egg mixture until well combined.

5 Check that the caramel has hardened in the dish. If not, wait until it has, and pour the milk mixture through a fine-mesh strainer into the dish. Place the dish in a larger roasting pan and fill it halfway with boiling water. (For safety reasons, you may want to place it on the oven rack before pouring in the water.)

recipe continues

6 Bake for 35 to 40 minutes, until the custard looks just barely set and still is quite jiggly in the center. Remember that it will continue to set up as it cools, and even more as it chills. Carefully remove the roasting pan from the oven (use oven mitts in case some of the hot water splashes out) and set on a cooling rack. After a few minutes, remove the baking dish from the roasting pan and cool completely. Cover and chill until ready to serve, at least overnight. Run a small, sharp knife around the edges of the dish to release the custard. Place a flat serving platter over the top of the dish and, holding them tightly together, flip over as a unit. Then remove the baking dish, letting the custard drop down to the plate. Serve right away or chill until ready to serve.

TIMING TIP:
The beauty of flan is that it must be made completely ahead of time and will keep very well for 2 to 3 days, until you unmold it. Store in the fridge, tightly wrapped.

HAZELNUT BROWNIES

MAKES 15

These brownies are more of a (almost) flourless chocolate cake than a typical brownie, thanks to the large amount of chocolate involved. Be very careful not to overbake them, and let them cool completely before slicing. If you want to make these gluten-free, omit the flour and double the ground hazelnuts.

½ cup (1 stick) unsalted butter, cut into pieces, wrapper reserved, plus more for greasing the pan

⅓ plus ¼ cup whole hazelnuts (2½ ounces)

7 ounces bittersweet chocolate, chopped

4 ounces unsweetened chocolate, chopped

4 large eggs

1¼ cups sugar

1 teaspoon vanilla extract

½ teaspoon kosher salt

¼ cup ground hazelnuts (1 ounce)

¼ cup all-purpose flour

Flaky sea salt

TIMING TIP:

The brownies can be made up to 1 day ahead.

1 Preheat the oven to 350°F. Butter the bottom of 9 x 13-inch baking pan using the butter wrapper. Press a piece of parchment paper large enough to go up the sides of the pan on all sides into the pan, running your hand across the bottom to adhere it.

2 Toast the hazelnuts for 8 to 10 minutes, until they smell toasty, the skins are popping off, and they are turning golden. Remove from the oven, leaving the oven on, and pour into a bowl. Cover the bowl with a folded dishcloth and let them cool. Rub off as much of the skin as comes off easily. Separate the nuts from the skins and discard the skins. Grind ¼ cup of the nuts in a food processor until fine. Crack the remaining nuts slightly using the side of a chef's knife, leaving some whole. Set aside.

3 Combine both chocolates and the butter in a metal bowl. Put about 2 inches of water into a saucepan that the bowl can sit in without falling in and bring to a boil. Place the bowl on top of the pot and turn off the heat. Stir occasionally until completely melted. Set aside to cool slightly.

4 Combine the eggs, sugar, and vanilla in the bowl of a stand mixer fitted with the whisk attachment and beat on medium-high speed until very fluffy, about 2 minutes. Add the kosher salt. Pour in the chocolate mixture and beat slowly to combine well.

5 Fold in the ground hazelnuts and flour. Let the batter sit in the bowl for 15 minutes, folding a few times. Transfer to the prepared pan, smoothing the batter evenly with an offset spatula. Sprinkle the hazelnuts over the top, pressing them in slightly. Lightly sprinkle the top with flaky sea salt.

6 Bake for 15 to 18 minutes, until just set. Cool completely and cut into 15 squares.

STRAWBERRY-CHOCOLATE TART WITH PISTACHIO CRUST

SERVES 8 TO 10

This tart is an homage to a favorite tart that used to be served at The Commissary in Philadelphia, where I worked as a teenager. I could and did often eat several Strawberry Heart Tarts during my shift, and never seemed to gain weight. What I loved most about them was the layer of chocolate under the creamy filling, which keeps the crust crisp indefinitely. Sweetened goat cheese and yogurt adds a tangy note to the easy filling. The crust is very simple and has the great advantage of not needing to be rolled out or blind baked. You might wonder why it's baked at such a low temperature. That's because this is more like a shortbread cookie dough, which needs to be baked slowly without browning.

FOR THE CRUST:

½ cup (1 stick) unsalted butter, slightly softened and cut up, plus more for greasing the pan

½ cup unsalted shelled raw pistachios

⅓ cup granulated sugar

½ teaspoon almond extract

½ teaspoon salt

1¼ cups all-purpose flour

FOR THE FILLING:

5 ounces soft, mild goat cheese

¼ cup plus 3 tablespoons confectioners' sugar

½ teaspoon vanilla extract

8 ounces 2% plain Greek yogurt

3 ounces semisweet or bittersweet chocolate, chopped

⅓ cup strawberry preserves

1 pound strawberries, hulled and cut in half or quartered if large

1 Grease a 9-inch nonstick tart pan with a removable bottom with butter.

2 To make the crust: Place the pistachios in the bowl of a food processor and pulse until finely ground and powdery. Transfer to a bowl. Add the butter and granulated sugar and pulse until well blended, scraping down the sides as needed. Add the almond extract and salt and pulse to combine. Return the pistachios to the processor and add the flour. Pulse until the dough comes together. Immediately press into the prepared tart pan and chill until firm, about 30 minutes.

3 Meanwhile, preheat the oven to 300°F.

4 Prick the crust with a fork and bake for 40 to 45 minutes, until just beginning to color. Transfer to a cooling rack. After 15 minutes, loosen the tart shell from the ring so it can be removed easily later. Cool completely.

5 To make the filling: In a stand mixer fitted with the paddle attachment, or in a food processor, combine the goat cheese, confectioners' sugar, vanilla, and yogurt and beat or process until well blended.

recipe continues

6 In a microwave-safe bowl, melt the chocolate in the microwave in 20-second intervals, stirring in between, until melted and smooth. (You can also melt the chocolate in a double boiler set over low heat.) Pour into the cooled tart shell and spread evenly using an offset spatula or the back of a spoon. Chill until the chocolate hardens.

7 In a small saucepan or in the microwave, heat the preserves with 1 tablespoon water until liquefied. Strain through a fine-mesh strainer into a medium bowl. Let it cool a little so it can cling to the berries better. Toss the berries into the preserves, tossing gently with a rubber spatula to coat well, then tumble them into the tart shell.

TIMING TIPS:

Tarts are always best broken into parts for prep, as by their very nature they are made up of separate components.

- Up to 2 days ahead: Make the dough and bake the shell.

- Up to 1 day ahead: Fill with the chocolate and chill until firm. After that, it can be stored at room temperature if the room is cool; make the filling and store it in the fridge.

- At the last minute: Fill the tart shell with the cream; glaze the strawberries and tumble into the shell. This is best served right away.

APPLE GALETTE WITH HALVAH FRANGIPANE

SERVES 6 TO 8

This galette is not overly sweet, and the subtle sesame flavors from the halvah and seeds come shining through. Halvah can be tricky to find—if Joyva bars from the candy, deli, or "ethnic" section are all you can find, they are fine for this, but for a real treat, order the best halvah you've ever had from Seed + Mill in Chelsea Market in New York (see page 356). Because this galette only calls for two apples, I use one tart (like a Granny Smith) and one sweet (like a Honeycrisp). If your apples are small, you will need three. Creamy and tart labneh (see page 16) makes a good dollop with this.

FOR THE FRANGIPANE:

4 ounces plain halvah, finely crumbled (about ½ cup)

2 tablespoons very soft unsalted butter

1 large egg, lightly beaten

1 tablespoon (packed) light brown sugar

¼ cup all-purpose flour

½ teaspoon vanilla extract

⅛ teaspoon salt

FOR THE GALETTE:

½ recipe Galette Dough (page 351)

2 large apples (about 1 pound), peeled and thinly sliced (about 4 cups)

⅓ cup granulated sugar, plus 1½ teaspoons more for sprinkling

2 teaspoons unsalted butter

1 teaspoon white sesame seeds

1 To make the frangipane: In a small bowl, combine all of the ingredients, and cream with a wooden spoon until smooth and well-blended. Chill until needed.

2 To make the galette: Preheat the oven to 400°F. Line a rimmed baking sheet with parchment paper.

3 Let the dough soften slightly until malleable enough to roll out, about 15 minutes. Roll out on a well-floured surface to ¼- to ⅛-inch thickness in a rough 12-inch circle. It doesn't have to be perfect. Place the dough round on the prepared baking sheet. Chill until firm, about 15 minutes. Toss the apples with the granulated sugar.

4 Spread the frangipane on the dough, leaving a 2-inch border. Arrange the apple slices on top, leaving a 2-inch border of dough. Sprinkle the fruit with 1 teaspoon sugar and dot with the butter. Fold the dough over to enclose the edges of the filling, patching any cracks. Chill again until firm.

5 Brush the crust with cold water and sprinkle with the sesame seeds and ½ teaspoon sugar. Bake for 40 to 45 minutes, rotating the pan halfway through the baking time, until the filling is bubbling and the crust is golden brown.

recipe continues

- Up to 3 days ahead of time: Make the frangipane and make the dough. Chill until needed.

- Up to 4 hours ahead of time: Roll out the dough and chill until needed, wrapped well.

- Up to 2 hours ahead of time: Assemble and bake the galette.

6 Remove from the oven and place the pan on a cooling rack. Run a long spatula under the galette to loosen it from any spilled juices, changing the position on the parchment (do this periodically during the cooling time to make sure it doesn't stick). Brush any spilled juices onto the top of the galette to glaze it as it cools. If you are lucky enough to not have any spills, dip the brush into the excess juices inside the crust and brush on top to give it some shine. Let cool for at least 30 minutes before serving to allow the juices to thicken and the crust to firm up. Carefully pick up the parchment by opposite corners, transfer to a serving plate, and pull out the paper. Serve warm or at room temperature.

PEACH CARAMEL GALETTE

SERVES 6 TO 8

I love making galettes because they are so easy and they appeal to the artist in me. They seem more open to interpretation than, say, pie, with less rigid parameters. I always keep a jar of caramel sauce in my fridge for emergencies—like you forgot about dessert and you have people coming over. A little caramel sauce drizzled over ice cream and a cookie and you're good. It keeps forever in a glass jar, so it comes in handy for adding another flavor dimension to my galettes, and it goes especially well with peaches.

½ recipe Galette Dough (recipe follows)

3 tablespoons all-purpose flour, plus more for rolling

4 tablespoons granulated sugar

3 ripe peaches

¼ cup Caramel Sauce (recipe follows)

Crème fraîche or vanilla ice cream

TO FINISH:

1 to 2 tablespoons turbinado sugar

1 Preheat the oven to 400°F. Line a baking sheet with parchment paper.

2 Let the dough soften slightly until malleable enough to roll out. Roll out on a well-floured surface to ¼- to ⅛-inch thickness in a rough 12-inch circle. It doesn't have to be perfect. Place the dough round on the prepared baking sheet. Chill while you cut the peaches into 16 slices each.

3 Sprinkle the dough with the flour and spread with your hand, leaving a 2-inch border. Sprinkle with 2 tablespoons of the granulated sugar. Arrange the peach slices in a single layer, leaving a 3-inch border of dough. Sprinkle the fruit with the remaining 2 tablespoons granulated sugar. Drizzle with the caramel sauce. Fold the dough over to enclose the edges of the filling, patching any cracks. Chill again until firm.

4 Just before baking, brush the crust with cold water and sprinkle with the turbinado sugar. Bake for about 40 minutes, rotating the pan halfway through the baking time, until the filling is bubbling and the crust is golden brown.

5 Remove from the oven and place the pan on a cooling rack. Run a long spatula under the galette to loosen it from any spilled juices, changing the position on the parchment (do this periodically during the cooling time to make sure it doesn't stick). Brush any spilled juices onto the top of the galette to glaze it as it cools. If you are lucky enough to not have any spills, dip the brush into the excess juices inside the crust and brush

recipe and ingredients continue

on top to give it some shine. Let cool for at least 30 minutes before serving to allow the juices to thicken and the crust to firm up. Carefully pick up the parchment by opposite corners, transfer to a serving plate, and pull out the paper. Serve warm or at room temperature with crème fraîche or ice cream.

CARAMEL SAUCE

MAKES ABOUT 1 CUP

Store in a glass jar in the fridge to serve over ice cream or add to pie and galette fillings. It will keep for a long time. Just rewarm before using to return to a liquid consistency. I usually microwave the jar with the lid off to warm it up, but you also could sit it in a saucepan of hot water.

1 cup granulated sugar

½ cup water

½ cup heavy cream

2 tablespoons high-quality cold unsalted butter

½ vanilla bean, split and scraped

Pinch of salt

1 Combine the sugar and water in a 1½-quart saucepan and stir to combine. Use a wet pastry brush to wet down the sides of the pan and cook over medium-high heat until the sugar is dissolved and the mixture is boiling, 2 to 3 minutes. Use the brush (keep the brush in a cup of water) to wet the sides of the pan again if there are any crystals clinging to the pan. Meanwhile, cut up the butter and measure out the cream and have them standing by.

2 Raise the heat to high. Cook without stirring for 8 to 10 minutes, swirling the pan occasionally and carefully, until the mixture starts to color. At this point, lower the heat a little and watch very carefully, continuing to swirl gently until it turns a deep amber color (it will start to smoke a bit).

3 Turn off the heat and immediately pour in the cream all at once with an oven mitt protecting your hand. It will sputter and expand temporarily. As it calms down, add the butter and whisk until smooth. Add the vanilla pod and seeds and the salt. Cool completely before using. Store any leftover caramel in a glass jar in the refrigerator for up to 1 month. Warm to a liquid consistency before using.

GALETTE DOUGH

MAKES ENOUGH FOR 2 MEDIUM GALETTES

Sometimes I make my dough by hand, and other times I use a food processor to help me cut in the butter. It kind of depends on how much I'm making. I like that a food processor cuts in the butter quickly, so it remains cold. While it is still in pretty big pieces, I transfer it to a bowl to work it a bit more with my fingers and add the water. If you want to do it entirely by hand, cut the butter into fairly thin slices so they are easier to break down using your hands. If using a machine, cut it into tablespoon-size chunks.

2 cups all-purpose flour

½ teaspoon salt

1 teaspoon granulated sugar

14 tablespoons (1¾ sticks) ice-cold unsalted butter, cut into pieces

¼ cup ice water, plus more as needed

Combine the flour, salt, and sugar in the bowl of a food processor. Pulse until combined. Add the butter and pulse until the largest pieces of butter are the size of quarters and nickels. It still should make a thumping sound when you pulse. Transfer to a wide bowl, and continue working the dough with your finger tips, flattening the butter pieces, and breaking down any larger pieces until they are approximately pea-sized. Sprinkle the ice water over the flour mixture while tossing with a fork. Knead lightly to mix evenly and bring the dough together. Add dribbles of water if it is too crumbly or if you see a lot of dry flour in the bottom of the bowl. Divide dough in half and place each half on a sheet of plastic wrap. Wrap tightly and press each into a flat disk. Chill until firm, at least 30 minutes and as long as 2 days ahead (or freeze for several months).

ROASTED STRAWBERRY-BASIL SHERBET

MAKES ABOUT 1 QUART

Sherbet is just sorbet with a little dairy added. Prepping this is as easy as making a smoothie, aside from roasting the strawberries in the oven first, which concentrates their flavor and eliminates any chance of iciness in the finished sherbet. It's divine when made with height-of-the-season strawberries, but even basic supermarket strawberries take on a more complex and concentrated character when roasted. While basil may seem like an unusual addition to a strawberry sherbet, it adds a complexity that's hard to identify and easy to like. The combination of the basil, vanilla, and strawberries creates an intoxicating perfume all its own.

4½ cups hulled strawberries, cut in half

1 cup plus 2 tablespoons sugar

½ vanilla bean, split and scraped

4 to 6 fresh basil leaves

1½ cups buttermilk

⅓ cup plain Greek yogurt (any fat content) or labneh

Pinch of salt

1 Preheat the oven to 425°F.

2 Stir together strawberries, sugar, and vanilla seeds and bean in a medium glass or ceramic baking dish. Roast for 15 to 20 minutes, stirring several times, until bubbling and the liquid is starting to reduce and caramelize.

3 Discard the vanilla pod and scrape the contents of the baking dish into a blender. Add the basil leaves and let stand for 5 minutes to infuse the basil. Add the buttermilk, yogurt, and salt and blend until perfectly smooth. Cool completely and chill very thoroughly, either by refrigerating overnight or transferring to a metal bowl and stirring over a bowl of ice water.

4 Freeze in an ice cream maker according to the manufacturer's instructions. Transfer to an airtight container and freeze until firm, preferably overnight. This keeps well for several days and even longer.

TIMING TIPS:

- Up to 2 days ahead: Make the sherbet base and chill; freeze the ice cream canister.

- At least 1 day ahead: Churn the sherbet and return to the freezer to firm up.

PARTY MENUS

I tried to make it easy for you to create your own menus by using the sections of the book. If you pick a Simple Starter, a Centerpiece, a Salad or Vegetable, a Starchy side, and a dessert, you should have a pretty good chance of coming up with a menu that works. Of course, try to keep seasonality in mind, and try to avoid redundancies or anything that would make for a less-than-harmonious combination. Also pay attention to whether the recipes are being cooked in the oven, on the stove, or completely ahead of time, and find a good and manageable balance. Use the Timing Tips given with each recipe to figure out how to get ahead, and no menu should be too much to manage! The recipes in the book were each created to stand alone, but if there is a redundancy in a menu (like cheese or nuts or olives in two recipes), feel free to leave it out on one of the recipes for better balance. Below you will find some good menus, just to give you an idea of how things can go together.

HARVEST FEAST
- Tomato Toast with Labneh and Harissa *(page 51)*
- Rosey Harissa Chicken *(page 111)*
- Summer Corn Pudding *(page 285)*
- Crispy Semolina Potatoes *(page 275)*
- Simple but Exceptional Green Salad *(page 238)*
- Apple Galette with Halvah Frangipane *(page 345)*

VEGETARIAN FALL FEAST
- Dukkah Grissini *(page 65)*
- Beet Hummus *(page 61)*
- Famous Kale Salad *(page 229)*
- Not-Fried Eggplant Parm *(page 199)*
- Quac 'n Cheese *(page 269)*
- Plum Buckwheat Bars *(page 331)*

ITALIAN-ISH DINNER
- Baked Ricotta *(page 59)*
- Whole Grain Cumin Crackerbread *(page 73)*
- Osso Buco Sugo with Orange Gremolata *(page 103)*
- Grilled Chicories and Lettuces with Melted Parm and Anchovy Vinaigrette *(page 247)*
- Chocolate Malt Semifreddo with Salted Candied Almonds *(page 325)*

GAME NIGHT WITH FINGER FOOD
- Crudités with Avocado Tahini Dip *(page 71)*
- Grandma Pie with Broccoli Rabe and Sausage *(page 169)*
- Hazelnut Brownies *(page 341)*

DEAD OF WINTER
- Charcoal Crackers and Black and White Cheese Board *(page 75)*
- Winter Citrus Salad with Red Endive, Avocado, Dates, and Olives *(page 219)*
- Modern Chicken and Dumplings *(page 117)*
- Whole Meyer Lemon Meringue Bars *(page 333)*

COZY NIGHT IN
- Kale Toast *(page 52)*
- Baked Turkey-Spinach Meatballs *(page 113)*
- Oven-Baked Polenta *(page 273)*
- Raw Cauliflower Salad with Warm Vinaigrette *(page 241)*
- Parsnip Sheet Cake with Cream Cheese Frosting and Home-Candied Ginger *(page 327)*

EVERYTHING BUT THE TURKEY
- Smoky Cheddar Crackers *(page 55)*
- Green Bean Salad with Tahini and Quinoa *(page 213)*
- Brussels Sprout Gratin with Speck and Rye Crumbs *(page 253)*
- Root Vegetable Tian *(page 255)*
- Caramelized Fennel with Citrus and Olives *(page 257)*
- Kabocha Candy with Yogurt and Toasted Pepitas *(page 251)*
- Butternut Squash Tart with Cranberry-Pomegranate Glaze *(page 317)*
- Multi-Nut Shortbread *(page 293)*

HEIGHT OF THE SUMMER
- Grilled Peas in the Pod, Edamame Style *(page 63)*
- Fish in Crazy Water *(page 139)*
- Fregola Salad with Oil-Cured Olives, Broccolini, and Salsa Verde *(page 271)*
- Any Fruit Crisp *(page 309)*

WARM-WEATHER BRUNCH
- Melon Toast *(page 50)*
- Flower Omelette Crepes *(page 177)* or Stress-less Cheese Soufflé *(page 185)*
- Shaved Rhubarb and Beet Salad with Rhubarb Vinaigrette *(page 235)*
- Roasted Radishes with Radish Green Pesto and Crème Fraîche *(page 263)*
- Cornmeal Thumbprints with Preserves *(page 299)*

SPRING MENU
- Whipped Ricotta Toast with Pickled Rhubarb and Grated Beets *(page 49)*
- Slow-Roasted Lamb Shoulder with Pomegranate Molasses *(page 107)*
- Freekeh Salad with Pickled Onions, Feta, and Herbs *(page 272)*
- Sugar Snap Pea and Radish Salad *(page 221)*
- Strawberry-Chocolate Tart with Pistachio Crust *(page 343)*

VEGETARIAN SPRING FEAST
- Burrata with Pickled Cherries, Sumac, and Basil *(page 69)*
- Mixed Peas over Whipped Feta *(page 223)*
- Meyer Lemon Gnocchi with Spring Vegetables *(page 189)*
- Roasted Strawberry–Basil Sherbet *(page 353)*
- Black and White Tahini Swirl Cookies *(page 301)*

EARLY SUMMER
- Blistered Shishitos with Avocado Crema *(page 67)*
- Za'atar Chicken Thighs with Grilled Peach and Crispy Couscous Salad *(page 119)*
- Shaved Asparagus Salad *(page 245)*
- Berry Brita Cake *(page 321)*

A SUMMER GRILLING MENU
- Smoky Eggplant Dip *(page 57)* with Whole Grain Cumin Crackerbread *(page 73)*
- Smashed Beet and Warm Goat Cheese Salad *(page 211)*
- Porchetta Chops *(page 87)*
- Summer Corn Pudding *(page 285)*
- Plum Buckwheat Bars *(page 331)*

ANOTHER SUMMER GRILLING MENU
- Roasted Tomato and Burrata Toast *(page 53)*
- Grilled Bohemian Steak with Garlic Scapes *(page 91)*
- Duck Fat Oven Fries *(page 279)*
- Peach Caramel Galette *(page 349)*

MOSTLY-ROOM-TEMPERATURE WINTER MEAL
- Castelvetrano Nibble *(page 56)*
- Spice-Roasted Salmon with Pickled Mustard Seeds, Citrus, and Herbs *(page 151)*
- Radicchio, Beets, and Cranberry Beans *(page 233)*
- Grain Salad with Many Flavors (That Holds Up for Hours) *(page 287)*
- Chamomile Flan *(page 337)*

SOURCES

FOOD AND KITCHEN

While I can and I do frequently order specialized items from Amazon, which makes it so easy for those who live in far-flung places to get their hands on hard-to-find ingredients, there are some items better ordered from the source.

CARISSA'S BAKERY

I love Carissa's Salty Soured Pickled Rye bread, especially for the topping for the Brussels Sprout Gratin on page 253. Lots of other people do too, which is why she now ships nationwide.

www.carissasthebakery.com

KALUSTYAN'S

Over the years, Kalustyan's has evolved from an Indian-focused spice and grocery store to a one-stop shop for any and all unusual and inspiring ingredient from every cuisine of the world. The shelves are overflowing with spices, grains, beans, lentils, rice, and more in seemingly infinite varieties. They also have an amazing variety of jarred and bottled ingredients, as well as fresh and frozen items. They have basic and unusual nuts and dried fruit in bulk. Basically, it's really hard to stump them. Even if you can't visit in person, they will ship you whatever you need!

https://foodsofnations.com

KING ARTHUR FLOUR

A great source for anything baking-related, but I always keep some of their baking parchment sheets in my kitchen. Parchment on a roll is fine, but I hate the way it curls up! These flat sheets fit perfectly in a half-sheet pan and come in white or natural. You can also order your silicone baking mat here, which you will need to make the Quinoa Almond Tuiles on page 303.

www.kingarthurflour.com

NEW YORK SHUK

New York Shuk is a small business making high-quality Middle Eastern ingredients including preserved lemons, preserved lemon paste, harissa, and rosey harissa.

https://www.nyshuk.com

RANCHO GORDO BEANS

Rancho Gordo grows and sells an amazing variety of heirloom beans, including cranberry beans.

www.ranchogordo.com

SEED + MILL

For the most delicious tahini and halvah, look no further than Seed + Mill.

www.seedandmill.com

TABLE

BLACKCREEK MERCANTILE & TRADING CO.

I love BCM&T's gorgeously smooth wooden pieces—especially the boards, in both regular grain and end grain. Their Blackline boards are wonderful for setting off anything you serve on them, and they are created using a natural blackening process, not pigments.

www.blackcreekmt.com

BLOOM

If you ever get to Sag Harbor, New York, visiting Mona Nerenberg at her beautiful shop Bloom is a must. She has a small but special collection of simple ceramics and other items for the home and table. Make sure to walk out of the back of the store, through the courtyard to the back house, where you will find a simple table set with Astier de Villatte ceramics and other items.

43 Madison St., Sag Harbor, NY 11963

631-725-5940

CHARIOTS ON FIRE

Beautiful housewares, but especially the highly collectible ceramics of Makoto Kagoshima, which grace both my table and the pages of this book.

https://www.chariotsonfire.com

FIELD COMPANY

The light, smooth, easy-to-season iron skillets from the Field Company are a sheer pleasure to cook and serve in. My 10-inch skillet gets used in a lot of recipes in this book.

www.fieldcompany.com

JANAKI LARSEN

I fell in love with Janaki's perfectly imperfect ceramic work when I was in Vancouver for a shoot. I visited her beautiful shop, Atelier St. George, and bought some treasured pieces, which were used in this book.

www.atelierstgeorge.com

www.janakilarsenceramics.com

JOHN DERIAN

This special shop in my neighborhood in New York City is a delight to visit. Among many other things, they have a wide assortment of Astier de Villatte pieces, which, with their cool white glaze that lets bits of the dark clay underneath, fits well with my wabi-sabi aesthetic.

www.johnderian.com

MONC XIII BY NATASHA ESCH

Another beautiful home design shop in Sag Harbor, New York, carries some of my favorite hard-to-find items, including K.H. Würtz ceramics, Cutipol flatware, and Blackcreek Mercantile boards and spoons.

www.monc13.com

ROMAN AND WILLIAMS GUILD

This incredible shop is the brainchild of award-winning designers and husband-and wife team Robin Standefer and Stephen Alesch. Here they share their incredible eye for beauty in unique, and often exclusive items for the table and home, many sourced from Japanese artisans.

www.rwguild.com

STAUB

I love Staub especially for its gorgeous Dutch ovens, roasting pans, and baking dishes. They make a wide range of shapes, sizes, styles, and colors, and they will last a lifetime.

www.zwilling.com/us/staub

TORTOISE GENERAL STORE AND TORTOISE

More collectible Japanese ceramics and objects

http://tortoiselife.com

ACKNOWLEDGMENTS

THANK YOU:

David Black, my agent, for taking me on, and for pushing me harder than I wanted to be pushed sometimes, but of course, you were right. And to everyone else who helped at DBA, thank you.

Andrea Gentl and Martin Hyers, aka Gentl & Hyers, thank you for agreeing to photograph my book. Having your unique eyes and hands on this made it so much better and exactly what I wanted it to be. Your talent cannot be put into words. Thanks for all the driving back and forth, and for the new rug.

Lucia Watson, my editor, thank you for wanting to keep my book and go on this journey with me. It's been nothing but a pleasure. Thank you for putting up with my strong opinions!

Avery Books, my publisher, for publishing my book! To everyone at Avery who has helped, especially Suzy Swartz, for always helping with swiftness and cheer, to Ashley Tucker, for your design—thank you for putting up with me! To Leda Scheintaub for being a thorough and kind copyeditor. To Anne Kosmoski, Lindsay Gordon, Sara Johnson, Katie Macleod-English, Erica Rose, Justin Thrift, and everyone else who helped make this book and get it out into the world.

Ayesha Patel, thank you for bringing your impeccable eye to the prop styling, and for seamlessly melding my personal collections with the borrowed and rented. Even when you couldn't be there, you were there in spirit. And to Joanie Danahy, thanks for filling in for Ayesha so beautifully, and for driving back and forth!

Frankie (Francesca) Crichton, thank you for your always cheerful and easygoing self, and for keeping track of so many versions of every photograph. Also, thanks for being my vegetarian focus group of one.

Pam Krauss, thank you for wanting and believing in my book. I'm sorry we didn't get to see it through together.

Rebekah Peppler, thank you for helping me in the early stages to organize my thoughts into something I could call a proposal.

Maryann Pomeranz (MVP), Maria Fantaci, and Yossy Arefi for testing recipes in your home kitchens so I can sleep at night knowing they worked for you too. Thank you for your excellent questions, and careful consideration to the details.

Pearl Jones, for spending so many winter days helping me develop recipes, and for assisting on the shoots.

Imogen Kwok, Laura Rege and Catherine Yoo, thanks to all of you for assisting me on the shoots. I could not have done it without your support, and in the case of Cat, your Excel skills!

Sami Ginsberg for assisting at the end, helping me with so many odds and ends as I finished the book, and for your amazing skills in so many areas, especially Photoshop!

Rosa Prieto, thank you for jumping in and doing dishes when we were running out of steam, and helping to distribute some of the leftovers.

Kristy Mucci, the greenmarket queen, for sourcing what I couldn't, and rendezvous-ing with my assistants so I could represent every season.

Stephen Doyle and Gael Towey, thank you for being such good friends and mentors, and for taking the time to look at my project and give your two cents, which is worth way more than that.

To everyone who generously lent or gave or discounted their gorgeous wares to be used in the photography: Meredith Bradford of Staub/Zwilling, RW Guild (I love you!), Mona Nerenberg of Bloom in Sag Harbor, The Field Company, Blackcreek Mercantile & Trading Co.

To all of the farmers and producers both from the Union Square Greenmarket and the many farm stands of the east end of Long Island who never cease to inspire me, thank you for working so hard to bring us so much beautiful produce to play with and nourish us. Special thanks and appreciation to Marilee Foster and Suzannah Wainhouse of Marilee's Farmstand, Jim and Jen Pike of Pike's, Amanda Merrow and Katie Baldwin of Amber Waves Farm, Balsam Farms, and of course Quail Hill Farm.

To my husband, Steven Kasher, for your discerning palate and endless appreciation for good food. Your unvarnished critiques and loving support helped me know what to keep (craveable) and what to toss. Without you, I'm nothing.

INDEX

Note: Page numbers in *italics* indicate photos separate from recipes.